34134 00020516 8

Leabharlainn nan Eilean Siar

WESTERN ISLES LIBRARIES

D0708136

Readers are requested to tak
possession, and to point out ₐ
to the Librarian.
This book is issued for a per
returned on or before the lates
of the period of loan may be granted wnen desired.

Back to the Front

Back to the Front

An Accidental Historian Walks the Trenches of World War 1

Stephen O'Shea

WESTERN ISLES
LIBRARIES
39804629

WITHDRAWN
940.4

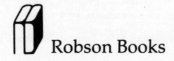

Robson Books

First published in Great Britain in 1997 by Robson Books Ltd, Bolsover House, 5-6 Clipstone Street, London WIP 8LE

Originally published in Canada by Douglas & McIntyre in 1996; published in the United States by Walker Publishing Company, Inc., in 1997

Copyright © 1996 Stephen O'Shea

The right of Stephen O'Shea to be identified as author of this work has been asserted by him in accordance with the Copyright, Designs and Patents Act 1988

Grateful acknowledgement is made for the assistance of the Canada Council and the British Columbia Ministry of Tourism, Small Business and Culture.

Excerpts from the following are reprinted with permission: *The Russian Album* by Michael Ignatieff; copyright © 1987 Michael Ignatieff. Used by permission of Viking Penguin, a division of Penguin Books USA Inc. *Goodbye to All That* by Robert Graves, reprinted by permission of A. P. Watt Ltd. on behalf of the Trustees of the Robert Graves Copyright Trust. '1914' by Rupert Brooke is reprinted by permission of Faber & Faber Ltd. *Tender is the Night* by F. Scott Fitzgerald, copyright 1933, 1934 Charles Scribner's Sons; copyright renewed © 1961, 1962 by Frances Scott Fitzgerald Lanahan. Reprinted by permission of Scribner, a division of Simon & Schuster, *The Ghost Road* by Pat Barker, copyright © 1995 Pat Barker. Used by permission of Dutton Signer, a division of Penguin Books USA Inc., *The Lost Voices of World War I: An International Anthology of Writers, Poets and Playwrights*, edited by Tim Cross; copyright © 1990 Tim Cross, used by permission of the University of Iowa Press.

Maps by Scott Blair, Mitchell Feinberg and DesignGeist

British Library Cataloguing in Publication Data
A catalogue record for this title is available from the British Library

ISBN 1 86105 149 2

All rights reserved. No part of this publication may be reproduced, stored in a retrieval system, or transmitted in any form or by any means, electronic, mechanical, photocopying, recording or otherwise, without the prior permission in writing of the publishers.

Printed in Great Britain by St Edmundsbury Press Ltd, Bury St Edmunds, Suffolk.

To my parents

Contents

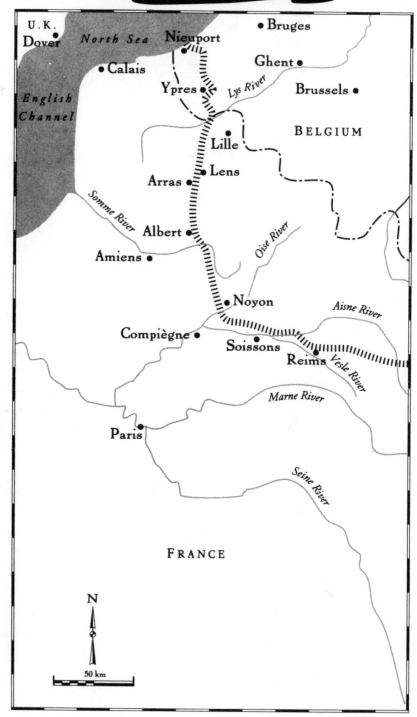

THE WESTERN FRONT

U.K.
Dover
North Sea
Nieuport
Bruges
Calais
Ghent
Ypres
Lys River
Brussels
BELGIUM
Lille
Arras
Lens
English
Channel
Somme River
Albert
Oise River
Amiens
Noyon
Aisne River
Compiègne
Soissons
Reims
Vesle River
Marne River
Paris
Seine River
FRANCE
N
50 km

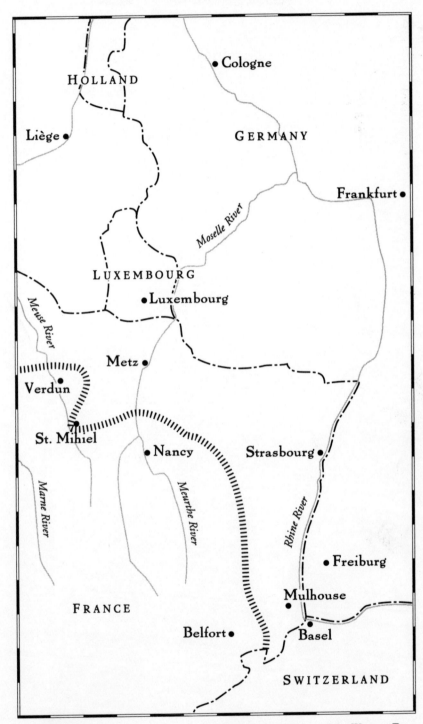

|||||| the trenches of the Western Front

Back to the Front

"I WENT BACK to the Front."

My dinner companion frowned slightly. He'd asked the simple, classic question—what did you do last summer?—and the answer he received was a puzzle. Now he'd have to play along.

"What front?" he said at last.

"The Western Front."

He nodded, relieved to have heard something vaguely familiar. "Is that like the Maginot Line?"

"Close," I said helpfully. "But you've got the wrong war."

We ate in silence for a few instants. I could almost hear the wheels spin: Western Front, Western Front . . .

"D-Day?"

"Nope."

His sunny California countenance creased in embarrassment. Here he was, a fellow freelancer in Paris, and some major European conflict had escaped his notice. What if he could interview me, get an assignment out of it? What if he could write our meal off as a research expense?

I relented. "The Western Front . . . *All Quiet* . . . The trenches . . . World War I . . ."

He almost spat a mouthful of couscous at me. "World War I," he said witheringly. "That's history!"

Ah yes, the ultimate put-down. A Baby Boomer lowering the boom. If a thing is history, it is a loser. Been there, done that, let's move on.

I felt bad for spoiling a pleasant conversation, because I knew that mentioning history in some company betrays a serious character flaw, like torturing canaries in your spare time. I understood his contempt: I too had started life with the view that history was something that began as a test pattern on a TV screen. Nothing of much importance had occurred before then. Moses, Christ, Columbus, *The Wizard of Oz* maybe, but nothing that could possibly rival the broadcast here and now.

In that we were not entirely unusual. Every generation is said to dismiss the experience of its predecessors as a sort of tedious overture humanity had to endure before the real divas stepped onstage. Ignoring, even forgetting, the past is much better than the alternative: being trapped by it, condemned to viewing current events as recurring events and thus fighting the same old feuds and wasting time in learning how and whom to hate. "History," Joyce had Stephen Dedalus say in *Ulysses*, "is a nightmare from which I am trying to awake." In my childhood years my peers and I were all fully awake; history wasn't even the ghost of a dream.

I grew up in North America, physically far from the quaint, the old, and the musty, where a sense of a past had almost been obliterated in the cause of the new. I write "almost," because vestiges of an earlier time had managed to survive. If I do a bit of personal archaeology, I can still hear a playground chant from the very cusp of memory, sung by my older brothers and me on dusty summer days in 1960:

> Whistle while you work,
> Hitler is a jerk,
> Mussolini has no weenie,
> Eisenhower has no power,
> Diefenbaker is a faker,
> Khruschev is a mischief maker.

How this geopolitical version of a Disney ditty got to preschoolers in southern Ontario is not important here. The Diefenbaker line showed we were Canadians; the Mussolini one, that we were little boys with the usual anxieties. That we judged this doggerel worthy of our repertoire meant that we had some idea of the enormities that had recently occurred in the adult past. We were letting intruders into our world away from time.

There were our parents, too. They could always be trusted to inject some cryptic reference into the normal day's round of weightless novelty. I once reached across the dinner table for an extra helping and was checked by a gentle paternal remark: "Austria was Hungary, so it took a piece of Turkey." I now know that the line, as playfully political as our rhyme on Khruschev, refers to the era around the Great War, the incomprehensible adult enormity preceding my father's childhood. At the time, however, the comment seemed to be just another example of the uncrackable code in which my parents chose to communicate. Like many children occasionally baffled by their elders, I put down such incidents to their not being me.

And they most definitely weren't. They had emigrated from Ireland in 1949, and were thus bearers of a sensibility at odds with the budding Boomers in their home. They, or at least their origins, represented History. Of the two main families of Irish immigrants to the Americas, the clannish keepers of the rebel flame and the clear-eyed seekers of assimilation, my parents belonged to the latter. Yet the mere fact of their "Irishness" contradicted the don't-look-back ethos reigning in North America at mid-century. They subverted the here and now simply by being themselves. Through them the reality of another place, Ireland, with connections, complications, and, however retrograde it seemed, a past that mattered to the present, could not be denied. No matter how many times we changed the channel, the shadow of something permanent always flickered on the screen.

We O'Sheas were a textbook example of an uprooted nuclear family. A large, extended clan lived inaccessibly across an ocean, and the whim of my father's employers sent us bopping from city to town to city every two or three years. Toronto, Montreal, Ottawa, Calgary, and a string of smaller towns in southern Ontario—Oshawa, Kingston, St. Thomas, Cornwall—formed the itinerary of our nomadism. Since there was never a hometown to which we could attach some fleeting identity or loyalty, we developed a virtual sense of place. It worked well with our approximate sense of time. I never dreamed that the two would come apart when I glimpsed the Western Front of the First World War. After that moment, the worm of context got into my ahistorical apple.

But not without difficulty, and not as successfully as the worm can penetrate, for better or worse, the overripe fruit of a European sensibility. Of the First World War I knew, vaguely, that my two Irish grandfathers had gone to France to fight the Germans for the British. This knowledge only confirmed my customary personal calculus: Europe = Confusing = Irrelevant. Others conspired to strengthen the notion of an indecipherable world. In late 1963, my second-grade music teacher in Calgary had her charges at St. Pius X elementary school stomp around a classroom and sing, "We Are Marching to Pretoria." Just why we little western Canadians were supposed to be enthused about going off to war—in this instance the Boer War of 1899—is as confusing to me now as it was then.

Adults were always springing surprises, some of which came from as far out of left field as my father's remark about Turkey. A week or so before having to feign martial ardour about those impudent South Africans, we were solemnly sent home from school in the middle of the day because the slain young president of the United States had been a Catholic. We didn't understand, but we didn't complain, either. A week or so before that, we were instructed to bring big bars of Ivory soap to class. These we carved into crosses, not out of parochial school piety but out of a yearly duty to change the art table at the back of the room into a soapy graveyard. The full implications of this grotesque exercise didn't occur to us, just as the macabre meaning of Halloween may never really dawn on most of us until the very end of life. In fact, November 11 seemed to be a sequel to Halloween, only far less fun and far more puzzling. There usually was some sort of poetry reading over the PA system in the morning, often John McCrae's "In Flanders Fields," followed by an extended art period, then a recess during which we got to compare who was wearing the best paper poppy. By eleven o'clock, the kid who had carved the most symmetrical soap headstone would get to arrange the cemetery in the back of the class. At lunch, all was mercifully forgotten, and this inexplicable intrusion—what could a "Flanders" possibly be?— into our cocoon would be, in the new sense of the word, history.

Things might have remained at that stage for me, at least with regard to the First World War, had I not been drawn back across the ocean that my parents had crossed at mid-century. In 1981, I moved to Paris and eked out a picturesque existence teaching English, subtitling French movies, and writing articles on trends, imaginary and real, for magazines and newspapers. The Boomer millennium had come and gone in the intervening two decades, and history, despite our reflexive indifference, had not stopped or ceased to count. From Washington in the mid-1980s came news of a theory grandly known as the End of History, but that turned out to be nothing more than an ideological chortle over the mounting problems of Communist regimes. The past, with its nightmare of nationalisms and ethnic hatreds, had stubbornly refused to give up its ghosts.

It was about this time that a friend and I took a winter weekend away from Paris to visit the barren fields of the Somme. He had let the worm gnaw all the way to the core of his apple: an Ohio Boomer, he had somehow landed up on the Left Bank as a graduate student of French history. I, fresh from reading an account of the battles of 1916, was the dilettante, out for a field trip away from the city. Although I had lived for about three years amid the old stones and streets of Paris, I still thought of history, whenever I did think of it, as something that happened in books, or, at best, on plaques affixed to buildings. My undergraduate education, the usual liberal arts mix of literature and history, had led me to believe that the past existed in the stacks of the university library. My graduate student friend thought otherwise—for him, it seemed to exist on maps. On the train ride north from Paris to Amiens, and thence to Albert, he unfolded for me a masterwork of anally fixated exactitude on which he had carefully shaded the positions occupied by the English, German, and French armies on different days in July of 1916. If we didn't see anything of interest, at least we'd know precisely where we were.

THE FIELDS EAST of the town of Albert were newly plowed. It was a cold December day, clear and crisp, and no snow lay on the deep brown earth. We stood on the crest of a long ridge that sloped eastward, down to the village of La Boisselle about half a mile distant. On each side of La Boisselle there were slight depressions—from the map we knew these sunken fields formed what the attacking British troops had called Sausage and Mash valleys. From our vantage point atop the ridge, the gently rolling countryside between the Somme and Ancre Rivers stretched out like a dark rumpled blanket. There was a jagged pattern on it.

In some fields the soil gave way to skittish traces of white, slashes of brilliance against the dun landscape of Picardy in the winter; in others, the chalk had completely taken over, changing what should have been a long swatch of moist dark earth to a blinding rectangle of whiteness. We looked at the fields stretching to the horizon in front of us, then back at the map. Then back at the fields. There was an uncanny similarity between the shading on the one and the splotches on the other. Wherever the fighting had been heaviest, the shelling hardest—wherever the murderous standoff of trench warfare had taken place—the ground was bleached with tiny chalk pebbles plowed up from its shattered subsoil.

The earth had not yet recovered from the Great War. This angry band of white, though irregular and intermittent in places, snaked across the land as far as we could see, as if someone had taken a styptic pencil to an immense wound. The chasm between us and the past vanished. We were looking at the Western Front.

I was stunned. This slice of history was not the safe, irrelevant stuff that gathers dust in some archive. This was staring me right in the face. We walked down the hill toward La Boisselle, across the ground, I would later read, where the soldiers of the Tyneside Irish division marched on the morning of July 1, 1916. Of the 3,000 who left the trenches that day, struggling under the seventy-five pounds of equipment with which the

British army saw fit to saddle each attacking soldier, only about 200 survived unscathed. By the time we reached the village of La Boisselle the litter of war had become apparent everywhere. On a hedge sat two tattered gas masks that looked as if they had been recently disentangled from some piece of farm machinery. In muddy trails scored with the twin tire ruts of heavy tractors lay a cache of rusting bullets and barbed wire embedded in the earth. Beside a fence post at the corner of a field, a small group of unexploded shells stood to attention, still laden with menace after a lifetime spent underground. Farmers had left them there, as part of the so-called Iron Harvest that every season's plowing yields. A government explosives unit eventually carts all the shells away—several hundred tons a year—and detonates them in quarries.

The village itself was a familiar succession of tan-colored bungalows of recent construction—French real estate developers grandly call them *pavillons*—that marked La Boisselle as a newly resettled hamlet. Only here the bland predictability of European exurbia suddenly took a turn for the ominous. In the midst of the bungalows with their backyard swing sets stood a vacant lot that could not be anesthetized into the present. It was an expanse of tall tortured mounds rising in unlikely and unnatural ways from a heaving plane of pockmarks and craters. The pale green fuzz of grass and weeds that covered each contour did not hide the violence that had once been done there. It looked as if a raging sea had been frozen, then made land. In between the Danger and Keep Out signs I spotted a small mountain bike, lying there as if some heedless boy had just popped a wheelie and then been dragged home for a spanking. The rear wheel turned slowly in the slight wind, its spokes glinting in the cold December sunshine. Seeing it comforted me.

That weekend on the Somme—we trudged all over the map—gave me a strange sort of thrill that I didn't fully welcome. I feared I'd fallen victim to the exuberant nihilism of the battlefield enthusiast, and that soon I would be whooping with joy at coming across a trench in the forest, or a skeleton behind a barn. There is a sort of macho romance to the futility of war, an attraction to seeing things fall apart, born of the same impulse that makes setting fires or watching the wrecker's ball such a fun pastime for so many men. Visiting sites of significant bloodshed— braking to gawk at humanity's biggest smash-ups—seemed a habit better left to groupies of the military. And I knew, or at least I thought I knew, that infatuation with uniforms and battles was entirely foreign to me, given a family animus that verged on the fanatical. A reflexive hatred of the army formed the sole, unarticulated legacy of my grandfathers' Great

War experience. In our home, career soldiers were routinely referred to as "professional assassins," and in the Vietnam War years of the 1960s and early 1970s our mother, her three sons in their teens, daily congratulated herself for not having chosen to immigrate to the land of the domino theory and the draft. Even the Boy Scouts had been suspect, their badges and uniforms seen as the thin edge of the warrior wedge.

But what if learning about history led me, against all odds, to a love of war lore? To a geek passion for guts and guns, to fetishism about medals and stripes, to furtive erection at the sight of fighter aircraft, to anachronistic anger over enemies never met, to hand-over-the-heart hypocrisy at monuments to massacres, to voyeurism disguised as compassion, to the fetid bath of patriotic cliché—what if it led, in short, to the wooden-headed fellowship of war buffs? If that's where it was leading, then there was no point in being a lapsed amnesiac. My dinner companion may have been right to despise me, after all. History is for the dead, or for rednecks. Perhaps I would become the expatriate equivalent of a Civil War reenactor who spends his Sundays playing Johnny Reb and pining for slavery.

Perhaps not. I felt that there had been something else out there, at the Somme, something other than a temptation to yield to a boyish love of destruction. I had seen it. The scar of the Front pointed to a curiosity that I did not know I had. In the months following that visit, reading brought home to me some of the connections between a generation long dead and my own, between those who witnessed the start of a century and those who would see it out. (Not that they are all gone: In March of 1995, the literary supplements of newspapers celebrated the hundredth birthday of Ernst Jünger, fourteen times wounded in the Great War and author of the classic German war novel *In Stahlgewittern*, or *Storm of Steel.*) If initially the code of the past seemed as hard to crack as the strange turns of phrase that had stumped me as a child, it eventually revealed itself to be a compelling language of irony, bitterness, and great beauty. I could scarcely believe that these loud, vital, angry voices, the voices of my grandparents' generation, could have been so easily forgotten, that their experience could have left its imprint on the earth itself but no trace in our minds. Or almost none. Familiar expressions coined at the time popped out at me—"over the top," "nothing to write home about"—and half-remembered, perhaps half-suspected, snatches of poetry rose up from the pages of anthologies. The sensibility seemed excruciatingly immediate, as mordant and disillusioned and undated as the latest world-weary wisecrack currently exchanged on-line by ponytail capitalists and their slacker offspring. The famous opening to Guillaume Apollinaire's poem "*L'Adieu du Cavalier"* ("The Cavalier's Farewell") speaks for a generation made sardonic by its experience in hell:

> *Ah Dieu! que la guerre est jolie*
> *Avec ses chants ses longs loisirs*
>
> (Oh God! what a lovely war
> With its songs its long idle hours)

The sarcasm sounds newly minted. Less well known, but just as sadly universal, are the great poet's entreaties as he lay on his deathbed, fatally weakened by war wounds, in 1918: "Save me, doctor! I want to live! I still have so much to say!" Apollinaire, to choose but him as an example, had stepped out of the cobwebs of a forgotten college curriculum and become an immediate presence for me. In glimpsing the Front, even more than a lifetime after the war had taken place, I opened the door to a haunted house full of invisible acquaintances.

Then there was, as I learned from perusing some of the excellent World War I histories published in the past twenty years or so, what can be called the Importance of the War. Had I read them before going on that winter weekend hike, I might not have tread so lightly around the Somme, content just to marvel like some idiot surveyor at the physical traces the conflict had left. The Great War is a great divide, as well defined a boundary as the Western Front was on my friend's shaded map. First, but not foremost, were the political changes it helped engender. Even an incomplete list of them goes on and on: the fall of the Romanovs, the fall of the Ottomans, the fall of the Hohenzollerns, the fall of the Hapsburgs, the rise of Soviet Communism, the dress rehearsal of American hegemony, the dismemberment of Austro-Hungary, the creation of Poland, the creation of Yugoslavia, the creation of Czechoslovakia, the return of Alsace and Lorraine to France, the birth of nationalism in Australia, the birth of nationalism in New Zealand, the birth of nationalism in Canada, the revolt, independence, and partition of Ireland, the guarantee of a Jewish national homeland in Palestine, the creation of Turkey, the birth of Arab nationalism, the fall of the monarchical principle, the extension of voting rights to women, the introduction of income tax, the introduction of Prohibition, the acceptance of total war, the rise of Fascism, the rise of mass pacifism.

However earthshaking that list might once have been, many of its items seem unimportant now because another world war followed—and because a lot of water has flowed under the bridge since 1918. Boundaries have been drawn and redrawn, and almost all norms of decency broken. There is, however, another list to compile on the Importance of the War, which I've made from other encounters during my post-Somme war book binge. This time the great divide of the Great War is in the mind, and some of the items may sound embarrassingly familiar to any of my peers who believed his/her worldview to have sprung spontaneously to mind, *ex nihilo*, during a station break. It is generally accepted that the Great War and its fifty-two months of senseless slaughter encouraged, or amplified, among other things: the loss of a belief in progress, a mistrust of technology, the loss of religious faith, the loss of a belief in Western cultural superiority, the rejection of class distinctions, the rejection of traditional sexual roles, the birth of the Modern, the rejection of the past, the elevation of irony to a standard mode of apprehending the world, the unbuttoning of moral codes, and the conscious embrace of the irrational. Admittedly, the emphasis once again is on destruction, on disintegration, but not of the exploding car crash variety deplored earlier. It is far more serious—more punk—than that, and to be fascinated by it may betray an inner malevolence greater than the one tapped into by the guys watching a demolition derby on cable. On this second list, with few exceptions, absence wins. Liberating, insecure, ironic absence.

I closed the books. The Western Front was out there, ready for my pilgrimage, my own private hajj. There was a lot to think about, a lot to look for. This book follows that journey, or rather those journeys, along the Front. In concrete, historical terms, the Western Front stretched from the North Sea on the Belgian coast to the border of France and Switzerland, some 450 miles, between the autumns of 1914 and 1918. I walked the length of it in the summer of 1986, precisely seventy years after the war's worst period of murderous immobility. It was the Front as it stood in mid-1916 that I then attempted to trace, the time of stupendous, static carnage that is now meant whenever the phrase "Western Front" crops up in conversation. Wherever possible my path kept to what had been no-man's-land, the treacherous moonscape lying between the German and Allied trenches, where the scar of barbed wire and shell holes disfigured the face of Europe. My first hike, from mid-July to late September, was succeeded in subsequent years by quick forays to different parts of the Front whenever I got the chance. I went back to the Front, again and again.

What follows, then, is a record of frequent visits to a vanishing metaphor, a scrapbook of journeys made between 1985 and 1995. I did not go to the Front to lay wreaths, or to say again what has been so well said by writers closer to the conflict in both time and temperament than I could ever hope or want to be. Stirring words are for speeches, not for travelers with sore feet, self-doubt, or eyes that seldom see beyond the present. At times I went to the Front as an amateur historian, at other times as a map reader, a literary tourist, a picnicker, a boyfriend, a trend hound on holiday, a curiosity seeker, a (I'll admit it) weekend war buff, a family researcher, a Canadian, a hiker, a married man, but always as a Boomer, trying to figure out why I was reaching for something beyond the horizon of living memory. Perhaps I did it out of an impulse to "mark the spot," as described in Michael Ignatieff's splendid family history, *The Russian Album*:

> I still cannot shake off the superstition that the only past that is real, that exists at all, is the one contained within the memories of living people. When they die, the past they hold within them simply vanishes, and those of us who come after cannot inherit their experience, only preserve the myth of its existence. We can mark the spot where the cliff was washed away by the sea, but we cannot repair the wound the sea has made.

Flanders

1. Nieuport to Dixmude

U BENT HIER. You are here. Or, fancifully, you are twisted. A municipal map of Nieuport, Belgium, tells me where, and perhaps who, I am. I have arrived in Belgium from Paris today, ready to set off on a summer-long hike down a metaphor. My light backpack contains a fistful of maps, a change of clothes, a bottle of mineral water, a couple of novels, a six-pack of chewing gum, and a notebook for collecting trivia. I have come back to the Front.

The First World War has been preying on my thoughts ever since I visited the Somme in the dead of winter. Throughout the following spring I invariably steered conversations toward the trenches, like a tiresome old soldier who wears out his listener's patience by telling and retelling the same stories. Now, in the summer of 1986, my remaining friends have given me a silver hip flask and a compass for my thirtieth birthday—in case, one of them says hopefully, I get lost in no-man's-land.

Thanks to the city map, however, I know where I am. Here. This is the spot where the Western Front began. From 1914 to 1918, you could walk from Nieuport, on the North Sea coast, all the way to Switzerland, approximately 450 miles if you followed the serpentine meandering of the trenches, without ever sticking your head above ground. Several million men hunkered down in two long, parallel ditches and tried desperately to duck the fragments of steel and lead that whizzed overhead for four years. It was a nightmare, a monumental exercise in folly. A generation of young men dug a sinuous graveyard from the sea to the mountains, and proceeded to bury themselves and their certainties in it.

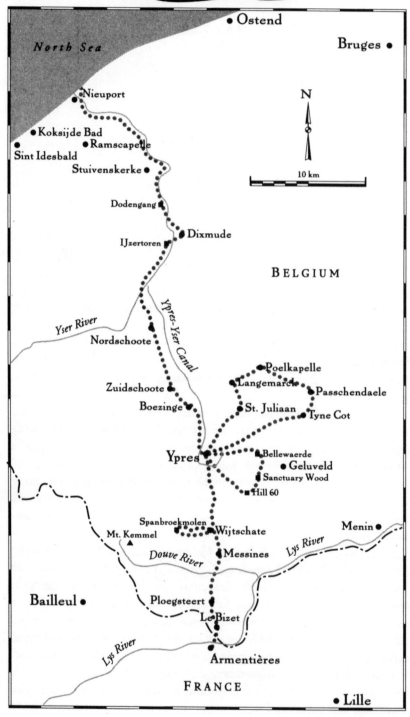

FLANDERS

North Sea

Ostend

Bruges

Nieuport

Koksijde Bad

Ramscapelle

Sint Idesbald

Stuivenskerke

Dodengang

Dixmude

IJzertoren

BELGIUM

Yser River

Ypres-Yser Canal

Nordschoote

Poelkapelle

Langemarck

Passchendaele

Zuidschoote

St. Juliaan

Tyne Cot

Boezinge

Ypres

Bellewaerde

Geluveld

Sanctuary Wood

Hill 60

Spanbroekmolen

Wijtschate

Menin

Mt. Kemmel

Messines

Lys River

Douve River

Bailleul

Ploegsteert

Le Bizet

Lys River

Armentières

FRANCE

Lille

N

10 km

•••• author's route

Nieuport—or as Flemish has it, Nieuwpoort Bad—is the place where they ran out of land.

I finish the last of my mayonnaise-smeared french fries and wander out of the shadow of the high-rise apartment blocks on Nieuport's main street. Trams click past with understated Low Countries efficiency. The loud colors of leisure rule the sidewalks. Clutches of beefy teens stroll the avenue in sweatshirts emblazoned in Ginza English: "Morgan Sisters Scoop Canada Best Hockey Wyoming" seems to be a favorite. At the point where the River Yser meets the sea there is a paved promenade overlooking a sandy beach. A fitness instructor is leading a group of laughing young girls through an aerobics routine as Madonna's "Papa Don't Preach" plays on an unseen loudspeaker. Beyond them, out to sea, a car ferry plows a gray-green path toward the horizon. This Belgian riviera, a collection of brave little resorts with names odd-looking to the untutored Anglo eye (Koksijde Bad, Sint Idesbald, Knokke, Heist, Nieuwpoort Bad), does not appear to be the type of place where epochal change could have occurred. Yet the girls are jumping and pumping on a spot where an era collapsed, and the Flemish-speaking families thronging the boardwalk tread a historical fault line.

Before the Great War, the thinking ran, this part of the world was a sunny Arcadia of perpetual progress, a sort of Merchant-Ivory drawing room with exquisite manners and delicacy of feeling. Europe was a summit of moral sophistication that towered over the bumpkins, dwarfs, and savages inhabiting the other continents. After the war, the world became a cruel, cynical place, riven by ideology, hatred, and bloodlust. And that was not all. Love itself had been extinguished in 1914. The fairest, finest summer to have graced Europe since the age of chivalry was followed by a century peopled by hollow men intent on mass murder. *U bent hier*, indeed.

The best-known utterance about the Great War, attributed to Edward Grey on the eve of the conflict, typifies the feeling. "The lamps are going out all over Europe," the British Foreign Secretary is supposed to have sighed as the armies began to march. "We shall not see them lit again in our lifetimes." After the war, after the fondly imagined good old days before 1914 were seen to be forever irretrievable, the sentiment became stronger. F. Scott Fitzgerald's *Tender Is the Night* contains a paragraph to that effect which has been so often quoted in studies of the war as to have become scriptural in its authority. Before I leave the shore at Nieuport to walk down the Front, the passage must be invoked. It will be my traveler's prayer. In the novel, Dick Diver visits the trenches less than a decade after the armistice and announces to his companions:

This western front business couldn't be done again, not for a long time
. . . This took religion and years of plenty and tremendous sureties and
the exact relation that existed between the classes . . . You had to have a
whole-souled sentimental equipment going back further than you could
remember. You had to remember Christmas, and postcards of the Crown
Prince and his fiancee, and little cafes in Valence and beer gardens in Unter
den Linden and weddings at the mairie, and going to the Derby, and your
grandfather's whiskers . . . This kind of battle was invented by Lewis
Carroll and Jules Verne and whoever wrote Undine, and country deacons
bowling and marraines in Marseilles and girls seduced in the back lanes of
Wurttemberg and Westphalia. Why, this was a love battle—there was a
century of middle-class love spent here . . . All my beautiful lovely safe
world blew itself up here with a great gust of high-explosive love.

BEYOND A TANGLE of road junctions and canals south of Nieuport the
countryside finally stretches out in front of me, that "great gust" at the
onset of the century having long ago blown off shore and out of memory.
If anything is borne on the wind this nineteenth of July, 1986, it is a few
stray embers from the blast at Chernobyl three months earlier, as explosive a symbol of human incompetence as any created by the military
mind. That too will fade into obscurity eventually, but not for another
generation or so.

For the moment, the simple glory of a blue sky forbids thoughts of
mud or war or oblivion. The flat, almost featureless plain of Flanders
looks neither threatening nor welcoming today, like a landscape you
could ignore from a speeding car. The morning sun beats down, present
and immediate. To my left the Yser, its banks two obedient concrete
strips; to my right, cow pastures drying pungently in the heat.

I could be anywhere, but I'm instantly reminded that I am not. The
traveler on the road out of Nieuport, south to Dixmude, is almost
immediately met by the vanguard of the sad column of memorials and
cemeteries that marches across northern France and Belgium. This con-
fetti of slaughter—an isolated graveyard in a farmer's field, a forlorn stela
beside a cow track, a rusted plaque in a forest clearing—lies lightly on
the landscape, a ubiquitous presence whose stone keening is now inaud-
ible to all but the very old. The first graveyard I come across is British.
Enclosed by a low, redbrick wall, it holds rows of off-white headstones,
each inscribed with a religious, regimental, or national symbol. Flower
beds have been planted and maintained, in keeping with the Commonwealth War Graves Commission's mandate to make gardens of its many
properties. I jot down the inscription of the first headstone I read. For

me, he'll represent the ten million other soldiers who perished in the Great War:

28237 Private
E. R. Cadogan
Lancashire Fusiliers
29th August 1917 Age 19
He died that we might live

To one side is a plinth embossed with a sword and engraved with a collective epitaph taken from Ecclesiastes: "Their name liveth forevermore." A sense of failure hangs in the air.

The line of high-rises on the coast shrinks to toy size as the day progresses. Ahead all is inoffensive pastoral flatness, except a point far to the south, where what appears to be an enormous water tower dances in the heat haze. Fields of beetroot and mustard come one after the other. If I stop and make a full 360-degree turn, a dozen or so tawny-colored steeples can be seen poking skyward, signs of distant villages. Aside from the cows grazing in a Zen trance near the road's edge, sweating packs of sports cyclists are my only occasional companions.

The meanders of the Yser lead me through a few villages with names longer and livelier than their main streets: Schoorbakke, Stuivenskerke. The unplanted borders of the fields between them, despite the heat of midsummer, still bloom with a profusion of wildflowers. Occasionally the homely company of buttercups gives way to a scarlet burst of poppies. I pick one, and am almost surprised to find the bloom does not conceal a lapel pin. My notebook closes over its lurid red petals, and I continue southward under a blistering afternoon sun. Soon I am limping, an urban tenderfoot already bested by a few miles of reclaimed marsh.

On the outskirts of Dixmude, I stop into a bar for a beer. Thoughts of rural Belgium are banished once my eyes adjust to the dim light. The bamboo-covered walls show posters of basset hounds, Tyrolean castles, and Venice's Piazza San Marco. A rendering of the Virgin and Child feeding mendicant pigeons looks over a collection of beery knickknacks scattered round the room. The one at my table, a porcelain statuette, takes as its theme the incompatibility of keg draining and male sexual arousal. Normally I would cluck appreciatively out of tavern etiquette, but not here, not in the expectant silence that has greeted my entrance. The Flemings at the bar, their eyes staring out of great steaks of faces, look as if they've just lumbered in from posing for Brueghel the Elder. There is a pause as they take my measure, then the room rings once again with their bellowed repartee. I like this jolly spot. It's called Dodengang—the Trench of Death.

Across from the bar is the Dodengang itself, a preserved stretch of trench that runs for about three hundred yards along the left bank of the Yser. The sandbags that make up its walls (the front wall was called the parapet; the rear, the parados) have been filled with cement, so that the fortification can now withstand the assaults of tourism. On the firestep, the platform from which soldiers fired over the parapet, a few wild poppies compete for attention with discarded Coke cans and potato chip bags. Like all trenches, this one zigzags in a saw-tooth pattern, to buffer the impact of explosions and to prevent an attacking enemy from having a clear field of fire should a portion of the trench be captured. Thus, the elaborate ditch was even more claustrophobic than it might have been, for the man in it could see only his traverse, that is, his section of the trench between two saw-teeth. He could of course step up and look out over no-man's-land, or behind his own lines, but that would be foolhardy. In the quiet months of the war that saw no great battles or offensives, the British army alone lost 7,000 men a week, what it termed "wastage," to snipers and random shellfire. Not all these casualties were from wounds, however. Rotting feet—called trench foot—and venereal disease took their toll as well.

I stand on the firestep and look out over the river and fields beyond it. There is scarcely a sound, except the odd plop of a fish in the water. Imagining the Front is difficult, if not impossible, even here in an old trench. A British officer, quoted in historian Martin Gilbert's *First World War*, wrote to his friend Winston Churchill in 1914 about a place like the Dodengang, in which "crouch lines of men, in brown or grey or blue, coated with mud, unshaven hollow-eyed with the continual strain, unable to reply to the everlasting run of shells hurled at them from three, four, five or more miles away . . ." The officer also described for Churchill the Western Front in its infancy:

> Imagine a broad belt, ten miles or so in width, stretching from the Channel to the German frontier near Basle, which is positively littered with the bodies of men and scarified with their rude graves; in which farms, villages and cottages are shapeless heaps of blackened masonry; in which fields, roads and trees are pitted and torn and twisted by shells and disfigured by dead horses, cattle, sheep and goats, scattered in every attitude of repulsive distortion and dismemberment.

The writer was a Fleming, but not of the Flanders variety. A British MP and a major in the army, Valentine Fleming died in battle in 1917, leaving behind a nine-year-old son, Ian, who would in turn bequeath James Bond to the world. The father, in his description of the Front, gives us the sad scene that would haunt the imagination of his peers until the end of their lives. Although immune to the glamour of violence, they would nonetheless encourage their children to go to war when the time came. The Dodengang stretches well into the twentieth century.

2. *Dixmude*

The main square of Dixmude is surrounded by a Germanic gingerbread of gabled houses. Its central Grote Markt, awash in a sea of parked cars, holds scrupulously maintained monuments to a Belgian general and to the man in the moon. The square's cobblestones are well scrubbed, uniform, obedient. The flowers in the flower boxes are petunias, the café tables are rigid plastic forms, and the radiating streets are lined with cookie-cutter redbrick rowhouses straight out of a British suburban sitcom. If Dixmude were a person, it would wear socks with sandals.

At the tourist office on the square, posters suggest that Dixmude is "The Heart of the Flat Country." Once my turn at the counter comes, I ask, in French, whether there are any vacant hotel rooms in town. After a pause, the blond hostess replies that everything is booked solid.

"What, nothing?"

"That's right," she says briskly, "nothing at all."

I ask her if there are any hotels in neighboring towns, whether I could get a bus to them. My French must have faltered, for she looks me in the eye and says, "Are you Belgian?"

When I tell her no, a transformation takes place. The wall of indifference vanishes. Concerned and motherly now, she leads me by the arm to a seat by her desk and asks me to wait a few moments. Of course we can find you a place to stay the night; Dixmude is crowded for the holiday weekend but we can phone around. Please, make yourself comfortable, m'sieur.

Thus I learn the dangers of addressing a Fleming in Belgium's other official language, without so much as an excuse-my-French. This proof of animosity between Belgium's Flemish-speaking Flemings and French-speaking Walloons gives me a guilty little thrill—having grown up a Canadian, I feel at home whenever I encounter bickering over language. The French speakers of Belgium used to have the upper hand in business, finance, politics, and the arts of the nation, but now demographic trends and economic changes have tilted in favor of the Flemish speakers, who are tired of being portrayed as oafs by the Walloons. That age-old habit of derision has long since spread south to France, where the telling of Belgian jokes is now a national pastime. These are often enjoyably stupid, as in the story of the public address system at Paris's Gare du Nord: "The train for London departs at 8:15; the train for Berlin departs at 9:15; and the train for Brussels departs when the little hand is on the ten . . ."

Such jokes don't go down too well in Flanders, especially if told by a Walloon. Understandably, militant Flemings want respect; unfortunately, their loudest voice is the Vlaams Blok (Flemish Block), the kind of truly repulsive party of racist xenophobes that European political culture excels at producing. In Dixmude, the Great War plays a leading role in the Blok's theater of ethnic rage. What, from a distance, I took to be an enormous water tower wavering in the heat haze turns out to be a twenty-seven-story-tall memorial to the First World War that doubles as a shrine for the extreme Right. The IJzertoren (Yser Tower), a great brown truncheon rising out of the plain, looks the part.

Originally erected to honor Belgian soldiers who died on the Yser, the tower gradually became a rallying point for local patriots. Flemish veterans of the First World War claimed that their fallen comrades had been wantonly sacrificed by the Belgian army's French-speaking officer class. Thus the Yser war monument automatically became a symbol of aggrieved nationhood. This was especially true after March 15, 1946, when the original IJzertoren was unceremoniously blown up, allegedly by anti-Flemish dynamite. The spectacular act of vandalism, spurred by indignation over the pro-Nazi sympathies of many Flemish nationalists during the Second World War, naturally engendered more resentment. Using the masonry from the original tower, the people of Dixmude constructed on the site a modest peace arch. Beside that the massive new IJzertoren rose, inaugurated in 1962 by a bevy of bishops and old soldiers. On its side is an acrostic:

A
V V K
V

This stands for *Alles voor Vlaanderen, Vlaanderen voor Christus* (All for Flanders, Flanders for Christ), a mix of Musketeer and Crusader sentiment that pushes the correct reactionary buttons for the extremists who hold rallies here. They are sometimes joined by like-minded fellows from France, Britain, and Germany in gatherings at the foot of the tower where, presumably, everyone compares skull tattoos and trades Adolf and Benito bubble-gum cards.

I feel distinctly queasy as I pay my money to ascend the IJzertoren. Here in Dixmude, the Old World seems incurably steeped in old ways, and the contemplation of the past reserved for people bearing grudges. I have barely begun my journey and already I find myself wondering whether visiting the Western Front merely adds another small brick to the edifice of Reaction. Perhaps it's better to ignore history, for history is too often used as a defense of the ignoble. The know-nothing ugly American exists, but so too does the do-nothing ugly European, who constantly invokes the past as an excuse for his present. We've always done it this way, so it must be right; we've never had your kind living amongst us, so we can't allow you to stay; my father hated your father, so I hate you.

I share the elevator ride with a small boy and his parents. We are enclosed in the heart—the dark heart—of the flat country. The problem of history and hate continues to nag. When the cult of the past involves a war, the freedom to speculate shrinks, for the more destructive the activity, it seems, the more zealous its curators. Even far from the battlefield in North America, remembrance of wars past regularly brings out the thought police. Veterans' groups act as self-appointed censors of large swaths of history, shrieking like outraged virgins whenever the record is challenged. In Canada in 1992, veterans tried to quash a TV documentary about the Allied bombing of Germany in the Second World War. In 1995 the Smithsonian Institution canceled its Enola Gay exhibit under similar pressure. Intolerance came disguised as warrior virtue.

The museum at the top of the tower, organized around the central shaft and composed of mementos evoking life in the trenches, is dusty and deserted. The Fleming family and I head for the windows to look out over a patchwork of green meadows and redbrick villages lying far below. Guy de Maupassant once said that he liked the view from the Eiffel Tower because it was the only place in the city from which he couldn't see the Eiffel Tower. The same holds true, *mutatis mutandis*, of the prospect from the IJzertoren. To the north is the blue blanket of the sea. To the south are the first timid signs of relief in the Flanders plain. A modest, wooded ridge rises beyond the distant spires of a large town. The scene is disingenuously ordinary, for the town, Ypres, and its surroundings form one of the most terrible landscapes of the twentieth century.

I take the elevator down. The distasteful connotations of the tower have faded, as have visions of aiding the mastodons of conservatism by pursuing this journey. War, French Premier Georges Clemenceau is supposed to have said in the wake of a battlefield debacle, is too important a matter to be left to the generals. The same could be said of the past. It needn't be surrendered to the nostalgic and the intolerant, to the ugly European, to the frat boys of neo-fascism, or to the antidemocratic mullahs of military memory. The past belongs to everyone. It's too important to be left to the professionals.

3. Dixmude to Ypres

Strange popping noises punctuate my walk out of the village of Nord-schoote on the road to Ypres. Pfft! Pfft!

Silence.

I take a few more steps, then hear them again: Pfft! Pfft! The detonations are loud but slightly muffled, as if coming from a great distance. Is it hunting season? Murder month? Has some well-armed cuckold come home too early?

I squint into the flat afternoon light, searching for a better explanation out in the pale green mantle that unfurls to the horizon. My bewilderment is noticed and misinterpreted as telescopic lechery. A couple of girls bent over double at some vague agricultural task straighten up and wave at me from the middle of a field. I wave back, embarrassed.

Pfft! Pfft!

The usual parallel about distant echoes is now inescapable. What had been a silent landscape now rings with this faint cannonade, like a far-off and feeble remnant of one of the most deafening dins in all of history. With every step southward, toward the villages of Zuidschoote and Boezinge, I walk toward what was once known as the Ypres Salient, a great C-shaped curve in the Western Front. Seldom, if ever, has any place on earth been rocked by so many millions of pounds of whizzing steel and high explosives.

For four years the Germans held the low ridge to the east of Ypres. Their lines were on the outside of the C. Inside that letter, bulging out toward them, were the British and their allies, an entire army of sitting ducks. They could be fired on from the front and from either side by an enemy who had the distinct advantage of holding the higher ground.

Pfft! Pfft! The sound seems to be growing louder the farther south I go.

The Ypres Salient was a remarkable shooting gallery. Both sides took part in hellish artillery duels that tore up the waterlogged ground and transformed it into a foul seething swamp. The Salient's defining moment was the week of July 25 to July 31, 1917, when the British army fired off 4,283,550 shells (or 107,000 *tons* of metal) along a front twelve miles wide, then had its infantry try to wade through—in the rain—the ensuing soupy morass in the face of sustained machine-gun fire. Defining, because this place is one of the three or four on the Western Front, along with Verdun, the Chemin des Dames, and the Somme, where the criminal stupidity of the First World War still seems manifest, even after the passing of eighty years.

But I'm getting ahead of myself, in more ways than one. I sit down by the road outside Boezinge and massage my feet. A squadron of mosquitoes arrives from a nearby puddle to keep me company. The mysterious pops continue fitfully, farm dogs bark, cars whoosh past, the bugs start biting. What am I doing here?

No, that's the wrong question. What were the British and the Germans doing here?

PFFT! PFFT!

Two shots were fired at 10:34 A.M., on June 28, 1914, in front of Schiller's Delicatessen in Sarajevo. Gavrilo Princip, the nineteen-year-old Bosnian Serb holding the gun, mortally wounded Franz Ferdinand, the Habsburg heir to the imperial throne of Austria-Hungary, and his wife, Sophie. When they died, about half an hour after Princip had blasted away at point-blank range, the nineteenth century entered its death throes. The event was a fluke: The archduke's driver made a wrong turn onto Appel Quay and had to back up, right into the sights of the scrawny Serb student with the world-historical mission. But for the chauffeur's inept driving, the continent-wide car wreck of the next four years might have been avoided.

Earlier in the morning of that June 28, the victims had been celebrating their fourteenth wedding anniversary. Since Sophie's soon-to-be-spilt blood was not blue enough—she did not have the requisite degrees, or *quartiers*, of nobility—to be accorded formal honors at the Viennese court, her doting archduke of a husband made a point of going to places where she could be given royal treatment. Sarajevo was just such a city. As every protocol martinet in central Europe knew, when Franz Ferdinand acted in a military capacity, in this instance as Inspector General of the Austro-Hungarian army on a tour of the Bosnian capital's garrison, he— and his wife—had to be given the full panoply of feathered deference, decorous bowing, and stylized scraping that Habsburg vanity required. Franz loved his wife, and the cream-puff perquisites of his office.

Princip loved his cause. June 28, 1914, was also the 525th anniversary of the Battle of Kosovo, the resounding defeat that Serbs still perversely celebrate as their nation's brush with greatness and respectability. Today they might mark the occasion by gunning down demonstrators—as they did in Sarajevo, to open the latest bout of barbarity in Bosnia; in Princip's day the anniversary usually called for beetle-browed acts of sedition against foreign overlords. In this the Bosnian Serbs were helped, surreptitiously, by their brethren in Belgrade, who had enjoyed independence in a sovereign Serbia (or "Servia," as it was often called) ever since an earlier conflict had wrested their territory from the control of the Ottoman Turks. And everyone in Europe, then as now, got excited when real estate changed hands.

In fact, all five of the Great Powers—Britain, France, Russia, Austro-Hungary, Germany—were talking Turkey. The Divan, as the Ottoman court was known, had once controlled the Balkans, but Turkey was now the so-called "Sick Man of Europe," a tottering empire no longer able to restrain its restive peoples. As outsiders greedily looked on, insiders weakened the Ottoman presence in Europe. A vocal, dissident faction, impatient with the dotty despots in the Topkapi Palace, agitated for modernization under the name of the Young Turks, a term that entered turn-of-the-century English to describe any collection of lean and hungry hotheads.

This Balkan cocktail of Young Turks (many of whom were Bosnian Muslims), angry Serbs, and smitten Habsburgs was the brew that sent the Old World on its self-destructive bender of 1914–18. Even though Prussian Chancellor Otto von Bismarck had famously adjudged the Balkans undeserving of "the bones of a single Pomeranian grenadier," and every political commentator worth his postprandial cigar had pointed out that, *pace* the English humorist Saki, the benighted region produced more politics than could be consumed locally, it was indeed the mountainous, hidebound, backward Balkans that ushered in—and would later usher out—the twentieth century.

To review: Austria was Hungary, so it took a piece of Turkey. The piece was Bosnia-Herzegovina, annexed in 1908. The powers-that-reclined in Istanbul, enfeebled by recent wars and undermined by the Young Turks, could do nothing to prevent their former possession from slipping away. Serb nationalists in the region were not so listless—they, like most Europeans, knew that Bosnia's latest landlord was far from robust. Istanbul's empire might be a frail old man, but Vienna's was no youngster either, the government of its eighty-four-year-old Emperor

Franz Josef renowned for comic opera intrigues and mind-numbing bureaucracy. Serb nationalists in Belgrade and Sarajevo, like their descendants Slobodan Milošević and Radovan Karadžić, saw a power vacuum and dreamed of filling it with a Greater Serbia. The most radical of them formed *Ujedinjeje ili Smrt* (Union or Death), a terrorist group also known as the Black Hand. Run by Colonel Dragutin Dimitrijevic, a loose cannon in the Belgrade government, the organization abetted would-be assassins wherever they served the cause of Serbian nationhood. Dimitrijevic, a bald colossus who today would not look out of place wrestling on TV, went by the name of Apis, the potent bull in the pantheon of ancient Egypt. Apis supplied Princip and his fellow conspirators with the guns to do the dirty deed in Sarajevo. Thus it was Apis and his bloody-minded Black Hand, the template for all the semi-official dirty tricks squads to have enlivened recent history, that delivered the ultimate insult to the spluttering autocrats of Austria.

I PUT MY socks and boots back on and walk through Boezinge. Someone has had the good sense to plant shade trees in the middle of the village. Boezinge was once a hallowed name in the French region of Brittany because thousands of Bretons fought in the fields to the north and west of here. Who else passed this way? French, Senegalese, Algerians, Moroccans, Portuguese, Indians, Chinese, Thais, Irish, Scottish, Welsh, Austrians, Bavarians, Saxons, Prussians, South Africans, Australians, New Zealanders, Canadians, Americans—a roll call of battalions brought to this corner of Belgium because of a murder in the Balkans. It was not the proverbial "shot heard round the world" (that, according to Ralph Waldo Emerson, occurred in Lexington, Massachusetts, in April 1775), but Princip's bullet of June 28, 1914, had the distinction of being the first of billions to be fired in the Great War.

Still, the original question remains unaddressed—why were the British and Germans here, in this shooting gallery Salient? What could have linked the fate of the two nineteen-year-olds: Princip, the trigger-happy Bosnian Serb, and Private Cadogan, the British teenager buried in Belgium? British soldiers took to singing a pithy answer to such questions. The tune is *Auld Lang Syne*:

> We're here because we're here
> Because we're here
> Because we're here

We're here because we're here
Because we're here
Because we're here.

Sing it to yourself, and you'll see what a satisfying explanation it is. There were, of course, official reasons.

When the authorities in Vienna learned of Franz Ferdinand's murder, they saw a golden opportunity to squelch the upstart on their southern border. Foreign Minister Leopold von Berchtold, the man most at fault for the ensuing debacle, issued the Serbian government a blisteringly severe ultimatum, the terms of which were tantamount to surrendering sovereignty. The advisers of Serbia's King Peter, suitably cowed by the Habsburg tantrum, agreed to comply with all of the demands contained in von Berchtold's ultimatum save one—the order giving Austrian police a free hand on Serbian soil. Rather like an old man buying a red sports car, the Austro-Hungarian empire then declared war on Serbia. By telegram, in French. It was 1:00 p.m., July 28, 1914.

The story now leaves the precincts of south-central Europe to involve the rest of the continent. Over the years a system of alliances had developed to transform international affairs into a shifting, intrigue-ridden round of diplomatic skirmishing that gave a civilized veneer to the cutthroat commercial rivalries of the time. Crises in Morocco and the Balkans came and went in the first decade of the century, causing mustaches to moisten and horses to snort, but large-scale wars had always been averted. The game of diplomacy was wonderful and glamorous and cosmopolitan and aristocratic, but in the summer of 1914 it fell apart. The well-bred grandees in the chancelleries and foreign offices drafted their customary cables and issued their usual exquisitely worded warnings, all to no avail. In its final, prewar stages, diplomacy slipped out of civilian control to fall in step with the implacable logic of military timetables. When that happened, the traditional ruling classes of Europe became history, in the Boomer sense of the word. They had delivered their citizenry into the maw of the industrial battlefield. At war's end, they would not be forgiven.

The road to the Western Front began in the east. Austria's bullying of Serbia induced Russia to order the mobilization of its troops. Pan-Slavic nationalists in Petrograd (as St. Petersburg was then called) viewed the Slavs of the Balkans as their protégés. The armies of Czar Nicholas II headed by the millions toward the western borders of Russia. Germany, the industrial and military powerhouse under the somewhat loopy leadership of Kaiser Wilhelm II, was aghast. The government in Berlin had foolishly given its ally Austria a "blank check"—that is, a guarantee of assistance no matter what the outcome of its saber-rattling policy toward the Serbs. Now, panic-stricken at the results, Germany demanded that Russia stop its mobilization.

This was easier demanded than done. Mobilization was a machine years in the planning that required massive resources to effect quickly, so you couldn't just stop it halfway and run all the troop trains backward— unless you were willing to leave yourself defenseless in the ensuing chaos. Naturally, Russia refused to do this.

Not that getting your army up to strength and poised on your borders necessarily meant you were going to war. When France, an ally of Russia at the time, began mobilizing in the last days of July, it was preparing for hostilities, not starting them. Likewise Austria-Hungary, Russia, Serbia, Great Britain, and Turkey. This may seem like hairsplitting, but it's not—there's a big difference between pointing a pistol at someone and actually shooting him. In only one country was this distinction not made: Germany.

In the 1890s a Prussian military planner, Count Alfred von Schlieffen, had rightly surmised that Germany might one day have to face hostile armies in both the east and the west. He, like all German policy makers, feared *Einkreisung*, or encirclement. Positing that his country could not wage a victorious war on two fronts at once, Schlieffen masterminded a scheme whereby the Kaiser's armies would deliver a knockout blow to France, then race over the rails to deal with the Russians. Speed was of the essence for the Schlieffen Plan. When German fighting forces mobilized they would automatically blast their way into France. And, to get there, they would surprise everyone by marching through neutral Belgium. So what if this bald violation of treaties brought in Britain against them? As a German military planner had once said of the prospect of the British sending their small professional army to the Continent: "If the British land, we'll arrest them."

THE TOWN OF Ypres draws nearer, both in this narrative of 1914 and on this day in 1986. The spires of churches and civic buildings are now clearly visible to the south, pointing skyward in artificial medieval splendor.

Pfft! Pfft!

The detonations are too loud to ignore. I make one last detour off the road to plumb the mystery of the Salient pops. A small, boxlike object lying a few paces away emits a deafening Pfft! Pfft! as I approach. How humiliating. The source of my World War I blasts is a scarecrow speaker, placed in the ground to startle birds away from freshly seeded fields. Do the people of Flanders like playing mind games with obsessed hikers? First the Dodengang bar; now this. I return to the roadway, convinced the pops are beginning to sound derisive.

Still, the Flanders I've come to see has not entirely disappeared. Beside the Ypres-Yser Canal, almost in the shadow of a traffic cloverleaf, another weirdly immaculate British cemetery awaits inspection. A plaque informs the traveler that this is the Essex Farm Cemetery, where John McCrae visited the makeshift grave of a friend on May 3, 1915, noticed some poppy blooms blowing in the breeze, and then became inspired to write "In Flanders Fields." In so doing the doctor from Guelph, Ontario, made this spot emblematic of the Great War for a large part of the English-speaking world. Originally published in *Punch* to great acclaim, the poem is now pointedly unloved by literary critics and anthology compilers. Of the final stanza's famous exhortation, which begins "Take up our quarrel with the foe," Paul Fussell, in his peerless *The Great War and Modern Memory*, has written: "We finally see—and with a shock—what the last six lines really are: they are a propaganda argument—words like *vicious* and *stupid* would not seem to go too far—against a negotiated peace."

Despite the critical abuse, the sentimental old poem has shown great staying power in popular culture. It, along with the songs "It's a Long Way to Tipperary" and "Over There" and Remarque's novel *All Quiet on the Western Front*, may be said to form the final fading pages in the scrapbook of First World War cliché. As such, the Essex Farm Cemetery, its beribboned wreaths shivering in the wake of onrushing afternoon traffic, now doubles as a shrine to a vanished syllabus. The cannons of the Salient have long been silenced, as has its canon.

THE SCHLIEFFEN PLAN laid out the route of attack. The bulk of the German army—its right wing—would swing through Belgium, skirt the Atlantic coast, pass west and then south of Paris. By doing this it could eventually encircle the French armies that, Schlieffen had once again correctly surmised, would be busy throwing themselves at well-fortified defensive lines to regain Alsace and Lorraine. Indeed, since the debacle of the Franco-Prussian War of 1870, in which France had lost Alsace and Lorraine, the general staff of its army had thought of little else but recovering the two provinces from the Germans. Out of this keen sense of injured pride came a military doctrine that elevated the attack to an almost quasi-mystical status. Attacking *à outrance* (to the utmost), no matter what the terrain or the strength of the opposition, entailed wearing the dashing but conspicuous red trousers and blue coat of the infantryman and running directly at enemy machine-gun fire, presumably protected from injury by one's warrior insouciance, or *élan*. Such were the pitifully inadequate tactics taught at elite French military academies. Their strategic thinking, which had been dignified by the name of "Plan XVII," called for remorseless, predictable, frontal attacks into Alsace and Lorraine. As in 1870 and 1940, in August 1914 the French were hopelessly outsmarted by the Germans.

Under the command of Joseph Jacques Césaire Joffre, an avuncular officer with a seemingly boundless appetite for casualties, the French army went to the slaughter, launching attack after attack à outrance until entire battalions were annihilated. In the summer and fall of 1914, France lost as many men on the battlefield as the American army would in all of the twentieth century. Their conscript army was thrown away by incompetent generalship. In the month of August alone, more than 210,000 Frenchmen died in the headlong offensives of Plan XVII. The bloodbath was more than appalling, it was absurd.

Joffre blamed his subordinates. He demoted dozens of generals and sent them to the city of Limoges for reassignment: whence the French verb *limoger* for any high-profile firing. According to many accounts, Joffre's imperturbable demeanor in the face of horrific losses sometimes reassured but more often repelled. The sacredness of the general's stomach—Joffre always had two well-cooked, uninterrupted feasts a day, no matter how dire the military situation—contrasted dramatically with his callow disregard for the lives of his soldiers.

While Joffre minded his digestion and sent tens of thousands to their doom in the east, 750,000 Germans were walking toward France from the north. As the Kaiser's armies advanced through Belgium, they carried out a highly publicized policy of *Schrecklichkeit*, or "Frightfulness," meant to discourage any attempts at civilian resistance. Hostages were taken and shot, and cities were burned, a brutal overture for the total war to come. The Belgians became a nation of refugees, crowding the roads south to France and the boats over to England. Of the hundred thousand or so who reached Britain, the most famous of the lot never really landed there at all because he was, in point of fact, fictional. Like his unfortunate compatriots, Hercule Poirot, Agatha Christie's sleuth, was chased from his homeland by Schrecklichkeit. (Why else would a Belgian detective be living in London?)

The Belgian refugees were welcomed as heroes. In Britain enthusiasm for the war ran high. Shopkeepers with German surnames had their businesses patriotically looted, and, in just the first month of a recruiting drive for a volunteer army, half a million young Britons rushed to sign up to avenge what was called "poor little Belgium." It is difficult to imagine the naïveté of expectations, the trust in one's country, the excitement of being young in that summer of 1914. Rupert Brooke, genteel England's undisputed golden boy for both his godlike looks and his felicitous way with words, came to symbolize the vaguely homoerotic ideal of youth in arms. Previously he had been the athletic, intelligent, effortlessly irresistible upper-crust Brit, a sort of ur–Calvin Klein male; now he was a noble Galahad off to grapple with the awful Hun. The opening to the first of Brooke's "1914" sonnets, once committed to memory by a nation swooning over his early death (in 1915), then subsequently ignored out of embarrassment at the work's politically incorrect martial ardor, deserves to be cited at least one more time before it no longer catches the heart. The end of the nineteenth century is speaking directly to us when Brooke limpidly writes of August 1914:

> Now, God be thanked Who has matched us with His hour,
> And caught our youth, and wakened us from sleeping,
> With hand made sure, clear eye, and sharpened power,
> To turn, as swimmers into cleanness leaping,
> Glad from a world grown old and cold and weary,
> Leave the sick hearts that honour could not move,
> And half-men, and their dirty songs and dreary,
> And all the little emptiness of love!

On August 23, 1914, a small force of the British army fought the advancing Germans at Mons, Belgium. It was the first time the British had fought in Europe since defeating Napoleon at nearby Waterloo, ninety-nine years previously. Although ludicrously outnumbered, since neither the French nor the British command had yet figured out that the main German offensive was coming through Belgium, they held off their attackers for a full day before beating a tactical retreat. The engagement, minor in comparison to the suicidal French maneuvers in Lorraine, nonetheless loomed large in the collective imagination of the British Isles. My favorite of the many Mons stories concerns the preparations for the first battle by a British sergeant, as related in oral historian Lyn Macdonald's *1914*. Ordered to post four lookouts to warn of an eventual German attack on the town, the officer sets up only three and is later forced to explain his negligence to an enraged superior officer: "I'm sorry, Sir. I didn't think it necessary to post one. The enemy would hardly come from that direction. It's private property, Sir."

This quaint attitude, straight out of a Galsworthy novel, would change radically in the following weeks, becoming scarcely contained panic. The British and the French fell back in desperation as the size of the German onslaught coming from the north dawned at last on the dim minds sharing dinner with Joffre. The French commander, unflappable as ever, ordered a full-scale retreat so that his shattered armies could regroup and finally do something other than die in futile assaults in the east of the country. In the meantime, the Germans continued their march south and came closer and closer to Paris. When Alexander von Kluck, the commander of the now tired 350,000-man corps on the extreme right of the German lines, elected to go east rather than west of the French capital and cross the River Marne, the reinforced Allied legions wheeled about and attacked. The Battle of the Marne raged from September 6 to 9, and involved more than two million men. The Kaiser's armies, overextended and far from their supply lines, blinked first.

The giant German attacking force then retreated northward, to the heights overlooking the next major river: the Aisne, in Champagne. There they dug trenches, set up machine-gun nests, and mowed down waves of infantrymen foolishly ordered to take a run at the German lines. They could not be budged. It was late September 1914. Realizing, temporarily, that the best way to defeat a dug-in army was not to attack it head-on, the Allied generals had their exhausted troops attempt flanking movements—that is, they tried to swing around and attack their opponents from the side. This led to a series of fierce battles up through northern France and eventually back into Belgium, as each adversary frantically tried to encircle the other. It came to be known as "the Race to the Sea," but was more akin to a zipper closing. With each failed flanking movement, the armies dug in, extended the miles of trenches, and moved farther north to attack again.

In Flanders they hit the sea. It was the end of October. The German high command sensed that, at Ypres, the ragged British lines that were just forming could be easily smashed. It was their last chance to thwart *Stellungskrieg*, or the war of position that the framer of the Schlieffen Plan had so single-mindedly striven to avoid. The Kaiser came to watch. His officers, anticipating the Aryan prose of a German army a generation later, issued the following message to their troops on October 30, 1914:

The breakthrough will be of decisive importance. We must and therefore will conquer, settle forever the centuries-long struggle, end the war, and strike the decisive blow against our most detested enemy. We will finish the British, Indians, Canadians, Moroccans, and other trash, feeble adversaries, who surrender in great numbers if they are attacked with vigor.

They did not succeed, but only by a hair-breadth. In one particularly dramatic moment during the murderous melee, a British commander rounded up a squadron of cooks to plug a gaping hole in the lines to the east of Ypres; in another, a major launched a foolhardy counterattack because he had not enough men left alive to mount a credible defense. Both tactics worked, stalling the German assaults at a critical juncture and thus thwarting their plans for a rout. There would be no break-through, ever.

It was late November 1914. The digging started in earnest from Nieuport to Switzerland. The Western Front went underground, as did an unimaginable number of young men killed in the three-month-old war. British propagandists, stunned by the near extermination of the 100,000-man force sent across the Channel in August, searched for a symbol to keep civilian enthusiasm at a fever pitch. They found one in Ypres. It would have to pass for the infantry's apotheosis, a sort of Anglo Alamo in the muddy slough of Flanders. Only here the fort would not be overrun, the enemy would not get through the gates. No matter what the cost, Ypres would not be surrendered.

Thus was born the Salient, the death trap into which the English general staff would place its citizen army. A German officer remarked that British soldiers were "lions led by donkeys."

4. Ypres

Ypres. Ieper. Eee-pruh.

The problem with Ypres is its name. A place name, especially one connected with war, should have enough syllables to withstand constant barroom repetition. Wounded Knee, Normandy, Nagasaki, Waterloo: all words that easily roll off the tongue and into memory. Not so this little Belgian city. Ypres's recent history is not only unspeakable, it is unpro-nounceable, which may explain why the town's epoch-making role has faded to almost total obscurity. The British soldiers of the time obviated the problem altogether by calling the place "Wipers."

Not that the Great War made the city's name. As with all places along the Western Front, there was life here before 1914. The city's fame once rested on its reputation as a wealthy cloth-making center during the High Middle Ages, when it was the rival of nearby Ghent and Bruges. Ypres, or Ieper, its Flemish name, has supposedly given us the word "diaper," derived from *tissu d'Ieper*. Its later notoriety, connected with the other extreme of life, finds expression in the rare word "yperite," which reappeared in newspapers of the 1980s as stories reached the Western press of poison gas being used against the Kurds of Iraq. Yperite is dichlorethyl sulfide, a variant of the mustard gas that in 1917 began wafting regularly over the Salient. The people of Ypres live with that suffocating legacy, just as the people of Lynchburg, Virginia, can now profess a belief in due process of law without the slightest trace of self-consciousness.

Far pinker than I was a few days ago in Nieuport, I wander toward the center of town in search of a local who can point me to a cheap hotel. A saintly gent, on realizing that I speak no Flemish, puts his bag of groceries down on the sidewalk and mimes a series of directions that lead me to the impressive main square of Ypres. I enter it in the shadow of the reconstructed Cloth Hall, a faithful replica of the original fourteenth-century edifice destroyed in the Great War. One hundred twenty-five yards in length, the great gray building once sheltered the stalls of prosperous burghers who sold their linens for export throughout Europe. In its spiky Gothic majesty, the hall looks more like a parliament building—like the old label on HP steak sauce, in fact—than a garment district warehouse. A soaring bell tower, two hundred feet tall, rises from its roof and overlooks the cafés and beer terraces in the wide embrace of the square.

In the tourist office I read that stuffed cat toys are thrown from the top of the bell tower during the city's riotous little *Kattestoet*, a spring festival said to date all the way back to the year 962. Live cats used to go splatting down onto the cobblestones until the festival of 1817, when squeamish town fathers forbade such gory mediaeval exuberance. Now ersatz cats are hurled from on high. Either option sounds more amusing than hanging out with skinheads at the base of the IJzertoren.

A pleasant feeling of disorientation steals over me. After reading at length about Ypres in the First World War, I half expect the place to have disappeared. Such a vanishing act happened once before. At war's end the city was a heap of rubble, and some wished it to remain that way. Churchill, never at a loss for memorable rhetoric, said of Ypres, "A more sacred place for the British race does not exist in the world," and then went on to suggest that it continue to be nonexistent. He and other proponents of object lessons saw in the ruins of Ypres a permanent theme park, where visitors would come to admire the destructiveness of modern warfare.

In the same spirit, the Michelin tire company shrewdly produced touring manuals to the regions devastated by the Great War, complete with "before" and "after" pictures of architectural marvels leveled by bombardments. This tsk-tsk tourism became very popular immediately after the armistice and ensured the success of the fledgling Michelin guides. The 1919 edition for Flanders, entitled *Ypres: un guide, un panorama, une histoire*, teases the reader with its pictures and detailed descriptions of buildings and artworks that could no longer be seen. Page after page contrasts prewar and postwar snapshots: here a church, there an empty lot; here a charming village street, there a road bordered with tree stumps; here an imposing chateau and its garden, there a dusty expanse filled with rusting sheets of corrugated metal. Even more jarring are the pictures of the countryside. Invariably, a jalopy is shown driving through a moonscape devoid of any distinguishing feature save for a rough wooden sign indicating where some village used to be. When the Western Front was still fresh in everyone's memory, it fascinated more for what it had destroyed than for what it had created.

Eventually, 1919's screaming swath of nothingness was silenced by new construction. When the civilians of Flanders returned to where their homes had been, there was no debate over whether the province should be left as a Churchillian war wonderland. Reconstructing a distant past was deemed the best way to blot out the recent past. Along with the Cloth Hall (which was finished only in 1964), a new old cathedral rose from the rubble, the tomb of the influential prelate Cornelius Jansen dusted off and displayed once more for admirers of his Catholic version of Calvinism. Architects studied the "before" pictures—like those in the Michelin guides—and set to rebuilding along the main arteries of the town. Where preexisting buildings were found wanting in historical cachet, their newer versions came with a few more gables, or turrets, or whatever. In the process of re-creating a world, exactness mattered less than effect. The Flemings even had the Germans pay for rebuilding the town's seventeenth-century fortifications—even though the Germans had just shown the great walls to be useless in defending the city. The place became virtual.

The British saw Ypres as a mausoleum. The stupendous profligacy with which those in command had wasted lives in the defense of this Belgian backwater called for an extravagant peacetime riposte. Well before the armistice, the authorities in London ordered elaborate and expensive plans drawn up for commemorations, graveyards, statuary, and the like. A new sacredness, a civic religion, would have to be invented to ward off mounting nihilism—all the suffering had to be made legitimate so that those in power would not be blamed. Thus was born the modern war memorial, a mix of accountancy exactitude and the notion of universal victimhood. Determine the correct tally of the dead, etch their names in stone, and avoid the sticky question of responsibility by implying that such a regrettable calamity occurred independently of human agency. At Ypres, the British invented the twentieth-century response to war. By commissioning a stone ledger of the lost, the State, through its very punctiliousness, can be absolved. Visitors to the Vietnam memorial in Washington will recognize the device.

Not only was Ypres a mausoleum for hundreds of thousands—there are more than 150 British graveyards within walking distance of town—it also came to be viewed, paradoxically, as the last outpost of the pre-1914 era. Between the two world wars, Ypres was filled with pubs and chip shops and chapels catering to veterans and relatives, nurses and clergymen, teachers and schoolboys. Now that Anglo aspect of the town is as dusty and distant as the Vietnam memorial will be a couple of generations hence. As I look around the main square, I'm disappointed that there are no buskers playing "Tipperary" on penny whistles, and that there are no corny old *estaminets*—the Great War word for soldiers' taverns—in sight. What can be seen, off to the east in a gap in the reconstructed city ramparts, is an archway known as the Menin Gate. It is one of two enormous monuments the British erected on the Western Front; the other towers over Thiepval, in the Somme. Under the long marble vault of the gate, which resounds with the thunder of passing traffic, are the names of 54,896 soldiers of Britain and its empire who disappeared in the mud around here between August 1914 and August 1917, and whose bodies were never found. As for the rest of the war—September 1917 to November 1918—the official tally of those Britons and colonials with no known grave in the Salient is 34,984. Their names are inscribed on panels at the Tyne Cot cemetery near Passchendaele.

Every evening at eight o'clock, the traffic is halted at the Menin Gate while members of the Ypres Fire Department play "The Last Post." I have attended the brief ceremony three times. There were usually about six to ten of us at the monument, milling about awkwardly in anticipation of the Belgian bugle boys. Once I looked up at the sea of inscriptions and saw a group of names that were distinctly non-European: the missing soldiers from a regiment raised in Bhopal, India. The Salient that gave the world poison gas honors the ancestors of its recent victims. On another occasion, I exchanged quizzical glances with a young woman who was clutching to her breast Siegfried Sassoon's *Memoirs of a Fox-Hunting Man* (Sassoon's work and Robert Graves's *Good-bye to All That* were the most popular of the thousands of British war memoirs). Her male friend gripped her waist tightly. The last time, nothing occurred. My mind wandered, and I thought of the mussels I was going to have for dinner.

Ceremonies of this sort, with their pathos of unfocused mourning, often leave participants with a twinge of guilt for feeling unmoved. Yet it is faintly ridiculous for later generations to murmur stock phrases about sacrifice and suffering as if we knew what they originally meant. Many of those who experienced the Great War were just as uncomfortable with such ritual utterances and performances. My paternal grandfather, Daniel, who saw Ypres in flames as an Irishman in the British army, hardly ever spoke of his Great War experience, even though he had spent four years in the trenches, lost an eye to a sniper's bullet, and sustained a shrapnel wound in the leg from which he never fully recovered. He died, prematurely, in 1940, unwilling to divulge his war stories to his children. Words did not suffice.

THE KNOWLEDGE OF Daniel's silence makes St. George's Memorial Church, a small officers' chapel built opposite the Ypres cathedral, look all the more peculiar to me. Raised by private subscription in the 1920s, mainly from the alumni of Eton (on whose playing fields, according to the Duke of Wellington, the Napoleonic wars were supposed to have been won), the sanctuary is an odd blend of thin-lipped High Anglican grief and fetish-house ostentation. Its sober redbrick exterior gives no hint of the totemic wordiness within. Everywhere in St. George's there are inscriptions—on brass plaques, carved pews, stained-glass windows, statues, busts, flags, banners, wood panels, fonts, railings, handles, floor tiles, radiators, gratings—as if a flow of words, a permanent logorrhea, could somehow offset the reality of slaughter. To dry eyes at the dawn of the twenty-first century, the sanctuary resembles an AIDS quilt as a tool of memory.

Like the Menin Gate, however, St. George's is now a museum of mourning, no longer moored to any direct human experience. Almost all of the people who composed the wordy tributes on the walls, floor, and ceiling of the church are no longer alive to appreciate or explain their significance. We can only guess at the depth of feeling behind each phrase. What, if anything, would we have written on the walls of a place dedicated to the disappearance of our peers? How would we distinguish, in a telling phrase, one twenty-year-old from another? "Played a mean guitar." "Had a problem with authority." "Awesome hang-glider." "Headed for med school." The sample I scribbled down seems almost contemporary, until the tag at the end:

THE SANCTUARY STEPS AND PAVEMENT
ARE GIVEN BY NANCY Q RADCLIFFE
PLATT IN EVER LOVING AND PROUD
REMEMBRANCE OF HER BROTHER
JOHN ROCKHURST PLATT
LIEUT R F A (T) KILLED IN ACTION
AT ZILLEBEKE MARCH 27, 1916
CAPTAIN OF THE OPPIDANS
ETON COLLEGE 1909
SANS PEUR ET SANS REPROCHE

A pamphlet picked up in the Cloth Hall's Salient Museum reports that some in the grieving English upper classes went so far as to invoke King Arthur in their search for spiritual solace. In Vera Brittain's once avidly read *Testament of Youth*, she writes of losing her fiancé, her brother, and two friends—her entire coterie of male companionship—in the war. That type of wholesale trauma was too great to be handled by the Anglican Militant style alone. Whereas many visitors to Ypres took out their Ouija boards, others resorted to mysticism concerning their nation's founding, just as the French developed a full-blown fixation with Joan of Arc.

According to legend Joseph of Arimathaea, the fellow who took Christ's body down from the cross, brought the Holy Grail to Britain, and from the wooden staff Joseph carried with him a thorny shrub had sprouted in Glastonbury, which is the English town, as every well-read pot-head used to know, with the strongest claims to having been Camelot. It was a shoot from this growth in Glastonbury that some distressed English patriots had seen fit to bring to Ypres and plant near St. George's in the 1930s. If true—the story of planting a shrub in Ypres, that is, not the Grail—the tale says more about the shock of the Great War than any description of memorials or inscriptions. Going back to Arthur and company is more than a reach. It's grasping at supernatural straws in an attempt to lend dignity to cataclysm.

As with all good illustrative stories, this one should not be confirmed. Nonetheless I spend a Monty Pythonesque hour poking around the neighborhood of St. George's in a quest for Arthurian shrubbery. As is only fitting to a seeker of an object akin to the Grail, I come up empty-handed, even after trespassing into the defunct schoolyard adjacent to the church and knocking loudly on every door in sight. I find neither guide nor guardian, and am, in the end, pleased to leave legend undisturbed. As I cross the street in the evening air to head back to the cafés in the main square, I notice another sign of the English presence in Belgium. A Ladbrokes turf accountant—i.e., off-track betting shop—looks out onto a little corner it shares with St. George's. Solemnity has its limits, even for British pilgrims to Ypres.

I close the door in my hotel room and see one last inscription from this city of words. Finally, a message in Ypres that makes me smile:

> To our Guests,
>
> We wish to inform you about the fact, that each Saturday, there is a PARKPROHIBITION from 0 A.M. till 1 P.M., on the Marketsquare, because of the weekly saturdaymarket.
>
> If you are by car, we ask you to take account of this prohibition, to avoid that the police will drag your car away.
>
> > With our greetings
> > for a joyfull stay
> > The Direction

5. Langemarck to Passchendaele

The cashier at the supermarket drums her fingers on the conveyor belt as I fish for coins. I'm stocking up on speculoos, the Belgian ginger snaps that have warded off hunger during my hikes around Ypres. In the past few days I've been staring out over fields that look as if they need a good ironing, so subtly and unnaturally uneven are their surfaces. The woods tell the same secret story. Once off the shaded bridle paths, I come up against the bracken of rusted barbed wire and spent bullets. Memorials, both public and private, stand alongside every country lane; from any viewpoint the observant visitor can easily pick out at least one or two links in the long chain of monuments and graveyards, a sinister gap-toothed smile against the dark green countryside. I inspect the inscriptions, pop a speculoos, then sit on the ground and lean against the cool stone surfaces to powder my shrinking blisters. The heavy hiking boots have been temporarily jettisoned for black Keds, the khaki canvas backpack abandoned in the hotel room, the red woolen socks left bleeding in the sink. Above, a great gray cloud bank glowers over the Salient.

The aptly named speculoos accompanies me in my idle conjectures. How many thousands of stories connected to this land have been lost? What can I possibly be looking at, when I look at this stela, this column, this marker? Has the experience of so many millions been reduced to some overgrown granite headstone in a farmer's muddy field? It occurs to me, as I glimpse the russet town of Passchendaele on a far-off ridge, that the First World War took place in color, not in the black and white of the photos in history books. That this wet sponge of a sky was their sky, that this sweet bird song was the same as the one they heard in their muddy ditches. Yet a speculoos, for all its other qualities, is hardly a madeleine. Memories do not come flooding back to someone trained to disregard the past. More frequently, the cares of the moment crowd in to assert their rightful place in the consciousness.

Like right now, as I fumble with my Belgian francs in a supermarket of the village of Langemarck. The farmers' wives waiting in line behind me look on tolerantly, a conservatory of faded floral prints allowing a radish-faced man into their midst for the morning. Outside, in the parking lot, the women's endomorphic menfolk sit somnolent behind steering wheels, secure in the knowledge that shopping is beyond their ken and beneath their station. Clearly, in my eagerness for speculoos, I have transgressed.

In this countryside, however, just being alive, in good health and good spirits, seems to be a transgression. The few miles I covered this morning, northeast from Ypres to Langemarck, confirmed that impression. A knot of busy roads leading to an expressway eventually gave way to sloping fields, scrawny woodlands, and a windmill standing alone in a meadow. Here it was, inevitably, the "Windmill of Death," a much-bombed observation post in the war. Signs along the way indicating Cheddar Farm and Oxford Road, former British strongholds, alternated with barns and farmhouses built on the concrete remains of old pillboxes, the curious name given to fortified firing positions. A well-tended corner garden near the hamlet of St. Juliaan turned out to be a memorial for more than 2,000 Canadian war dead. A column depicting a soldier, his arms crossed and his eyes downcast, stands beside evergreen bushes trimmed to look like artillery shells. In old trench maps, this area was known as "Vancouver."

The Canadians, along with their Algerian, Breton, and Belgian allies, took the brunt of a surprise poison gas attack around St. Juliaan, the first of its kind on the Western Front. At about five in the afternoon of April 22, 1915, spotters noticed a ten-foot-tall wall of yellowish-green mist floating down toward them over these fields. The technicians of the

German *Stinkpioniere* units had uncocked their deadly cylinders. Choking and coughing, the French colonials and Canadians stood in their trenches without gas masks, their lungs turning into wheezing, scorching sacks of pain. Men clambered above ground in the lethal fog and ran for daylight, terrified, pumping the gas already inhaled into their bloodstreams. By nightfall, thousands of youths lay gasping and dying in farmyards behind the lines, many of them in Boezinge, the shaded village in which I'd paused on my way into Ypres from the coast. Half the Canadians who survived the attack had to be sent home. Most of them would be permanent invalids.

Small wonder, then, that Langemarck is a dark place, even in the light of midday. The atrocity of 1915, however, was preceded by the tragedy of 1914. Once out of the supermarket, I walk past the redbrick façades on the main street and head to the town's principal attraction: a graveyard. For Germans, Langemarck marks the spot where *der Kindermord von Ypern*, the Massacre of the Innocents at Ypres, took place in 1914. The German war cemetery in the middle of town, unlike its Commonwealth counterparts in the countryside, is planted with large oak trees and resembles a shaded pasture suitable for a lovers' picnic. The grass grows long, and only a few headstones, roughly sculpted basalt crosses aligned in groups of five, are scattered about the enclosure. More than 44,000 bodies are interred in the Langemarck cemetery, the majority in mass graves. A pavilion at the entrance opens out onto a small plaza bordered by somber oaken panels listing the dead student volunteers buried here. As at the Menin Gate, the procession of names looks endless.

In the land between Langemarck and the village of Poelkapelle runs a straight and featureless road, just as it did during the days of the Kindermord. The massacre took place on either side of this road. The innocents in question were university students who had flocked to enlist in August of 1914. Before the war, many German youths had been sweetly idealistic, organizing themselves into hiking and nature groups known as *Wandervogel.* Their motto was *rein bleiben und reif werden* (to stay pure is to mature); their favorite activity, camping trips during which they would dance around bonfires, sing folksongs, and declaim poetry, hoping to establish a temporary community divorced from the demands of adult life, in much the same way as the far sillier men's movement of today aims for transcendence through a retreat into sweatlodges. The youths of the Wandervogel chafed at the constraints of custom and were understandably impatient with the discipline imposed by the bewhiskered patriarchs of Wilhelmine Germany. So when war came, thousands of Teutonic

Rupert Brookes saw it as an adventure that would allow an escape from a craven social order and an opportunity, at last, to act with heroic selflessness.

It did. In October of 1914, when the chances for a breakthrough in the Race to the Sea were slipping away, the German general staff sent thousands of untrained student volunteers to these fields as part of a last-ditch offensive. The British positions were to be smashed and the triumphant German army would scramble across country to the vital Channel ports. The military command spoke of "feeble adversaries" and "trash"; for the Wandervogel youths, their nationalist fiber stirred by the presence of the Kaiser, exaltation and eagerness were the real marching orders of the day. To find a modern-day equivalent, the Iraq-Iran war of the 1980s must again be cited, when whole divisions of Iranian martyrs flung themselves, lemming-like in their fundamentalist enthusiasm, at fortified positions near Basra. In 1914, much the same thing occurred. Whereas elsewhere in the Salient battle-hardened German troops nearly broke the British and Belgian lines, no such close call occurred wherever the student soldiers attacked. British war memoirs describe groups of massed teen-agers, arms linked and voices raised in song, walking across the fields as if on a Sunday outing. The power of purity, presumably, would sweep away all that lay before it.

Predictably, a curtain of lead met the students as they neared the enemy lines, and the Wandervogel songs were suddenly silenced. Wave after wave of volunteers followed, only to be mowed down methodically by British machine gunners, some of whom later voiced dismay over the scale of the carnage. Rarely would there be a more grotesque example of lambs being led to slaughter. If the Great War was the unhappy childhood of the twentieth century, then the Kindermord was the infant century's unanswered scream in the night. More than 150,000 German soldiers died that month. The story of the sacrificed youth of the Wandervogel, like the "lost generation" in British culture and *la génération creuse*, or hollow generation, in French thought, gradually took root in the German mind as news of the Kindermord and other senseless battles filtered home through the haze of official lying. Walter Flex's *Der Wanderer zwischen beiden Welten* (*A Wanderer between Two Worlds*), a novella about a Wandervogel youth killed early in the war, has been popular in Germany since its publication in 1917, the year the author died on a Baltic battlefield.

GASSING, THE KINDERMORD — the associations of these hours spent in the orbit of Langemarck are depressing. Despite foreboding about what lies

lies ahead this afternoon, I break into a smile when the village of
Poelkapelle finally appears. At its central crossroads there stands an
unusual statue of a stork in full flight. The monument honors French
flying ace Georges Guynemer, whose plane was shot down in the skies
above Poelkapelle on September 11, 1917. However strange the stork
looks, in perpetual mid-flap twenty feet above a traffic circle, the inscription on the base of the memorial seems even more bizarre. The language
of outdated chauvinism, a specialty of French war memorials, now
amuses more than it inspires. An excerpt:

> *Héros Légendaire Tombé en*
> *Plein Ciel de Gloire après Trois*
> *Ans de Lutte Ardente Restera Le*
> *Plus Pur Symbole des Qualités*
> *De La Race: Tenacité Indomptable*
> *Energie Farouche Courage Sublime*
> *Animé De La Foi La Plus Inébranlable*
> *Dans La Victoire . . .*

> (The Legendary Hero Fallen in the
> Full Glory of Flight after Three
> Years of Fiery Combat Will Remain
> The Purest Symbol of The Strengths
> of His Race: Indomitable Tenacity
> Fierce Energy Sublime Bravery
> Inspired by the Most Unshakeable Faith
> in Victory . . .)

It's likely that Guynemer, a twenty-three-year-old daredevil who had
already been shot down seven times before his fatal encounter over
Poelkapelle, might find this epitaph too pompous to describe his acceler-
ated, exhilarating life span. Like other successful airmen, Guynemer
reveled in scarcely credible risks—although for sheer combat mania few
could match Frank Luke, an American ace who died at the age of twenty-
one after making an emergency landing behind enemy lines. Luke emptied his pistol at the admiring German infantrymen on their way to take
him prisoner; naturally, they forgot their admiration and fired back.

Poelkapelle is made less lugubrious by its stork. The air force was the
only murderous innovation of the Great War to have received good
publicity. The ballet of aerial battle—English Sopwith Camels and
French Spads rat-tat-tatting through the skies against German Fokkers—
enchanted minds starved for a coherent narrative. The dogfight suggested
a life-and-death contest in which the individual had some say. The

conflict on the ground, with its machine guns, artillery, and mortars, was viewed as an industrial abattoir; the conflict in the skies, with its attendant legends of dashing chaps buzzing about in aeroplanes, silk scarves snapping in the breeze, came to be seen as the acme of glamour.

The glamour of war, destroyed when the horseman left the field to be replaced by the troglodyte in the trench, was a mystique badly in need of novelty. The aces, a new breed of warriors for the new aerial battlefield, met the modernist need perfectly. Before a peacetime aviator, Charles Lindbergh, appeared on the scene to establish his preeminence as celebrity airman of the new century, the names of Great War aces were well known to an adoring public, as was their tally of kills: the American Rickenbacker (23), the Canadian Bishop (72), the Frenchmen Fonck (75) and Guynemer (53), the Britons Mannock (73) and Collishaw (60). The one who has survived the longest in the public mind, thanks to Charles Schulz and Snoopy, is the German Manfred von Richthofen who, as the Red Knight (or the Red Baron) commanding his Flying Circus of aviators, was responsible for 80 kills. Richthofen was shot down over the Somme on April 21, 1918, either by Canadian pilot Roy Brown or by an Australian machine-gunner on the ground.

FROM THE SKY to the pits. The rest of today's walk will bring me to the worst of the Salient's imaginative landscape. Few places along the Western Front have witnessed such destruction as the countryside beyond Langemarck and Poelkapelle. In the windows of some farmhouses, displayed like religious statuary, are decorative arrangements of brass shells and steel shrapnel, burnished to brilliance and battered into domestic objets d'art. Munitions are this region's marble, a mineral resource that is available in limitless quantities. One house is sandwiched between two bomb craters, its garden shed a crumbling concrete structure with tapered apertures designed for the barrels of machine guns. A road sign nearby points to the southeast, indicating a destination two and one-half miles distant: Passendale. In English, the spelling is Passchendaele, and the meaning ranges far beyond the simple Dale of the Passion or, less literally, Valley of the Crucifixion. For the first generations of the twentieth century living in Britain and its Commonwealth, Passchendaele was a word that signified the abominable and the inhuman; in the sad, sickened middle age of that century, only one other word, Holocaust, would surpass it in the lexicon of horror.

The sun makes an unexpected appearance overhead, its warmth inviting me to snap out of my anachronistic funk. Yet it is difficult to contemplate Passchendaele without feeling anger, no matter how absurd that emotion may be. I know, for example, that every step I take in the next few hours cost thirty-five lives in October 1917. No other battle of the Western Front was fought under such appalling conditions. Worse yet, pig-headed incompetence was the cause of it all—and the man responsible still, inexplicably, has his statue and place of honor in London's Whitehall, while the deserters from this and other heinous battles were denied a posthumous pardon as recently as 1992. Thus Passchendaele also means iniquity. As I leave Poelkapelle and take a narrow farm track down into the valley, I know that here, more than ever, I am treading on metaphor.

What happened can be stated baldly: an army was forced by its own generals to drown in the mud. There are two oft-cited *mots* relating to the battle. One is an ordinary soldier's lament, taken up by Siegfried Sassoon: "We died in hell, they called it Passchendaele." The other is supposed to have been inspired by the improbably named Launcelot Kiggell, a British senior staff officer. Unwilling to venture near the Front during the fighting and just as unwilling to believe reports of conditions on the ground, Kiggell finally visited the oozing landscape of blood and mud after the guns had been stilled. He is said to have burst into tears and exclaimed: "Good God, did we really send men to fight in that?" His companion replied calmly, "It's worse further up." Passchendaele was a prolonged, futile massacre conceived by an inept military mind unmoved by suffering. The mind belonged to Douglas Haig, the commander in chief of British forces, and the debacle is officially known as the Third Battle of Ypres.

The campaign opened on July 31, 1917, with the aim of smashing the German position in the Salient and advancing more than twenty-five miles to capture the North Sea ports of Zeebrugge and Ostend. This plan, a breakthrough followed by a dash to the sea, sounds a lot like the scheme that led to the Kindermord, except for one crucial difference: the Kindermord occurred when the war was three months old; Passchendaele, when it was three years old. Thirty-six months of trench warfare had taught Haig nothing. In 1916, the year before Passchendaele, more than a million men had died at Verdun and on the Somme, and the ground gained by either side had been negligible. Yet Haig, a handsome medi-ocrity whose friendship with King George V had done wonders for his career, spoke of racing across whole provinces in a single week. Eerily immune to experience, he even foresaw the cavalry galloping across open fields to the sea, as if the machine gun had yet to be invented and the years 1914, 1915, and 1916 had never happened. The tactics to be used, masses of men trudging across no-man's-land in the hope that the enemy's barbed-wire defenses had been wiped out by shellfire, were identical to those employed in past fiascoes, except for one difference: more artillery would fire more shells than at any other time in history. This, Haig believed, was the decisive innovation that would carry the day.

The million British soldiers who had been sitting in Flanders for three years knew otherwise. Anyone who had spent time in the trenches saw that heavy shelling turned the earth around Ypres into a glutinous bog, where large pools of groundwater alternated with expanses of viscous mud. In peacetime, an elaborate system of canals and polders had been used by farmers to keep the ground dry, but much of that drainage network was destroyed during the first three years of the war. The Salient was notorious on both sides of no-man's-land for its rat-infested, impassable muck. Yet this is where Haig chose to stage his magnificent artillery barrage. As one commander, quoted in Leon Wolff's classic account of the campaign, *In Flanders Fields,* wrote of Haig's choice: "To anyone familiar with the terrain in Flanders it was almost inconceivable that this part of the line should have been selected. If a careful search had been made from the English Channel to Switzerland, no more unsuitable spot could have been discovered." Moreover, as all mud-splashed soldiers realized, the early-autumn rains in Flanders usually turned the Salient into a swamp.

Objections were overruled, and Haig, a dangerously stupid man, prepared his offensive. Charts drawn up by junior officers to warn where large lakes of water would appear in the aftermath of artillery bombardments were sent back from headquarters with the annotation, "Send us no more of these ridiculous maps." Talk from Haig of cavalry charges, as germane to trench warfare as the crossbow, unnerved senior officers so much that they shared their misgivings with David Lloyd George, the British prime minister. Lloyd George, already heartily sickened by the Somme, received assurances from Haig that if the number of casualties climbed too high and the number of square miles gained stayed too low, the offensive would be stopped—before it became a colossal suicide. That was Haig's promise, and he broke it in so many different ways, with such devastating effects on so many individual lives, that my grandfathers' legacy of a reflexive hatred of the military seems entirely reasonable. How anyone who knows the history of the Great War can choose a career in the army remains a mystery.

On July 24, 1917, the British lined up thousands of guns along a fifteen-mile front, one every six yards, and sent eastward a solid, unrelenting rain of metal that lasted a week. The sound was a deafening, indiscriminate roar that the German soldiers, huddled within their many concrete fortifications, found a word to describe: *Trommelfeuer*, or drumfire. The earth, shattered and smashed, soon became sodden, as subterranean water welled to the surface and torrential rain began to fall. At 5:27 in the morning of July 31, when 120,000 British troops left their trenches, they were faced with a landscape of gray, milky mud. Contrary to Haig's expectations, if no one else's, not all the German first- and second-line forces had been annihilated. Machine guns were quickly set up and the classic First World War slaughter scenario reenacted.

The plan called for an advance of five miles in one day with minimum casualties. By the end of the second day, the attackers had gone only about half a mile, and 35,000 of their troops had been killed or wounded. Haig was urged to call the whole thing off, strike elsewhere, use surprise. Nothing doing. Elated by the advance, he ordered fresh troops into the Salient. New attacks were launched: August 9, 13, 16, 24, 27. Another 40,000 men lost, another mile gained, the ruins of Langemarck retaken. While Lloyd George raged impotently in London, Haig planned another massive attack for September, along a front half as wide so that the storm of steel would be twice as violent. The soldiers went over the top on September 20, gaining 900 yards and losing 22,000 of their fellows. On September 26, 1,000 more yards, 17,000 men lost. On October 4, 700 yards, 26,000 casualties. The armies had reached the outskirts of Poelkapelle, the land was a lunar bog, the rain came pouring down. Worse was yet to come.

IN THE VALLEY below Passchendaele today, there is a tall stand of trees beside a narrow irrigation channel that I hop over on my way toward the village on the ridge. In October 1917, the channel was fifty yards wide, a porridge-like pool snaking across a valley of mud craters. This was no-man's-land. The area behind the British lines, the few acres between Langemarck and Poelkapelle captured at such great expense, was so soupy that it took reinforcements heading up to the Front an hour to walk just 400 yards. Because of the swamp created by millions of shells, the hapless soldiers had to stay on the duckboards—narrow paths made of wooden planking—which, to worsen matters, the German artillery targeted at all times of day and night. Slipping off the boards sometimes spelled death. Infantrymen, stretcher bearers, gunners, pack mules, and horses—hundreds of unfortunates drowned in the darkness because of one false step. Once at the Front, newly arrived soldiers squelched through the muck in search of a crater rim, a dry spot, a hollow, a place to hide. Bloated rats feasted on bodies everywhere.

On October 5, 1917, the day after the British entered Poelkapelle, everyone knew that the 200,000 casualties of the past few months had been suffered for no good reason. Even in Britain, the smoke screen of misinformation in the press could not offset the stories being brought back by the wounded. In Flanders, the rain was now lashing down, the army was covered in mud from head to toe, infection was rampant, and men were cracking under the strain. Haig, undeterred, declared that Passchendaele was too important an objective to be left in German hands. Capturing the ports was long forgotten—if they could take the height of Passchendaele, all would be well on the Western Front. Criminally blind to the end, Haig ordered another attack.

The rest is almost too sad to recount. On October 9, an army slogged into the dawn light, some units near exhaustion after having struggled all night through the muddy blackness to get up to the front line. This time the artillery barrage had petered out into insignificance. Field guns got lost in the swampy universe, the recoil from their discharge burying their barrels deep in the mud. Heavy shells, fired from miles away, had gone through the ground as if it were Jell-O, exploding harmlessly below the soggy surface of the earth. The German defenders of Passchendaele were practically untouched. They opened fire at the thousands wading into view. Men jumped into shell holes, hid under corpses, cowered in the mud as all day long they were strafed by machine guns. The slopes became a charnel house, the wounded slowly dying as their strength gave out and they slid deeper into the pools of slimy water at the bottom of every crater. The few pillboxes that had been captured overflowed with the dead and wounded. Thousands were stuck in no-man's-land, drowning, crying, left to a horrible fate.

Near the bottom of the vale some resourceful farmer has made a duck pond out of a giant shell hole. There is a swing set beside it. The grass looks preternaturally green, even in this bright sunlight. I begin the gentle climb up to the village, only too aware of what happened here. Even after October 9, Haig refused to give up. Repeated attacks were ordered throughout the month. After the British came the Australians and then the New Zealanders, who lost 13,000 soldiers, killed or wounded, in a single murderous morning. The attackers' line inched forward in pathetically small increments as the rains continued and the mud grew fouler and the stench from the dead became unbearable. Finally, a contingent of Canadian soldiers entered the obliterated village of Passchendaele on November 6, 1917. The supposedly all-important position, for which so many had died in an amphibian nightmare, was later abandoned on Haig's order. Passchendaele was too exposed, a salient sticking out of the Salient. More than half a million men had been killed or wounded for nothing.

I stroll through a side street in the silent, treeless village. From the height of the little ridge, the fields I have just crossed look pastoral, inviting, as if one could almost imagine living in a place such as this. War cemeteries can be discerned in the distance, as can the spires of neighboring village churches. St. Aurodorus, an ungainly faux-Romanesque church built after the war, squats on a bend in the main road. A man in a black leather jacket nails a notice to its front door, then hurries off. Intrigued, I cross the street to read: "Passendale Moto-Cross." This definitely calls for a speculoos.

As I sit on a bench waiting for the bus back to town, an ice cream truck rounds the corner, bells ringing. The children of Passendale step out of doorways and run for their treats. There is shouting in the streets. The rays of the late-afternoon sun catch the hair of one boy, sending a sudden shower of gold down the barren thoroughfare that curves through the village and out along the crest of the ridge. My bus arrives. I get on and go back the seven miles to Ypres.

6. The Menin Road

I start out early one morning and stride through the Menin Gate. I go straight along the main road, east, my eyes smarting in the dusty wash of transport trailers as they growl their way out of town. On either side of the road are rowhouses, shuttered tight, gritty with exhaust.

I'm on the straight Roman road that leads from Ypres to the town of Menin (or Menen, in Flemish). This was the main drag of the Salient, the Ho Chi Minh Trail for British soldiers as they straggled up to the trenches in a night made lurid with flares and fiery explosions. Anyone who has glanced at the contemporaneous paintings of British artist Paul Nash will have an idea of this road's appearance in 1914–18: a flat, muddy track, littered with burned-out carts and carriages and bordered by a few forlorn spikes that were once shade trees. Now, I conclude too quickly, the Menin Road looks like any other secondary highway in Western Europe as it approaches a provincial market town. Faded billboards advertise warehouse discount outlets and a few subdivisions hunker down in a leaden suburban landscape.

It's only after the housing thins that I first notice the jarring sights in the tableau. There are too many signs in English, German, and French, too many crumbling concrete structures in the fields, too many weird stone road markers with helmets atop them. What should be an ordinary crossroads is announced, in English, as Hellfire Corner. The white directional signs for distant villages of the living are outnumbered by green arrows pointing to settlements of the dead: Sanctuary Wood Cemetery, Hill 62 Cemetery, Tyne Cot Cemetery. After my day around Passchendaele, none of these sights is welcome.

Fortunately, a giant purple mascot comes to my rescue. Off to my left, according to my 1919 Michelin guide, there should be a tank graveyard— a field where seventeen tanks were taken out by one German pillbox during the Third Ypres campaign. Instead, a purple creature stands there, directing wayward cars into a parking lot. A multicolored sign above an entrance gate states "Bellewaerde." Beyond that there are roller coasters, Ferris wheels, giant slides. Garish posters advertise "Florida Water Show," "Boomerang," "Pirates' Castle." I hear squeals of fright carried on the wind. Buccaneers are blasting a hole in time, racing over terrain with no other story to tell than the one remembered by the spectators. The Belgians have done more than build an amusement park here, they have fully reclaimed their land. This place is not for poppy tourists like myself.

I dodge a truck trundling up the grade past Bellewaerde to Geluveld and the vanishing point of this infamous ridge. The Menin Road, I decide, is too busy for the absent-minded pedestrian. I take a tree-lined road south, past golden fields into Sanctuary Wood. On its fringe is a ramshackle building, with Coke signs and dud munitions standing on guard at the door. I've heard about this place—a privately owned museum with a preserved stretch of trench behind it. The latter, a much reconstructed ditch snaking through the forest floor, looks as if it has never been completely dry. Soggy, unsightly, and, for purists about such things, unconvincing, the trench has nonetheless been the livelihood of three generations of the Schier family, on whose land the armies descended in 1914 to destroy everything in sight. Gradually the family's weapons and knickknack collections grew to strange and interesting proportions. When the German army came calling again in 1940, the clan of trench-keepers sealed off all their goodies in the cellar. Some of the bric-a-brac made from shell casings is now displayed in the museum's flyblown café, which resembles a garage sale of items from some Muscovite granny's sitting room. Mugs, ashtrays, trophies, picture frames, statuettes, plaques, planters, clocks, coasters, plates, devotional items—

the variety of junk impresses by its sheer volume. Within the museum, aside from a dank and musty room given over to rusted weapons, is a collection of war porn.

A central table in the Sanctuary Wood Museum holds ten or so wooden viewing devices that allow the war buff to study hundreds of revolting pictures of the carnage in the trenches. Ever since Matthew Brady popularized photos of dead soldiers during the American Civil War, the line between ghoulish prurience and graphic pacifism has been difficult to draw. I sense its presence every time I write about the history of this war, and hope not to overstep it. Deploring something at length is sometimes a useful disguise for wallowing in it, and there can be no doubt that the barbarity of the Great War has led to a culture of celebrating its sheer awfulness. In an otherwise sober guide to the battlefields I read the following about Sanctuary Wood's collection of gruesome pictures:

> They are a *must*. Each one has different glass slides that when viewed with persistence focus dramatically into sharp 3 dimensions. Here in this atmospheric environment is the true horror of war—dead horses, bodies in trees, heads and legs in trenches and, everywhere, mud, mud, mud.

The mud I understand.

I don't have the sensibility of a Brady, or a Weegee for that matter, so I avoid the war porn display in the Sanctuary Wood Museum. The Devotees of Salient Gore is not a club I wish to join. That people spend time poring over these distressing pictures is repulsive enough. As at Dixmude, I'm uneasy about the company I'm keeping. First it was the far Right, now it's the voyeurs. Again, I paraphrase Clemenceau: History is too important to be left to the geeks.

I leave Sanctuary Wood and head directly out into a farmer's field. Beyond is a bigger wood, then more fields. Since I'm so hung up on time, maybe I should lighten up on space. I intend to get lost. The bad feelings about the war porn display linger. Perhaps I wanted to see the atrocious photos and just wouldn't admit it.

The sunlight does nothing to dispel my gloom. An hour or two is spent zigging and zagging at random, crossing country roads, stealing around villages, jumping over ditches until I'm finally brought up short in front of a crazily deformed hill. Sheep are grazing in shell holes and mine craters, geese can be heard cackling from behind a fence. This is Hill 60, in which lie the bodies of scores of German and Australian tunnelers. There is no bicycle here, as at La Boisselle on the Somme, affirming the primacy of life.

As I pull out my map to get my bearings and find the shortest route back to town, a man appears from behind the hill. He has been cutting grass somewhere. He wears black shoes, black pants, and a black T-shirt. Over his right shoulder, he carries a scythe. He smiles as he passes me.

7. *Messines to Armentières*

A beer bottle goes whistling past my ear. I duck, far too late to dodge it if the thrower had had better aim. By the time I straighten up, the Toyota full of rowdies has swerved down the road out of sight. It is nine o'clock in the morning, and I have been persuaded to stop singing.

I ascend a gradual slope to the village of Wijtschate, or "White Sheet," as it was referred to in the British trenches. The slope, part of the modest but murderous highland that ringed the British positions, is known to history as the Messines Ridge, so called because the town of that name, south of Wijtschate, was at the centerpoint of an offensive. This time the operation was a British success, for the simple reason that the attackers blew the German lines to smithereens. The surprise lay in nineteen gigantic underground bombs. Miners brought over from the collieries of Britain, and from New Zealand and Canada, had spent almost two years digging under no-man's-land to the German trenches, sometimes more than half a mile away. As if that task were not grim enough, they then had to spend weeks hauling great loads of unstable ammonal explosive through the dark, suffocating tunnels to set the trap.

At 3:10 A.M. on June 7, 1917, the mines were blown, several million pounds of explosives in all. The blast was clearly heard in London, the windows in several tony Belgravia drawing rooms, it is said, nearly shattering as the shock wave from Belgium buffeted the southern counties of Britain. First World War histories are fond of stating, with a sly kind of pride, that the Messines operation produced the largest man-made, non-nuclear explosion in history.

Whatever its rank in the percussive pecking order, the blast obliterated hundreds of young Germans outright and left the survivors in the front line deafened, dazed, and terrified, unmanned by the telluric forces that had swallowed up their comrades. The British artillery then began shelling the German lines, and the troops advancing through the fiery light show of the predawn hours met little resistance. The lines shifted two to three miles in a single morning—the British captured the shattered ridge—before the customary stalemate once again took hold. Haig, thrilled by this modest gain but forgetting that it had required two years of painstaking spadework, was emboldened for the next stage of his offensive, which culminated in the Passchendaele debacle.

THE LANDSCAPE BEGINS to change as the shallow basin around Ypres gets left farther behind. Past Wijtschate rows of mature trees stand out in the middle distance. Away to the west a few wooded hills, some more than 350 feet tall, are clearly visible in the plain. Mont Kemmel is the nearest prominence, home to hiking trails, campgrounds, and a French mass grave. Nothing in this countryside is innocent of Great War associations. In the gentle undulations between Mont Kemmel and Wijtschate, aside from the bleached dominoes of Commonwealth gravestones, lie the giant craters from that 1917 blast, which are now used as swimming holes and fish hatcheries. The largest of the lot, called Spanbroekmolen, or the Pool of Peace, has been left to the elements as a sort of perpetual conversation piece. Bushes now grow around its perimeter and visitors are invited to contemplate the stagnant murk of the water's surface. Nearby, behind a prosperous-looking farmyard, is the small Lone Tree Cemetery. On the night of the big boom, Spanbroekmolen detonated a quarter of a minute later than its eighteen fellows. Several hundred unlucky Irishmen were already up and over the top when the rain of debris from this 91,000-pound explosion fell from the sky. Hence the cemetery, which holds eighty-eight graves.

I reach Messines. Its unsightly church stands out like a black eye in the blameless blue sky. The original, ruined church was the subject of sketches by Corporal Adolf Hitler, who spent much of the war in the trenches on this ridge. I pause in a café to make notes and put my feet up on a wicker chair. A chain-smoking twelve-year-old wordlessly serves me a coffee, holds out his hand, then pockets my coins, all without once meeting my eyes. This must be the Paris of Flanders.

The land drops off suddenly south of Messines into a succession of golden fields. The scene seems anonymously pastoral, but this stretch of land is anything but nameless. In the valley lies a still-active western front of Europe, this one far more enduring than that dug by the ghosts of 1914. Here the tiny River Douve separates the Flemish province of West-Vlaanderen (West Flanders) from an enclave of the Walloon province of Hainaut. On one side of the stream is Germanic turf; on the other, Latin. This linguistic front runs through Belgium and Luxembourg, separates Alsace from Lorraine, then meanders through the Swiss and Italian Alps before finally confronting another line, that of the Slavs, in the Balkans. In western Europe, the Latin-Germanic divide was lastingly established when Charlemagne's heirs sliced up the pie between Salic Goths and Ostrogoths in A.D. 843. The treaty giving rise to this age-old western front was signed—where else?—in Verdun.

As I cross the small bridge spanning the Douve, I'm stepping on both *een brug* and *un pont.* Ahead are *un arbre* and *une ferme*; behind, *een boom* and *een boerderij.* Birds wheel back and forth, becoming *oiseaux* or *vogels* in turn; clouds overhead change from Flemish *wolken* to French *nuages.* Not that much else changes, even if I do expect to see more gold chains and fewer spiky haircuts as a result of crossing the cultural divide. I am reminded of going from Ontario to Quebec over the Ottawa River, except that here in Flanders it is the French-speaking side that holds out the promise of greater familiarity. Although Flemish may be English's first cousin (or *cousin germain*, as French so aptly puts it), I feel more at home with my north Latin in-laws, having spent a dutiful Trudeau-led boyhood in quest of French-English bilingualism. The next time I'll cross this line, at the only other point of intersection between the two fronts, is eight weeks away in the Vosges Mountains, where the French spoken on the western slopes gives way to the Alsatian on the eastern.

Almost immediately on leaving Belgium's linguistic divide of the Douve, I enter the trees of Ploegsteert Wood and encounter the monuments that mark the southern extremity of the Ypres Salient. Two large stone lions sit before a rotunda on which the memorial makers, once again seeking absolution through accountancy, have etched another long list of young men whose bodies were never found. The proud felines, I assume, were placed there to cloak the grisly proceedings with imperial grandeur. The trick may have worked once, in the glory days when the sun never set on either gin or tonic, but it doesn't any longer. Now the reference to a defunct empire, here in a Belgian grove, seems pathetic. The lions' time had passed even when they were being sculpted—it was precisely because of the Great War that the dominions of the Empire distanced themselves from Britain. There remained, of course, links between crown and former colonies, some of which survived as tenacious throwbacks well past the mid-century mark. I need only think of my second-grade teacher teaching us Boer War songs in the shadow of the Rocky Mountains.

An elderly New Zealander couple befriends me in the neighboring Hyde Park Corner Cemetery. Our acquaintance doesn't start off well, as conversation quickly bogs down in Commonwealth cross-purposes. The man, fearful that a Yank like myself will mistake them for Australians, insists on telling me several times that he and his wife are Kiwis. Fortunately, she interrupts him.

"Look at that," she says, pointing down at what seems a standard headstone. "It's disgraceful."

I read: "A Soldier of the Great War Known Unto God," the euphemism coined by Rudyard Kipling to describe an unidentifiable body. It's a phrase etched on countless headstones along the Western Front. I'd always thought it rather elegant.

"And over there," she continues, gesturing to another row of headstones.

Her husband walks a few paces, squats down, and starts to weed the grass. I begin to understand.

"They've really let the side down. In France, they've done a lovely job, but here . . ." At the thought of imperfect gardening her voice trails off in disgust.

This is the couple's third trip to the old battlefields. Each time, they have tried to keep the groundskeepers of the Commonwealth War Graves Commission "on their toes." It's a hobby.

Messines, they go on to tell me, was the scene of a heroic New Zealand action in 1917, and is thus a well-known name in the antipodes. Ploegsteert Wood, in which we stand, is famous for two things. It once held the house where Churchill did his brief tour of duty in 1915, and it still holds a gigantic unexploded mine from the 1917 offensive. It used to hold two, but one exploded in 1955, apparently detonated by a stray thunderbolt striking a tree. The remaining mine has yet to go off, and no one has volunteered to go digging for it.

The New Zealanders climb back in their car and drive off north to give the gardeners of the Salient graveyards a hard time. I strike out south for France, setting a fast pace for these last few level miles. Once out of the woods I head through the village of Ploegsteert, where a woman with a sad smile hands me a pamphlet protesting a proposed hazardous waste depot in the area. First a time bomb, now a toxic dump—this is not a blessed corner of creation.

Half an hour later, border bars and discount shops begin to thicken along the roadside. Le Bizet, once a dormitory town for Belgian laborers who toiled in the brickworks across the way in France, now lives off a few French bargain hunters and day-trippers. At the border crossing, my status as disheveled pedestrian is immediately noticed and judged suspect. I'm waved over into a French customs office where, of the five young men in uniform, only one is not playing with a lighter, reading the paper, or listening intently to AM radio.

My arrival in the shed creates a stir. The backpack is emptied, and the search for illegal drugs almost instantly abandoned once the nature of my belongings is seen. My silver hip flask earns admiring wolf whistles. The linguist of the five correctly guesses it contains Irish whiskey, given the "O" in my last name. This inspires two others to crouch before me for a mock scrum—France and Ireland play every year in the Five Nations rugby tournament—that is interrupted by a shout of "*Putain!*" One of the boys has found on my maps the obscure border post where he is to be transferred. Just the other day he was trying to tell the others about it, and they didn't know where it was.

His explanations are cut short. A dignified man enters the shed. He has swept-back gray hair and is wearing an understated blue suit. He greets each officer individually, then turns to me, unsure of what to do next. He glances down at my boxer shorts on the table, which seem to help him come to a decision. He shakes my hand, utters a perfunctory "*bonjour,*" then turns on his heel and walks out.

Seeing my puzzled face, a customs officer explains: "*Maire adjoint. Socialiste.*"

ON THE WAY into the deputy mayor's town, Armentières, I see a directional road sign pointing to nearby Bailleul. During the Race to the Sea in 1914, the townspeople of Bailleul fled in terror, and the retreating German army let the inmates of an insane asylum run free in the deserted streets. This incident, which inspired film director Philippe de Broca's classic pacifist farce, *King of Hearts*, is not difficult to dredge up from memory after spending time in the Bizet customs post. Inmates still run a few asylums in French Flanders.

I walk into the large town square of Armentières, a paved expanse used as a parking lot. Somewhere a reconstructed belfry chimes out the time. A few cafés give out onto the square, the clings and clangs of their pinball machines adding to the late-afternoon carillon. The city, once famous as a party town for British troops, was leveled in the fighting of 1918 and hastily reconstructed afterward. A song, "Mademoiselle from Armentières," became an anthem for soldiers in this sector, its countless verses—raunchy or polite, depending on the audience—always concluding with the chorus, "Hinky-dinky (or "Inky pinky") parlay-voo." There are worse ways to end a visit to Flanders:

> Mademoiselle from Armentières, parlay-voo?
> Mademoiselle from Armentières, parlay-voo?
> Your eggs and frites, they give us the squits.
> Hinky-dinky parlay-voo.

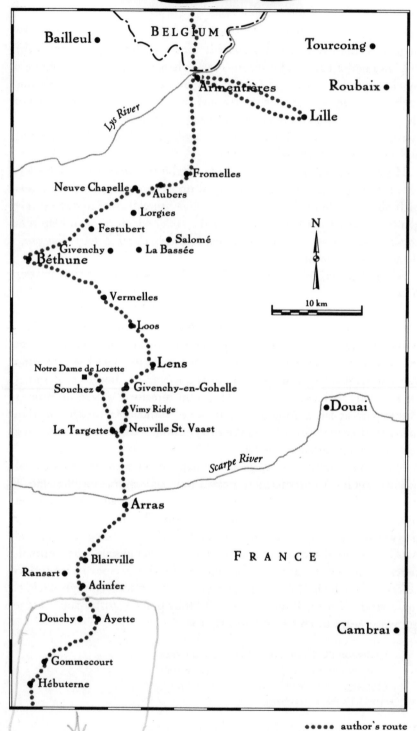

ARTOIS

BELGIUM

Bailleul •

Tourcoing •

Roubaix •

Armentières

Lille •

Lys River

Fromelles •

Neuve Chapelle •

Aubers •

Lorgies •

Festubert •

Salomé •

Givenchy •

La Bassée •

Béthune •

Vermelles •

Loos •

N

10 km

Lens •

Notre Dame de Lorette ■

Souchez •

Givenchy-en-Gohelle •

Vimy Ridge ▲

• Douai

La Targette •

Neuville St. Vaast •

Scarpe River

Arras •

Blairville •

F R A N C E

Ransart •

Adinfer •

Douchy •

Ayette •

Cambrai •

Gommecourt •

Hébuterne •

••••• author's route

ALBERT

Artois

1. Lille to Aubers to Neuve Chapelle

THE RAIN FALLS. Armentières becomes a puddle in search of the hole in my shoe. I take a commuter train to the capital of French Flanders, Lille, and put off for a day my journey south to the slag heaps of Artois. I bring a book with me, *Pride and Prejudice*, and read it in a restaurant. Elizabeth tells Darcy to take a hike just as it's time for me to go back to the Front and do the same. I forget to look at Lille.

Ten years later Lille will be an aspiring Europolis, a showcase of shiny technology parks and shopping centres. The high-speed train that goes under the Channel will stop at a glitzy, glassy station in the middle of town. Lille as a satellite of Brussels, a suburb of London, a city in eastern Kent—all notions that would cause its most famous son, Charles de Gaulle, to turn over in his tank. Expressways and express rail lines stream west of Lille toward England. The tiny cemeteries and memorials in the fields near Armentières, St. Omer, Bailleul, and Hazebrouck flash past the windows of the TGV trains like places not really seen. The very speed of passage mocks the unmoving behemoth that once lay over the countryside. No-man's-land is crossed in seconds, as coffee is poured and another Eurobun buttered. The Chunnel shall one day fog the British memory of war, for much of their national myth-making is tied up with going abroad to fight, with sailing out to meet the foe. What meaning "fair stood the wind for France" or "there's some corner of a foreign field / That is for ever England," when making the once fateful trip takes less time than crossing London on the Underground? The notion of France will have been rendered domestic. Wogs no longer start at Calais, Wogs 'R' Us.

Somewhere in this land rich in anachronistic borders and fronts is yet another invisible line, the shared boundary of Flanders and Artois. The current *départements* are Nord and Pas de Calais, but the long-standing regional names serve the purposes of this account better, for they conjure up a history, a sense of the past. Roughly speaking, Artois is the upland separating the forests of Picardy and the basin of Île-de-France from the great northern European plain beginning in Flanders and continuing through the Netherlands, Germany, and Poland. Yet the boundary that matters most, I tell myself as I study my maps in puzzlement, is the line of the Front. To be more precise: the Front as it was in 1916, the year of utter stalemate, the Front I have set out to see. In 1917 and 1918 the lines moved considerably in northern France, making any retrospective hike down no-man's-land an event for a zigzagger of Olympian stamina. With that in mind, a few miles south of Armentières I declare myself to be in Artois.

In fact, I have just entered a different type of buffer zone: suburbia. A landscape of bungalows lies ahead. On the road surface are speed bumps or, as French highway slang has it, "sleeping policemen." Somehow it's more satisfying to drive over them that way. I assume that the residents of this subdivision work in Lille, the big city, and not Armentières, the small town, because the dogs I encounter here are quivering little neurotics, more fashion accessories than faithful companions. Thus the preemptive tactic I've been using to confuse charging farm dogs—I bark first—fails miserably. These inbred suburbanites obey only their nerves. One toy-sized beast barrels out of a front gate, unimpressed by my bared incisors, and lets off a volley of yaps that drills deep into my inner ear. The two of us stand our ground in the narrow street, snarling theatrically at each other. I finally let loose a howl and lunge forward. The beast skitters back through the gate, its barking all the more furious for having given way to a bigger opponent. I move on, but not before glimpsing the curtains of the bungalow's front room fall back into place. So I'm not good with dogs, lady.

The tract housing thins and the cemeteries start cropping up again. The land is riddled with roads and tracks laid out in a grid pattern. There are far more people living here than in the countryside of Belgian Flanders. Farmhouses have been gentrified, rowhouses decorated, and a few garden sheds left in artful disarray. I pass several abandoned brickworks, testament to a once thriving industry. Catholicism's taste for the big gesture also appears. The crossroads around here are just that—roads with crosses. At several junctions, there are man-sized crucifixes on which are nailed extravagantly suffering Christs, like butterflies under glass. They look down at me as I sweat in the morning sun.

At a hamlet called Fromelles I pass a roadside Calvary that's not on my map. Kitty-corner from Christ there's a country café, which I enter to ask directions. Behind the counter a woman in a blue paisley smock watches bugs affix themselves to a long strip of flypaper. She glances up as I close the door behind me.

"Are you looking for a job? Because there aren't any to be found around here."

I think briefly about the *King of Hearts*, then shake my head. I tell her I'm looking for the road to Aubers.

This doesn't cut it as a ploy to change the subject. She tells me that unemployment has hit the area hard. Her daughter can't find a job and "might even have to go to Lille." I point out that Lille is only a dozen miles away. The café lady is not interested in geography. She tells me that unemployment is a scourge for young people today.

A man of about seventy comes in the door, smiling and ready to engage in debate. I like him instantly. He's wearing a gray tweed cap, a blue and white zip-up sweater, and navy-blue polyester bell-bottoms. He greets the café owner deferentially, as if he's conferring a prize on her, then fires a question at me that I can't quite understand. The French language streams out of his mouth, in a singsong accent I've never heard before. This is the legacy of the *chti* (pronounced "shtee"), the patois of northern France. The old man is what's called a *chti'mi*: He speaks French the way a Welsh auctioneer would speak English. On the third time around I understand what he's saying.

"Vous êtes oisif, m'sieu?"

He's asking me if I'm idle. I look at him, then at the café lady, suspecting that they're some sort of non sequitur tag team.

When I admit to loafing, I learn that today is a wonderful day for the idle—and that the old man has a wonderfully idle life. His wife in the city, his children gone, no one around the house, he can go and relax in the fields with his newspaper. Sometimes he sits up and reads it, sometimes he just lies down and covers his face with it. You can never be too careful with the sun. Especially at this time of the year. If you're not careful, you can get sunstroke. That would be unfortunate, for then you couldn't read the paper, could you?

He stops for a breath.

The three of us spend an enjoyable Socratic moment together, the old man posing questions then running away with the answers. When it's time for me to resume hiking, my two companions, satisfied that I'm idle but not looking for a job, direct me to a cow track leading to the village of

Aubers. I promise, nodding my way out the door, to stay in the shade as much as I can, to avoid sunstroke, to enjoy idleness, to take a bus if I get tired, to profit from my youth.

AUBERS, WHICH CAN be made out in the distance, sits on a slight rise in this transitional area between Flanders and Artois. In May of 1915, the British tried to storm the rise, to prove to their French allies that they were willing to take casualties. In that respect the attack was a success. They were mowed down by machine guns, and about 12,000 men were lost. At Fromelles, in 1916, it was the Australians' turn. Advancing without reinforcements, they stormed the German trenches, then were cut off, surrounded, and massacred. In some Australian battalions, more than 80 percent of the men were killed.

The pastures between Fromelles and Aubers are dotted with the crumbling remains of pillboxes. Beside one of them, as if just placed there, is a bouquet of fresh flowers. There is no card.

The flowers in the field hint at the profusion of blossoms in the handsome red village of Aubers. Despite the old man's opinion, his is not a village of the indolent. The houses, neatly rebuilt from the heaps of broken brick that were left after the armies had moved off in 1918, look well maintained and welcoming. The Front, a strip of Europe where nothing is old, where most things were reconstructed on the cheap in the 1920s and 1930s, has thus far been a succession of sad villages and soulless towns. Aubers seems determined to shake off the past, or at least cover it up with flowers.

At a fork in the road below Aubers, signs indicate the way to "Salomé" and "Lorgies." Both destinations sound like a good time, but my route lies elsewhere, down a gentle grade to the southwest, toward the village of Neuve Chapelle, another name in the annals of folly. The British made a successful surprise attack here in 1915. It was a surprise despite themselves—they did not have enough shells to launch a long preliminary bombardment and thereby give away their intentions. In one morning, they took the town and even managed to break through into the countryside beyond it. The 1,400 Germans holding the lines at Neuve Chapelle could not withstand the onslaught. They were outnumbered thirty-five to one.

Then the British stopped, as a result of the indescribable confusion reigning in the command structure. Reinforcements were sent up far too late, officers in adjacent units did not answer to the same commanders, and communication became a tangle of orders and counterorders. For most of the afternoon of March 10, 1915, there was a gaping hole in the German lines, but it was not exploited. Tens of thousands of men sat on the ground smoking, waiting to be told to go forward. The generals, as can only be expected of Great War stories, ordered the attacks renewed long after the Germans had had the time to shore up their defenses. Slaughter ensued. The Germans counterattacked and regained much of the yardage they had lost.

This did not play well in Britain, where expectations had been raised by reports of early success. The war, rejoiced the editorialists, was almost won. A scapegoat was needed for the reversal of fortune. Since the generals, John French and Douglas Haig, could not very well blame themselves and didn't dare blame the thousands they had just sent to their deaths, it was thought best to lay the whole thing at the doorstep of the British worker. There had not been enough artillery shells, army spokesmen declared, because the British worker was a shirker who spent all his time getting drunk. That was why Neuve Chapelle had been a disaster. The civilian government dutifully ordered British pubs to lock up in the afternoons, a law that remained on the books until 1989, when Prime Minister Margaret Thatcher decided that the threat to the war effort was over.

OUTSIDE NEUVE CHAPELLE, in a quiet semi-suburban street near the ruins of a lethal fortification known as the Quadrilateral, the locals appear to have launched a lawn gnome war. Dwarfs, trolls, and *schtroumpfs*—smurfs, in English—stand in competitive quantities before a row of recently built houses that coincides with the farthest advance of the British line. Aside from the gnomes, the only statuary of note is in the village itself. At a bend in the road is yet another Christ in agony, a replacement for a more famous fellow sufferer. The Portuguese, who held this part of the Front in 1918, were so surprised by a German attack during the spring of that year that they fled Neuve Chapelle without the legless crucifixion scene they had been lugging around with them for good luck. Happily, this so-called "Christ of the Trenches" was found after the war and restored to them. The villagers had to settle for a new Christ, which they erected at an unmissable spot on the highway leading out of town to Armentières.

That Christ is not, however, at Neuve Chapelle's most striking crossroads. Just west of the village, on the way to the town of Béthune, is an unprepossessing old inn called the Auberge de la Bombe. The name is just a coincidence, the owner tells me in the parking lot. I'm not

convinced but say nothing—our immediate surroundings are too dis-
tracting. Near la Bombe is a Portuguese military graveyard, a reminder of
the 1918 surprise German attack. Beside it, dominating the junction,
stands a large memorial with gray granite tigers and lotus blossoms rising
up from the dusty fields. Delicate stone latticework and Sanskrit lettering
run down the side of twin pavilions. This is the principal Indian memorial of the Western Front. Troops from India were in the vanguard of the
Neuve Chapelle fiasco of 1915, betrayed by the incompetence of their
colonial overseers. I try to get a closer look at the structure. Wherever
there are large stone felines, I've noticed, there is usually a British
embarrassment. The louder the roar, the emptier the tribute. The gate
is locked.

I get a lift into Béthune from the innkeeper of the Bombe, a man in his
forties. Signs for cemeteries in Festubert and Givenchy, outposts of no-
man's-land, flash by on the roadside. I ask him what he thinks of Indians
and Portuguese coming to die in his grandfather's backyard.

He whistles and says, "Unbelievable. This place is still unbelievable."

2. Béthune to Loos to Lens

Béthune, explains the driver giving me a lift in from the strange
crossroads at Neuve Chapelle, is a *ville bourgeoise*. Lens, the other big
town in the area, is a *ville populaire*. Which means that the one houses the
owners, and the other, the workers. Which also means that you can't have
fun in Béthune.

I tell him that during the First World War there was a famous brothel
in Béthune, called the Red Lantern.

He looks at me and says that if it's still there, he hasn't found it.

I'm let off in the central square, an improbable collection of skinny
shop façades and bunkerlike bank fronts. A medieval belfry, reconstructed after the Great War, stretches skyward over a midsummer crowd
sucking down colorful drinks. The tall tower is the town's pride, a symbol
of the city's freedom from feudal obligations. In the Middle Ages, the
burghers of Flanders and Artois erected belfries to cock a snook in stone
at churchmen and nobles.

Times have changed, and the burghers have become bourgeois. My
lift-giver was right about this being an uptight place. Along the sides of
the square files a procession of *baise-beige* couples out for a stroll before
dinner. Baise-beige ("fuck wanly") is the rude recent permutation of
bcbg, a slang term about social climbing that stands for *bon chic bon genre*

(roughly, "preppy and presentable"). To be baise-beige is to exude clean-cut smugness, to look askance at anything that tradition has not conse-crated, to ignore rather than inquire. Fortunately for Béthune's soul, the town's well-scrubbed decorum is easily breached. Every now and then a wreck of a car from the mining district south of town guns its way through the main square, music blaring and sports pennants trailing in the breeze. The strolling window-shoppers, as if obeying an unspoken agreement, affect not to notice these intrusions, preferring to continue comparing accessories and offspring, even if the effort entails raising their voices. The arrangement seems to suit everyone concerned, both the baise-beige on the sidewalks and the working-class heroes in their cars.

TIME TO FOLLOW those heroes. I look at the map: I am heading out of Béthune, a town 130 miles directly north of Paris. I'm walking southeast to Lens, along a road that runs straight as a geometer's dream, through a gray, treeless plain punctuated by conical slag heaps and brooding red-brick villages. In the distance, the skeletal remnants of machinery at a pithead stand out against a metallic sky. The town of Vermelles appears, its streets a succession of cherry-colored *corons*, the compact rowhouses once home to black-lunged miners. This is Germinal country, Zola in the provinces. Successive generations of families lived and died on this bleak Artesian plain, their menfolk going deep underground to extract coal for the heavy industries of Lille, Tourcoing, and Roubaix. The factories and foundries have long since closed, as have most of the mines. Their great dark mounds of spoil now shoulder an unlikely mantle of weeds that shifts and shudders in the wind. The plain is silent.

Except for this roadway. Trucks, buses, cars hurtle over the blacktop; capricious clouds of dust whirl in their wake. I scan the horizon for the first signs of Lens. Eyes sting, ears ring. If there are any other pedestrians on this stretch of road, they must be out of their minds. I bend my head and walk on, the hot breath of diesel never absent for more than a minute. Every time I glance upward, it seems that I'm looking at the word "Fruehauf," rubbery and dirty, on the rear tire mudguards of onrushing transport trailers. Occasionally I glimpse a signpost for an incongruously named British cemetery: Quality Street, Philosophe. The landscape is such that only graveyards provide levity. For the next few miles, the past will be more interesting than the present.

THE YEAR 1915 started well enough. The spontaneous Christmas truce of 1914, during which soldiers on opposing sides clambered into no-man's-

land to exchange gifts and compare family mementos, seemed an augury
of decency on the Western Front, even if the skies conspired to make the
winter one of the most execrable in living memory. In northern France,
from October 25, 1914, to March 10, 1915, there were only eighteen days
without rain. The misery of millions of men, standing in cold and muddy
ditches for months on end, can only be imagined.

The German supreme commander, Erich von Falkenhayn, one of the
few farsighted generals of the war, saw that total victory was now
impossible, given the failure of the daring Schlieffen Plan. Falkenhayn
concentrated his main offensives on the Eastern Front, hoping to knock
the Russians out of the war and force the French and English into a
negotiated peace. On their Western Front—for it is to the west of
Germany, after all—the armies of the Kaiser dug deeper into the earth,
poured concrete, and got ready for a long siege.

The French, under Joffre, thought differently about the coming year.
Or rather, they didn't think, they just attacked, again and again and
again. The carnage of 1914 repeated itself, only this time the action
didn't take place principally in the lost provinces of Alsace and Lorraine,
but in the newly occupied regions of Champagne and Artois. Behind
their ever-strengthening defenses, the German army controlled some of
the major industrial centers of the north—Tourcoing, Roubaix, Lille,
Lens, Douai, Cambrai—as well as 90 percent of France's iron ore production, 80 percent of its steel, and 40 percent of its coal. There could be
no respite as long as troops of the Kaiser stayed on French soil. This
pressure to act, understandable in light of the national emergency, was
unfortunately matched with abysmal leadership. With the exception of a
few enlightened instances, the tactic of head-on, massive assault was
maintained, as if no lessons could be drawn from the 454,000 French
battlefield deaths of the previous year. Joffre, ever imperturbable, seemed
not to care.

The French army attacked across the freezing, open spaces of Champagne in February of 1915. Perhaps a mile was gained, and 50,000 French
soldiers killed. In March, the British, eager to show their battle willing-
ness despite their smaller numbers, attacked at Neuve Chapelle. In April,
the Germans opened their gas canisters for the first time, at St. Juliaan in
Flanders, and won a few acres of the Salient.

The following month the French readied another grand offensive.
Undaunted by the Champagne debacle, the general staff drew up a plan
of attack for Artois. The plan called for storming the heights of Vimy
Ridge and Notre Dame de Lorette and then rushing over the plain of

Artois to the city of Douai. The result was predictable: a couple of miles gained, four ruined villages recaptured, and 102,500 French soldiers killed in forty days. The injured and maimed numbered three or four times that. The extent of the carnage, let alone its horror, is nauseating to contemplate.

The conscript pool was deep. After a summer spent licking its wounds, the French army went on the offensive once again. In September, October, and November 1915, Joffre ordered repeated assaults, in precisely the same regions where his tactics had proved so futile in the spring. One needn't possess hindsight to recognize the work of a dunderhead. Predictably, the same prodigious bloodletting resulted, but this time only a few hundred yards of wasteland were the reward. In Champagne, a whole swath of villages were destroyed so utterly that after the war they were never rebuilt, and the scarred land around them was turned into firing ranges for the French army.

In Artois, the British attacked to the north of the French positions. They lost 60,000 men, killed or wounded, around the town of Loos, in an offensive that briefly became a byword for butchery. The German defenders called one scene *Das Leichenfeld von Loos*—the Corpse-Field of Loos. Machine gunners had a wide-open shooting gallery as masses of men were ordered to walk toward them over the plain. Of 10,000 sent over the top on the second day, fewer than 2,000 survived. The Germans, who, as their regimental history has it, "fired till their barrels burst," felt so bad for their foe that they unilaterally imposed a truce to let the hordes of injured British soldiers crawl back to their lines. Yet this battle's ignominy has faded, at least from a short list of remembered debacles, simply because the disasters of 1915 pale in comparison to those of 1916 and 1917. In the Great War, there was an escalation in command incompetence.

In MY JOURNEY to Loos over that same Leichenfeld, the road from Béthune to Lens has calmed somewhat since the morning, now that the sacred lunch hour has descended on the land. My Fruehauf-waving tormentors have entered their *routier* restaurants, ready for the thumping big meal that French truckers habitually down at midday. The remaining cars on the highway, rusty and in need of paint, rush past at irregular intervals, many of their drivers wide-eyed at the sight of a plodding pedestrian. At a rise in the road, I duck into the Loos British Cemetery and Memorial, ascend a few stone steps in the visitors' pavilion, and come out onto a rooftop platform. From here I have an unobstructed view of the battlefield.

To the north is the plain of Gohelle, its name apt in its last syllable. It stretches for eight or so miles toward the town of La Bassée, featureless, flat, empty, ringed with slag heaps. There are no villages on the plain, and the crops, whatever they were, have been harvested. The prospect is of endless vegetal stubble stretching to a horizon crowned with distant pimples of dirt. At a military cemetery in its center is the terrain where the British, in a famous incident of the Battle of Loos, gassed themselves blind. New to the vagaries of what was euphemistically termed the "accessory" and impatient with the unhelpful readings of army anemometers, the generals behind the lines ordered the gas released against the wind. The toxic cloud filled the British front and support trenches, so the attackers went forward, wheezing and dying. Nearer to my vantage point is the spot where a youth named Peter Laidlaw, in a fairly unbelievable act of bravery, jumped up into no-man's-land, ripped off his gas mask, and marched back and forth across the front line, playing the bagpipes to rally his fellow Scots. The kilted young men rose up from their ditches and rushed to their deaths in the green fog.

To the southwest, in a hollow a mile and a half down the main road to Lens, is the small town of Loos. From my viewing platform in the cemetery Loos looks like the gateway to Mordor. Two mountainous heaps of coal dirt loom behind it, identical twins several hundred feet tall. They are pitch-black, perfect cones, their silhouettes uncannily regular. This landmark is the *Double Crassier*—the double slag heap, a touch of the apocalyptic in an already inhuman landscape. On September 25, 1915, members of the London Regiment ran at full speed down the hill from where I now stand toward that crassier. It was a paradigmatic moment of the Great War. Despite the bullets, gas, and barbed wire, they advanced joyfully—because they were chasing a soccer ball. It is estimated that 1,200 of them fell, dead or wounded, within the first hour.

Robert Graves tells another tale of the Battle of Loos that has entered the canon of Great War lore. The poet, then a twenty-year-old officer with the Royal Welsh Fusiliers, came to the front lines as exhausted troops streamed back from no-man's-land, gassed, injured, and shellshocked. In an oft-cited passage of his memoir *Good-bye to All That*, he tells of one story he heard from a survivor:

> When his platoon had run about twenty yards he signalled them to lie down and open covering fire. The din was tremendous. He saw the platoon on the left flopping down too, so he whistled the advance again. Nobody seemed to hear. He jumped up from his shell-hole and waved and signalled "Forward." Nobody stirred. He shouted: "You bloody cowards, are you

leaving me to go alone?" His platoon-sergeant, groaning with a broken shoulder, gasped out: "Not cowards, sir. Willing enough. But they're all f——g dead." The Pope's Nose machine gun traversing had caught them as they rose to the whistle.

Not all the gruesomeness of 1915 occurred on the Western Front. At sea, the British liner *Lusitania* was sunk by a German U-boat, and the American lives lost (128 of the 1,198 drowned) did no good for the Kaiser's image in the eyes of the giant neutral democracy. By the end of 1915 American capital had begun to bankroll the British and French war efforts, and the tide of public opinion swelled in favor of intervention at about the same rate as Allied indebtedness grew. The other German propaganda blunder of the year was the execution in Belgium of the forty-nine-year-old British nurse Edith Cavell. Having freely confessed her crime—helping Allied soldiers get out of German-occupied Belgium —she was shot in the early-morning hours of October 12, 1915, despite a long and loud campaign for clemency by American and Spanish diplomats in Brussels. So great was the international outcry, from neutrals and belligerents alike, that a startled German military command ordered all further executions of women civilians commuted or postponed. Two years and three days later, it would be the turn of Margaretha Geertruida MacLeod Zelle, better known as Mata Hari, to face a French firing squad. There was no outcry this time, just the beginning of a sultry legend. Aged forty-one at the time of her execution, the dancer and spy for the Germans eventually eclipsed Cavell as the most celebrated woman of the First World War, which may be taken as a comment on the relative glamour of their respective professions.

Although the other fronts are beyond the scope of this journey, it's worth noting that 1915 was also the year of Gallipoli. In an attempt to open another front, the British hatched a scheme whereby a landing in Turkey would lead their troops to Istanbul and beyond. Badly planned, atrociously executed, and needlessly prolonged, the Gallipoli campaign was another of the war's great foul-ups, a particularly graphic example of lost opportunities and wrong decisions made at the wrong time. Gallipoli's legacy, the memory of thousands of volunteers from Australia and New Zealand—known by their army corps' acronym, ANZAC—trapped on a narrow shoreline throughout a sweltering summer and fall, served as fillip to the anti-imperial nationalism down under. When Australia eventually becomes a republic, its Bunker Hill will be recognized as ANZAC Beach in Turkey.

As for the beach's defenders, 1915 marked the full flowering of the Young Turks movement. Mustafa Kemal, the founder of modern secular Turkey, was among the gunners on the heights above Gallipoli. The year would thus be a glorious one for the Young Turks, were it not for the other event that took place in their homeland. In 1915, the authorities in Istanbul began the wholesale slaughter of the country's Armenian population. Genocide ushered in the twentieth century.

Now IT IS the past that has become intolerable to contemplate. I turn away from slag heap and cemetery and walk through Loos into Lens. Despite its name, Lens is not photogenic. The place was obliterated in the war, then rebuilt with no pretensions to coherence. Here, the squat corons of Germinal were eventually outnumbered by the high-rise *cités* of immigration, the suburban housing projects in which the misery of modern France is hidden.

Saturday night, however, knows no frowns. The young are out in force downtown, showing a regard for come-hither fashion that would make a Parisian blush. I sit in a café and put my feet up, content to forget the truly awful pizza I've just ingested by watching the passing parade of tanned *rondeurs*. This is a serious scene. Oh, to give up walking and own a cosmetics counter in Lens—I could retire on the memories. A movie theater empties a wave of adolescent hipsters onto the sidewalk, and soon the air fills with the electric crackle of a French crowd exchanging quadruple social kisses. Souped-up subcompacts roar out of parking lots, voices rise and fall as car radios pass within earshot. From one, I hear the familiar drone of "Papa Don't Preach." Only then do I remember where I am. The Western Front.

3. Vimy to La Targette

> Un vêtement qui dort
> Est un vêtement mort

> (Clothing asleep
> Is clothing dead)

Poetry stares out at me from the window of a Lens dry cleaner's. It is a white, flat morning, and the road out of town leads past a row of corons with doors open wide to let out the beery funk of Saturday night. In the redbrick thresholds hang slim strips of grimy plastic that feebly suggest villa life in some sunnier land. The strips sway slightly in the exhaust that wafts into living rooms from the main road.

I skip into a backyard and begin my shortcut to Vimy Ridge. A heap of workings from an abandoned mine must first be climbed before gaining the greener slopes. The black dirt shifts and subsides under my boots— it's like climbing a granular sand dune that has been treated with tar. Even the local dogs think I'm demented, their barks ceasing abruptly once I take to the black hill. On the map it looked so simple.

By the time I reach the main square of the village of Givenchy-en-Gohelle, my once pristine Front-walking outfit—green sweatshirt, gray denim trousers, tan leather hiking boots—has become a sooty mess. I look ready for a minstrel show. At a riding school on the very edge of the battlefield, a young lady on horseback glances over at me in horror. Somehow this is not how I pictured my visit to Vimy Ridge.

DIFFICULT AS IT may be for older Canadians to believe, most of their younger compatriots grew up not knowing what Vimy Ridge represented. Carving soap crosses and wearing red poppies were somehow related to *The Longest Day*, not to a place called Vimy. Granted, there was a Vimy Street in every Canadian town, but that coincidence could always be shrugged off as some archaic phenomenon needing no investigation.

Long after making this hike, I called a Paris-bound friend in Toronto and asked her to bring me Pierre Berton's *Vimy*, a lively account of the 1917 battle.

"What was the name again?" she asked.

"Vimy. Like Vimy Ridge."

"Vinny?"

"No, Vimy, for Chrissakes!"

"Pierre Berton wrote a book called Vinny?"

And so on. The memory has been washed away far more thoroughly than any similar effacement of the words "Somme" or "Verdun." This is all the more peculiar since both of those battles represent decay and decline. The Somme spelled the end of the British century, and Verdun broke the French for the century that followed. Vimy, on the other hand, is a positive concept, the foundation myth of a country. Vimy was the Canadian Lexington, the moment of a national coming of age. Monuments were thrown up all over Canada in honor of Vimy Ridge and the troops of the Great War. The national government building in Ottawa has a "Peace Tower" in front of it, a tall, mock-Gothic belfry erected to commemorate the 65,000 Canadian dead of the Great War. The memory of Vimy thus informs the symbolic architecture of the Canadian confederation. The Parliament—the totem of national unity—is a mausoleum.

What happened on the heights of Vimy was quite simple, and quite bloody. One hundred thousand Canadian soldiers successfully stormed a heavily fortified German ridge on the snowy Easter Monday of 1917. The place was thought to be impregnable, but overwhelming artillery barrages and meticulously rehearsed attack tactics had been ordered by Arthur Currie, the British Columbia real estate agent and sometime embezzler in command of the Canadian troops. Currie's methods combined to dislodge the Germans from a height that they had successfully defended against all comers in previous battles. Flushed with victory, the Canadians tried to press on beyond the ridge but were cut down by German reinforcements rushed in from Douai with machine guns and artillery. The capture of Vimy was the sole tactical success in a two-pronged Allied offensive that would come to grief around the Scarpe River in southern Artois and end in utter catastrophe on the hills of Champagne.

Today the place is a showpiece of Canadian nationalism in the middle of an unlovely corner of France. An enormous two-tined Dalmatian marble monument rises up from a vast lawn. Into these two pylons and their base Walter Seymour Allward sculpted a score of larger-than-life allegorical figures to represent attributes of the nation and the emotions of its citizens. Grief is the figure most photographed. She looks over a commanding view of the plain to the east, with its slag heaps marching away at regular intervals to the industrial complexes of Douai. The perspective is surprisingly panoramic, as if one had climbed a tall mountain in the company of Grief. The Canadian soldier at the time must have felt the same way.

Behind the well-tended lawn is a well-tended battlefield, several acres of mine craters, shell holes, and trenches having been preserved under a soothing cover of greenery. Signs direct visitors to keep off the grass, which most do. Yet the frozen bedlam of the site only serves to excite small boys into aggression. As I head to the men's room to wash off my Givenchy grime, a child jumps from a trench and squeals, "*Coucou, je vous attaque!*" ("Look out, you're under attack!") I cringe, much to his enjoyment.

Underneath the battlefield, a Canadian college student leads visitors through one of the tunnels that formed the subterranean city the attackers inhabited before their assault. There are rail lines, dormitories, casualty clearing stations—and everywhere a dank odor of damp rock and old fear, mixed in with a trace of moldering cloth uniforms. I will later recognize this as the lingering smell of the Great War. The throat catches and the chest constricts. This subtle scent in the troglodyte part of the ridge seems truer to the memory of the Front than the fresh air of the battlefield park.

Once back outside in no-man's-land, I pick up a Canadian government handout about Vimy at the information kiosk. My eyes fall on a phrase describing the Great War as "very costly in terms of lives and wounds."

When I reach the pines planted on the park's perimeter, I turn to look at the trenches and monument one last time. Vimy surprises me. It departs from the discretion usually associated with Canada. The nationalism displeases but is inevitable given the imaginative importance of this spot for earlier generations. As a theater of memory, however, the setting is peerless. I don't leave proud to be a Canadian; I leave even more wary of anyone in a uniform.

THE LAND SOUTH of Vimy, although reclaimed from the war, exhibits its scars through its abundance of cemeteries. Outside the village of Neuville St. Vaast, the jumping-off point for many of the Canadian troops in 1917, there is a hamlet called La Targette. The name is fitting. Two cemeteries sit side by side: French, from the offensive of 1915, and British, from that of 1917. Across the road is an inn with a mural on its outer wall evoking Napoleonic exploits. Whereas the British graveyard is gardenlike and domestic, the French resembles a parade ground of crosses and serial numbers. Despite these national differences, the evocation of waste is the same.

Farther up the road yet another cemetery awaits. I recognize the Volksbund Deutscher Kriegsgraberfürsorge (the German War Graves Commission) logo on its gates from my visit to the Kindermord graveyard at Langemarck. There are 37,000 burials here. I step out of the entrance pavilion and onto the overgrown lawn of somber black crosses and tall trees. There is a Romantic strain to this place, alien to the French functionary or the British gardener. Many of the graves hold no crosses. I jot down the inscription on the first one of these that I approach:

> Leopold Aronsohn
> 18/8/1917
> Musketier

There is a star of David alongside the name. Others, in their hundreds, show the same symbol. These are the saddest graves of all the sad graves in La Targette. To die in a senseless war for a country that would soon want to rob you of life—there can be no worse trap set by the twentieth century. Twelve thousand Jews died in the German army of the First World War.

Perhaps it was better to die here in Artois and never to have known of the coming evil. Historian Martin Gilbert recounts that during the Great

War there were three Austro-Hungarian field marshals and eight generals who were Jewish. (The Allies, by contrast, had but one prominent Jewish officer—General John Monash, the head of the Australian Imperial Force.) In 1943 one of the Austro-Hungarians, Field-Marshal Johann Georg Franz Hugo Friedlander, was deported to Theresienstadt, the Bohemian garrison town where the imprisoned Gavrilo Princip had spent his last days twenty-five years earlier. Friedlander was herded into the Theresienstadt ghetto, then taken to Auschwitz in 1944, from which he never returned. His ultimate fate was shared by hundreds of thousands of other Jewish veterans.

Alfred Lichtenstein, a Prussian Jew, was spared such knowledge. As an artist and satirist, however, he did have a keen sense of where the Great War was leading. Lichtenstein died in Picardy in 1914. His poem "Abschied" ("Off to the Front") is the only appropriate response to this massing of cemeteries at La Targette and Neuville Saint Vaast and Vimy. The prose translation is by Timothy P. Morrow.

> *Vorm Sterben mache ich noch mein Gedicht.*
> *Still, Kameraden, stört mich nicht.*
>
> *Wir ziehn zum Krieg. Der Tod ist unser Kitt.*
> *O, heulte mir doch die Geliebte nit.*
>
> *Was liegt an mir. Ich gehe gerne ein.*
> *Die Mutter weint. Man muß aus Eisen sein.*
>
> *Die Sonne fällt zum Horizont hinab.*
> *Bald wirft man mich ins milde Massengrab.*
>
> *Am Himmel brennt das brave Abendrot.*
> *Vielleicht bin ich in dreizehn Tagen tot.*

> (Before my death I still must write my poem.
> Quiet, comrades, do not disturb me.
>
> We're off to war; death is our bond.
> Oh, that my sweetheart would stop wailing.
>
> What do I matter; I'm glad to go.
> My mother is crying. One must be made of iron.
>
> The sun sets on the horizon.
> Soon I'll be thrown into a gentle mass grave.
>
> The sun in the sky glows dusk red.
> In thirteen days I may be dead.)

I leave the cemetery, eager to get to a city of the living.

4. *Notre Dame de Lorette to Souchez to Neuville St. Vaast*

I left Vimy and La Targette too quickly nine years ago. I had gotten only half the story.

I shift down into third to ascend the rise of Notre Dame de Lorette. It is late August 1995, and I tune in to BBC long wave on the car radio. Reports from Bosnia say that NATO warplanes are bombing Serb positions in the hinterland of Sarajevo. A military spokesman comes on to say that all is going well, that all targets are being hit, that lives are being spared. I pull into a parking lot. This is not the place to be listening to army publicists.

In front of me stretch seemingly endless rows of crosses, marking the graves of those who died in Joffre's repeated attempts to take this hill and Vimy Ridge in 1915. There are more than 19,000 French soldiers buried here. Looking over these acres of spiky, waist-high crosses is like looking over fields of unharvested wheat. The image that comes to mind is of the grim sower, not the reaper. Roses flower at the foot of each of the thousands of crosses.

In the middle of the cemetery squats a monumental eyesore of a church, built in the Romanesque-Byzantine style favored by French clerics in the early decades of this century. Sacré Coeur on Montmartre in Paris is a similar hilltop blemish; here, however, the stone is not a blinding white, as it is there, but a dark, dirty gray, the color of despair, of northern France in November. In front of the church of Notre Dame de Lorette stands a tall lighthouse built of the same ashtray-gray stone. Inside this tower are caskets for an unknown soldier of 1914–18, an unknown soldier of 1939–45, an unknown French resistance fighter, an unknown Holocaust victim, an unknown soldier of the Indochinese War, and an unknown soldier of the Algerian War. They lie on top of an ossuary—a depository of human bones collected from the surrounding battlefield. It is estimated that this unseen, unknown pile accounts for another 30,000 men. On an exterior wall an inscription reads in the exalted tastelessness of French martial commemoration:

> *Ossements Qu'Animait Un Fier Souffle Naguère*
> *Membres Epars, Débris Sans Nom, Humain Chaos,*
> *Pele-Mele Sacré D'un Vaste Reliquaire*
> *Dieu Vous Reconnaîtra, Poussière des Héros*

> (Bones Once Inspirited By A Proud Breath
> Sundry Limbs, Nameless Remains, Human Chaos
> A Scattering Made Sacred In A Vast Reliquary
> God Will Know You, Dust of Heroes)

The road downhill leads to Souchez, a town in a hollow between Notre Dame de Lorette and Vimy Ridge. Given its unfortunate location between these two strategic Artesian heights, the town has a history of being obliterated. Its tourist office, grandly called the European Peace Center, tries to encourage visitors to visit the hokey military museums of the area. From its panoramic café, there's a supremely dismal view of the Double Crassier at Loos. Nowhere is there a mention that the small height above Souchez was visited by Henri Barbusse, the author of one of France's enduring Great War novels. His enormously influential *Le Feu* (*Under Fire*), published in 1916 and winner of the Prix Goncourt, described the sickening conditions of the fighting around Souchez. In his forties when the conflict engulfed Europe, Barbusse volunteered in the hope of establishing a socialist millennium, then gained recognition by being one of the first combatants to get his denunciation of the war's quotidian horror into print.

Before Barbusse's novel, many accounts of the war had still been caught up in the intoxicating myths of sacrifice and common cause. Even the avant-garde toyed with militarism. The Futurists, led by Italian visionary Filippo Tommaso Marinetti, had trumpeted the virtues of war because they saw it as a way of sweeping away the old and bringing in a brave new machine age. In 1915, the year Barbusse was in the hell of Souchez, critic and author Wyndham Lewis dismissed Marinetti and his voluble, drum-pounding Futurist followers as "boomers."

"The future," says Bertrand the soldier in *Le Feu*, "the future! The work of the future will be to wipe out the present, to wipe it out more than we can imagine, to wipe it out like something abominable and shameful." In this passage, Barbusse unwittingly brings Futurist boomers and future Boomers together. We of the future have wiped out the past— not because it's shameful, but because it's irrelevant.

I GET BACK in the car and head south. To my left is the gentle slope leading up to Vimy Ridge. The Canadian tuning fork peeks over the pines. I know what a weird landscape the trees are hiding. Ahead of me the highway rises slightly, to a crest where the city of Arras can be seen in the distance. At this vantage point the road threads its way between a monument to Czech volunteers and a memorial to Polish soldiers. The route out of Souchez is thus yet another unheralded and unlikely international meeting place, like the Indian-Portuguese complex at Neuve Chapelle. On this road, however, the cosmopolitanism goes a few steps further. It is here that several important sequences of another French-language war classic, *La Main Coupée* (*The Severed Hand*), take place. The author, Blaise Cendrars, a Futurist poet of Swiss-Scottish parentage who was destined to become a one-armed French literary gadfly after the war, tells of attacking Vimy Ridge in 1915 at the head of a contingent of Moroccan Zouaves. It's as if this stretch of road has killed someone from every nation.

La Targette and Neuville St. Vaast flash into view. I know this stretch of road. I see myself, nine years earlier, coming out of the German cemetery, notebook in hand, backpack askew, the sheep droppings of Vimy still clinging to my boots. I hit the accelerator. It's time to leave this sad corner of Artois and rejoin my former self as I walk into Arras.

5. Arras to Hébuterne

Arras is a town of chimeras, an optical illusion. After the dead desert of Neuville St. Vaast and La Targette, it appears as an oasis, an outpost of ambiguity in a plain that tolerates none. The pride of the city are two enormous squares bordered by pale pink seventeenth- and eighteenth-century townhouses, the gables of their uppermost stories pierced by baroque oeil-de-boeuf holes, as if to let in the moonlight. The larger of the two squares, called the Grand'Place, stretches out before me like a darkened dreamscape. The long arcades at street level—the houses are supported by graceful sandstone columns—echo with the footfalls of people unseen, wraiths slipping quietly through the inky night. I join the stealthy parade around the old square, staying clear of the blue cobbled sea in the center. Headlights of passing cars pick out the columns ahead of me, the black ranks of their shadows pivoting away from the intrusive beams. Then the light is gone, and all is much blacker than before.

What do I know about Arras? I'm only just convinced that it exists. It used to be no more than a word, a Trivial Pursuit nugget of knowledge from Shakespeare. In *Hamlet*, Polonius unwisely hides behind an arras—and gets stabbed by his would-be son-in-law. Arras: a wall hanging, a place of concealment. Italians, a brochure informs me, call tapestries *arazzi*. The city's most famous son was known, by those too frightened to call him by name, as the *avocat d'Arras* (lawyer from Arras). Maximilien de Robespierre sharpened his merciless intellect in the literary salons of the Grand'Place, one of which hid its provincial origins under the moniker of Rosati, an anagram for Artois. Concealment, once again.

The municipal museum, bursting with civic pride about every conceivable hiccup of Arrageois history, hardly mentions Robespierre. Although the good burghers of the city seem slightly less baise-beige than their counterparts in Béthune, they must be embarrassed about their incorruptible offspring. My less inhibited guidebook leads me down a street past the inevitable belfry of the city hall. I stand in front of a decrepit old house and search for a marker, a sign, a plaque. I study the map, unsure of where I am. A concierge comes out of a doorway, sweeps a few microbes off her stoop, looks at me, then nods. I've got the right place. Maximilien used to live here, but he's since moved to Paris.

Arras: a secretive place, a façade for mayhem. It was in the Arras train station one night in 1872 that Paul Verlaine and Arthur Rimbaud got arrested for drunkenly pretending to be murderers and terrifying a crowd in the waiting room. Arras: a city where poets are feared. Below the city, hollowed out of the porous rock, there are miles of tunnels and interconnected chambers. In the four years of the Great War, entire battalions of the British Army took shelter from the shells crashing along this part of the Front. They hid out, like Polonius, screened by Arras. Just as the city hides itself. Years after first visiting Arras, I come across a Michelin 1919 guide in the same series as my guide to Ypres. I stare at the pictures in disbelief. I've been conned. The lovely old city that I had so admired, its squares and townhouses and bell tower—all is rubble or ruin. The old Arras of today is a mirage. Arras: a sleight of hand performed by French craftsmen.

A parting word on the capital of Artois from Siegfried Sassoon's "The General." The poem has two privates passing an officer on their way to the city. Aside from showing the prepositional discretion of a Brit—"did for them" means "had them killed"—Sassoon conveys the matter-of-fact bitterness of Great War veterans:

> 'He's a cheery old card,' grunted Harry to Jack
> As they slogged up to Arras with rifle and pack.
>
> But he did for them all with his plan of attack.

Arras: a place to pass through. Quickly.

SOUTH OF THE city, in the last stretch of the Artesian uplands, the countryside opens up, its aspect changing as a series of gentle ridges leads the way to the woodlands of Picardy. Slag heaps give way to hayricks, grimy corons to sugar beet silos. There is not a hedge in sight; the landscape folds and rolls under a warm sun, as golden as a flame. Steeples pop up in distant villages. Ransart, Blairville, Adinfer, Douchy. I am beginning to enter France as it is imagined by outsiders, the hawkers of the image of a rural Arcadia, an uncomplicated land of apéritif drinkers falling off their bicycles and scented women surrendering beneath poplar trees. The settings may change slightly—the poplars may turn to *platanes* and the chablis become pastis—but the myth remains the same. I half expect a *deux chevaux*, a snail-shaped Citroën love bug, to rattle past in the morning light, trailing a zephyr of accordion music.

The power of received ideas is so strong that sometimes one forgets that they had to originate somewhere. Peter Mayle strung together a charming chain of clichés in his books on Provence—but whence did such caricatures arise? How did they become so widespread as to be recognized by millions? Notwithstanding nuclear tests in the Pacific and fairly regular riots in the suburbs, France can still be sold to outsiders as a rural pleasure dome. Perhaps it is because so many young men—British, American, German—spent the most dramatic days of their lives in France, fighting in one of the world wars, that the country became synonymous with heightened experience, with irresponsibility, with sexual coming of age. Whether France remains thus, as these veterans disappear, is doubtful.

The Great War was, as a Schwarzkopf or Saddam might put it, the mother of all bullshit. Received ideas were manufactured. France and Belgium, the reluctant hosts to the Western Front, became the scene of millions of now forgotten falsehoods, either spun deliberately by the military and the governments and their press, or created by fantasts sitting idly in their trenches. The First World War can be said to have ushered in the industrialization of the lie. In a memorable passage from *Voyage au bout de la nuit* (*Journey to the End of the Night*), Louis-Ferdinand Céline has his narrator describe the tenor of wartime life in the city:

> Lie, copulate and die. One wasn't allowed to do anything else. People lied fiercely and beyond belief, ridiculously, beyond the limits of absurdity: lies in the papers, lies on the hoardings, lies on foot, on horseback and on wheels. Everybody was doing it, trying to see who could produce a more fantastic lie than his neighbor. There was soon no truth left in town.

The French called the flood of lies *le bourrage de crâne* (skull cramming). German papers told of how the French had dumped typhus into the water supplies of Frankfurt. French papers explained how German corpses smelled fouler than French ones. Trench life was lauded as a walk in the country—French illustrators took pains to show the billiard rooms and refreshment centers supposedly built into every dugout. There was talk of "Turpin Powder," a mysterious substance that when applied liberally would protect against poison gas and shrapnel. In a time when the truth was obscene, the wellspring of rumor never ran dry. One of the most famous tales concerned celestial intercession on the English side during the battle of Mons in 1914. Wrathful archers appeared in the sky above the battlefield and loosed their arrows against the Germans. The so-called Angel of Mons survived all debunkers, even when it was pointed out that the heavenly archer originated in a story published on September 29, 1914, by one Arthur Machen, member of the Hermetic Order of the Golden Dawn. His war fable, entitled "The Bowmen," encapsulated the middle-class metaphysic of late Victorian society and, like any good story whose time has come, was spread by word of mouth until it became established fact. Throughout the war, reports of German soldiers found dead of arrow wounds in no-man's-land were regularly given credence. The Angel of Mons was wartime Britain's equivalent of midwestern America's vanishing hitchhiker.

Most rumors were innocuous. In the winter of 1914, many Englishmen believed that more than a million Russian soldiers, recognizable from telltale snow on their boots, had been spirited from Scotland to the Channel ports in the dead of night. Even the most intellectually gifted believed this preposterous bit of wishful thinking: Bertrand Russell noted their passage in his diary. Other tales had more chilling effects. Of all the spectacular stories of German atrocities—a favorite was the Belgian priest tied up and used as a human clapper in a large church bell—few were more pernicious than the so-called crucified Canadian. An unfortunate sergeant was supposedly found out in no-man's-land, horribly nailed to a tree, or a wagon wheel, or whatever. That appalling story spurred Canadians to be the most sadistic fighters of the war, known for torturing and massacring prisoners. Or so rumor has it.

Fortunately, only the countryside deceives about the war now. What appeared to be lovely old churches in a French Arcadia loom up as brick and concrete monstrosities, topped by witch's hat steeples. The Front has been here. Outside the village of Ayette, a narrow country lane suitable for trysts turns out to be the driveway of a graveyard. There, worlds away from home, dozens of Chinese laborers lie buried, their British-issue headstones etched with aphorisms. "A Good Reputation Endures For Ever" is the most common.

The final few miles to Gommecourt and Hébuterne pass without incident. As I walk along a sunken road in the late afternoon, a group of inquisitive cows comes over to greet me, as if expecting me to moo them a story. I put my hand on the wire fence and instantly regret it—a shock runs through me. I walk on, facing down the occasional dog that bounds toward me for a brief spell of mammal communion. I'm reminded of my first steps into Artois. Here, along a road leading to Hébuterne, I have reached the end of one province. Tomorrow, I'll head south into Picardy, the Somme, and 1916.

PICARDY

Auchonvillers ● Hébuterne
● Serre
● Beaumont

Ancre River

Amiens ●

Somme River

Villers-Bretonneux ●

see inset

Vaux ●

Eclusier ●

Dompierre-Becquincourt ●
Fay ●
Estrées ●
Belloy-en-Santerre ●

Péronne ●

Chaulnes ●

Fouquescourt ●

Damery ●

Roye ●

Beuvraignes ●

Crapeaumesnil ●

Lassigny ●

Thiescourt ●

Noyon ●

Ribécourt ●

Bailly ●
Tracy-le-Val ●
Ollencourt ●

Compiègne ●

Rethondes ●

Nampcel ●

Aisne River

Laon ●

Soissons ●

Vailly-sur-Aisne ●
Chavonne ●
Soupir ●

Chemin des Dames

N

10 km

Inset:

Hamel ●
Ancre River
Thiepval ●
Courcelette ●
Pozières ●
La Boisselle ● Martinpuich ●
Albert ●
Contalmaison ● Bazentin ●
Fricourt ● Longueval ●
Mametz ● Montauban ● Ginchy ●
Carnoy ● Guillemont ●
Maricourt ●

●●●●● author's route

CHAPTER
4

Picardy

1. Albert

THE SOMME. THE mere mention of that river has sent generations of writers to their desks, eager to churn out something elegiac or haunting, a descriptive passage to be read in a whisper on the BBC. It's a convention of sorts—the rain in your eyes, the wind in your face, the empty, now silent, forever silent, fields. For the British, there is no more ironic landscape on the European continent. Put in the "S" word and everything becomes ominous, a reference to massacre, to horror and pain. The sun set over the Somme. The train headed east, toward the Somme. Near the Somme flowers bloomed. The Somme awaited them, tranquil and inevitable. However bland these sentences, they all possess, as some like to say, a subtext. They bespeak death, waste, doom, or folly. Somme suggests the fey, in the Scottish sense of one fated to perish soon. To get the same effect, American English might replace Somme with Little Bighorn, or perhaps My Lai, but these equivalents do not measure up to the psychic caesura implied in the word Somme. Much more so than Passchendaele, the lone syllable of the Somme sounds a death knell. For an era, a way of life, a certain optimism, an empire, a world. Somme is short form for Armageddon.

It is fitting that the Battle of the Somme occurred near a town called Albert. Although the town, initially known as Ancre, was renamed for its seventeenth-century owner, Charles d'Albert, the Duke of Luynes, Albert also happens to be the name of Queen Victoria's German consort. Prince Albert—in full, Albert Francis Charles Augustus Emmanuel of Saxe-Coburg-Gotha—was the man whose death at age forty-two, in 1861, made the black trim of perpetual mourning a badge of social virtue in the drawing rooms of nineteenth-century Britain. Although originally a steady, old-fashioned, bandstand-in-the-park kind of name, Albert eventually came to mean something else. From the Albert Memorial to Albert on the Somme, from the German person to the French place, from mourning to massacre, Albert came to mean British death.

In his *Missing of the Somme*, a meditation on British remembrance, author Geoff Dyer states that "every generation since the armistice has believed that it will be the last for whom the Great War has any meaning." There has always been, Dyer points out, a cult of posterity surrounding the First World War, even as it was taking place. Perhaps that is true only of Britain—in my experience, the urge to eulogize the calamity of the Great War had sputtered into nothingness long before I reached maturity. Nostalgia for empire had also vanished. Even while encouraging second-graders in Calgary to go marching to Pretoria, our music teacher neglected to remind us that we were growing up in the province of *Alberta*, a name that fairly drips with black crepe and stale crumpets. The teacher had overlooked the secret meaning of her surroundings; we, her eager charges, would never care to know of its existence. If we now cast about for benchmarks, for before-and-after moments, for the markers of our mental landscape at mid-life, we may talk about Hiroshima, 1945, or Dallas, 1963, or the moon, 1969, or O.J. on the freeway, 1994. But the Somme?

THE DINING ROOM of my hotel in Albert proves that it is possible to eat badly in France. Perhaps this is because of the town's British connection. On my plate a lonely fillet has swum bravely through the doughy chop of a white sauce, only to end up marooned on a shoal of cold rice. I pout for a moment, then tear at a piece of bread with my teeth, knowing that the theatrics of self-pity usually make me feel better. I chew, mollified, and become aware that the room is humming. Everywhere there is the low murmur of grazing Brits.

Eavesdropping reveals that there is serious war buffery abroad in Albert tonight. In the far corner, a tour group of elderly people engages in a respectful give-and-take with a man whom I guess to be Martin Middlebrook, the former Lincolnshire chicken farmer who, after first visiting the area on a whim in the late 1960s, became the consummate expert on the battlefields around Albert. His historical work, *The First Day on the Somme*, and his guidebook, *The Somme Battlefields* (compiled with his wife, Mary), are staggering in their detail and painstaking research. The group gets up and leaves the room as one.

Adjacent to my table sit a man and a woman in their late twenties who also seem to be advanced bellicists. I can hear their subdued argument.

"No, dear," the man says, "the *Minenwerfer* was called the Jack Johnson."

"Not the whizz-bang, then?"

"That was something else. More like our trench mortar."

"A coal box?"

"That's it."

"Are you sure?"

"'Course I am!"

I learn that these artillery duelists are on their honeymoon. He's a Great War nut, and she, as she confides over rice pudding, was "cracked" enough to marry him.

"You'll like Verdun," he tells me, describing how taken they had been with the piles of bones on view at the mass grave at Douaumont. "Very impressive. A hundred and thirty thousand skulls." She nods and smiles encouragement at me.

The lull doesn't last long. Another squabble over firepower flares up as soon as the new bride ventures an opinion about the caliber of the field guns they saw in a fort near Reims.

"But they were seventy-five millimeter! They had to be!" he says, exasperated. "The most famous artillery pieces of the war!"

"I don't think that they were—"

"They wouldn't bloody well display German cannon, would they?!"

I leave them, honeymooners happy to reenact the guns of August.

ALBERT TONIGHT LOOKS much different from my first glimpse of it on a winter evening. Then, flushed and frozen from a December day spent in the fields, where I had discovered the white scar of the Western Front, my companion and I entered the silent town just as its streetlights flickered into life. It had been a peculiar day of somber exhilaration and private imagining. I realized that history existed in space as well as time, that it did not take place in the classroom or on the tube or in the stacks of a library but in places like these, on the chalky downlands and hedgeless fields between the Somme and Ancre Rivers.

My companion, the Ohio Boomer with a love of maps, traced our route on a pizza that night: La Boisselle, Contalmaison, Fricourt, Mametz, then back to his fork, embedded in a cheesy fold at Albert. I listened and watched, amused by his irreverence yet dimly aware that these names once spelled oceanic grief for people now silenced by the passing of years. They also must have meant, paradoxically, life, in its most extreme and self-conscious manifestation. "France," Vera Brittain wrote in *Testament of Youth*, "was the scene of titanic, illimitable death, and for this very reason it had become the heart of the fiercest living ever known to any generation." Such a notion was hard to credit in this deserted town. Albert looked stolidly inert under a cobalt sky on that cold December night, its *Addams Family* town hall and railway station improbable reminders of its haunted hinterland. We felt no presences in the streets, no sign of that fierce living that Brittain spoke of—only the deep slumber of small-town France.

Now I'm hoping that the town might disclose a few of its secrets. I've been waiting for this reunion ever since leaving the shores of the North Sea at Nieuport. The childlike petulance with which I viewed much of Flanders, my adolescent revulsion on the heights of Vimy— all seem to be a necessary apprenticeship for this encounter with the soul of the Western Front. Surely I will feel some kinship, after having spent weeks treading a metaphor, with the presences who once made history here.

I slip out into the warm evening air and wander down the main street to Notre Dame de Brébières, the redbrick pilgrim church that once displayed one of the Great War's most celebrated travesties. Its tall steeple is crowned by a peculiar statue of Madonna and Child: Mary stands, holding the baby Jesus above her head, like a soccer player about to throw the ball in from the sidelines. An ideal target for bored German artillery-men, the statue, through successive bombardments in 1914 and 1915, gradually leaned farther and farther forward until it was perching pre-cariously below the perpendicular. To put it another way: If upright mother and upraised child began the war standing at twelve o'clock, they soon teetered over the void at four o'clock, ready at any moment to topple into the street far below. The two figures stayed that way for most of the war, defying gravity if not belief. It was only in the spring of 1918, when the Germans were occupying the ruins of the town, that a stray British shell brought down the Golden Virgin of Albert.

The restored statue remains funny-looking. Mother, now glowing in the last rays of sunset, still seems ready to chuck her burnished babe into the air. Her posture is supposedly one of presentation, as the child is shown to the shepherds, but resembles more a moment of separation, of abandonment, a tearing asunder of generations. The latter makes me think of the grandfathers I never knew, Daniel O'Shea and Bartholomew Conlon, and how their generation must remain a stranger to mine. My grandfathers must have glimpsed this strange sight too. What did they make of it? The statue, perched high atop its steeple, was visible from the British and German trenches to the east of town, especially at sunset, when the dying rays of the day picked out the gold of the statue and etched a fiery silhouette against the horizon. Who knows what they thought, Daniel and Bartholomew, as they tromped through these streets like so many hundreds of thousands in the British army? Daniel, who spent the entire war in the trenches, suffered a shrapnel wound in the leg at the Somme that was to bother him for the rest of his life. Later he would lose his left eye to the war.

Unlike Daniel, Bartholomew Conlon, my mother's father, had been a draftee. Not many in Britain and Ireland would escape the war's voracious demand for manpower. He had been working in Scotland when the conscription law was passed in 1916. Rebellion had also broken out in his beloved Dublin on Easter Monday of that same year—the day that Yeats's "terrible beauty" was born—but Bartholomew, like so many thousands of his countrymen, soon found himself clad in a British uniform. The ambiguities of being Irish were perhaps never clearer than at that moment. "England's difficulty is Ireland's opportunity" ran the newly coined Republican byword, yet countless Irishmen endured the hard, murderous slog in the mud of the Somme and the Salient. Bartholomew was fortunate enough to survive the great German Picardy offensive of 1918. He was interned in a POW camp following the Battle of Saint Quentin.

After the war, both young men returned home, Daniel to tailoring in Tralee, County Kerry, Bartholomew to drawing pints in a Dublin pub. The two were discreet to the point of pathological about what they had seen and heard in their years in France, and no amount of wishful thinking on my part can make it otherwise. The Kerryman died in 1940, the Dubliner in 1955, before I arrived on the scene, and long before I got it into my head to spend my spare time visiting the sites of their silenced youth. Here, in Albert, it has begun to dawn on me that the spottiness of memory and of transmitted experience can be put down not only to the willed timelessness of my generation but also to the deliberate forgetfulness of theirs. They did not want to talk, neither did we wish to listen. Emigration and the passing of a lifetime did the rest. In Michael Ignatieff's phrase, we survivors can "mark the spot" of their vanished experience, and not much else.

I walk away from Notre Dame des Brébières, disappointed now with the weird Madonna on high. At least for the moment, I have stopped trying to wring affinities out of the unevocative streets of modern Albert. In the central square opposite the town hall, helping me to get my mind off my failure, a reassuringly loud small-town carnival is being held. The Albertins are out in force. At one booth a large and unhappy goose is being raffled off in aid of an agricultural charity; at another, a bullet-headed fellow sells sausage by what appears to be the kilometer. Ever the voyeur, I go to watch the local teens on the bumper cars and see them enact their concussive country foreplay: I like you, I give you whiplash, let's go neck. Inevitably, "Papa Don't Preach" blares from an unseen speaker.

At the counter of a café-bar called Chez Ginette, I am welcomed into a circle of camaraderie presided over by Patrick and his leather-laced girlfriend, Marie-Claude. My out-of-town exoticism calls for an immediate round of watery beer, and my status as a plenipotentiary of the Anglo-Saxon world automatically qualifies me as an expert on music of the sixties and seventies. Patrick, a thirty-four-year-old roofer disdainful of the present, asks me in quick succession if I like Jimi Hendrix, Janis Joplin, and Jim Morrison. Three nods from me set off yet another explosion of hospitality, and two chasers of cognac are set up in front of us. "They don't know what music is," Patrick says conspiratorially, gesturing to a group of youngsters lost in a cloud of cigarette smoke near the back of the café. "All the good music is in the past." My objections are overruled as Patrick plays Hendrix's *Star-Spangled Banner* on an air guitar while wailing out the tune through twisted lips.

About half an hour later, when the conversation has stalled somewhere between Procol Harum and The Who and Patrick has retreated to the men's room, a girlfriend of Marie-Claude's looks up at me and asks, "Why did you come to Albert?"

"Nineteen-sixteen," I reply, gamely.

She looks at Marie-Claude in alarm.

"The Great War," I add.

She turns back to me and says incredulously, "The war of 'fourteen? The English, out there? The dead?!" Her hand sweeps toward the entrance of the bar.

I nod, embarrassed. Marie-Claude steals a glance at her friend, impressed by her erudition. The friend is shaking her head in an eternal gesture of womanly condescension. I don't even try to explain. I could have mentioned the little boy's bike on the trenches and craters of La Boisselle, but I don't. Not now.

Patrick returns, humming the song "Venus."

NINETEEN-SIXTEEN, I should have told her, marked the turning point. Before that year, the intelligent and sensitive might have seen a reason for the war, might have had confidence in their country's leadership, might have placed faith in the army hierarchy. Afterward, that was impossible. It was the year that finally polished off the certainties of the nineteenth century, that made hope laughable, that sent God reeling in the minds of the ordinary man and woman. Before that time, poets could write about the nobility of sacrifice, parsons about the divinity of the cause, and propagandists about the imminence of victory, with a fairly reasonable expectation that their readerships would believe them. After 1916, skepticism and cynicism emerged triumphant. Nineteen-sixteen was the year that Fitzgerald's "great gust of high-explosive love" blew one last time across the continent of Europe. Thereafter, it was just the explosives.

The year began in the usual Great War manner. Joffre's general staff, seeing that no good had come of their costly offensives of 1915, decided to repeat their mistakes. The British, chastened by catastrophe at Gallipoli, agreed to follow Joffre's lead and concentrate all their efforts on the Western Front. A Loos-like operation would be tried again, on a larger scale. Thus, the Allies planned to launch massed attacks on fortified German positions and suffer astronomical casualties in the hope of pushing the invaders back a few miles. A poor, pathetic, inept, murderous strategy, but it was all that they had.

Falkenhayn, chief of the German war machine, produced a far more diabolical variant of Haig and Joffre's dreary offensive credo. He wanted neither to advance nor to retreat—he simply wanted to kill as many Frenchmen as possible, thereby demoralizing his opponents and forcing them to come to terms at the negotiating table. To his credit, Falkenhayn planned on sparing the lives of his own soldiers, a revolutionary concept among the spendthrift generals who commanded the millions in the trenches. In order, as he blithely put it, "to bleed France white," Falkenhayn chose to attack the point of the Western Front that he guessed the French would move heaven and earth to defend: the hills above Verdun. The story of 1916 thus shifts away from Picardy, east to Lorraine. As a symbol of French territorial integrity, the northeastern city of Verdun, the age-old divide between Latins and Germans, was peerless. Falkenhayn had no intention of taking Verdun; he just wanted the French to die in front of it. Attrition, a nice, inoffensive Latinate word derived from the idea of wearing down through rubbing, is the term used to cover this horrendous reality.

On February 21, the German army took the initiative away from the Allies for 1916. After an unexpected stream of explosive metal had rained down on the exposed French trenches, the Germans raced across the snowy hills to finish off the stunned survivors in the front line. French conscripts fell back in confused retreat, outmanned and outgunned. Verdun was in danger. Would the French fight back to protect it?

That question is not as stupid as it seems. The sad truth was that the town of Verdun and its fortifications served no appreciable military purpose in trench warfare—and the French generals knew this. The fate of Belgium's forts in 1914, isolation and then encirclement, had shown French military planners that their forts to the north of Verdun were more of a death trap than a defense. But Falkenhayn gambled that the French would throw good sense to the winds and perish in droves in defense of a symbol.

The assumption was correct. Pulled out of his bed in the middle of the night for the only time during the entire four and a half years of war, Joffre was ordered by Prime Minister Aristide Briand of France to hold Verdun, no matter what the cost. The French would fight for a trope. Almost 400,000 would die. The French decision to take back every sorry shell crater north of the city represents the most grotesque example of style winning out over substance in modern history. Not surprisingly, it has been held responsible for many of the ills that beset France in the decades that followed. The French collapse of 1940 and the subsequent disgraceful adherence to Pétain's brand of fascism have been rightly laid on Verdun's doorstep. From there, it is but a small step to see Verdun at the root of an immature political culture that elevated another general to the status of godhead and still prefers fanciful pronouncement to factual achievement. Verdun was the original lie of France in the twentieth century, and the biggest lie of a war whose sheer volume of untruths ended up shaking the beliefs of all but the most benighted.

Nineteen-sixteen thundered on. As if obeying some dadaist urge, German commanders eventually wandered into the same bog of irrationality. Falkenhayn's original strategy of attrition was abandoned. The armies of the Kaiser were ordered to take Verdun. The result: 400,000 Germans dead for a militarily insignificant goal, and Verdun remained in French hands.

As France and Germany sank deeper into this pit of pointless self-destruction during the spring of 1916, the other major player of the Western Front, Great Britain, remained unscathed. This would change with a vengeance. Joffre, his armies bleeding for a metaphor, called on

Haig to launch the great joint Allied offensive originally planned for early in the year. The Somme, a difficult terrain over which to attack, was selected because it was the region where the British lines hooked up with the French. Even if, given the mess at Verdun, there wasn't going to be a large French contingent involved, the need for a show of Allied unity overrode any strategic considerations. Appearances, the curse of 1916 and of an Old World gone senile, had to be maintained.

The initial attack took place on July 1, at 7:30 A.M. Subsequent waves of soldiers were ordered over the top throughout the morning. It was the biggest fiasco in British military history. No amount of apologetic casuistry can ever absolve its authors, Generals Henry Rawlinson and the ever-reliable Douglas Haig. Within a matter of hours, perhaps minutes, 40,000 British soldiers had been wounded and 21,000 killed, many of them within sight of their own trenches. No fighting force on the Western Front would ever lose so many so quickly, and for so little. Eighty years of ever-increasing detachment now separates us from that astounding morning, yet it still beggars understanding that the murderous boobs in charge of the British army were allowed to go unpunished. The war crime of Passchendaele still remained fifteen months in the future, yet the result of Rawlinson's and Haig's willful ignorance of trench warfare, even after the disaster at Loos, was plain to see. By noon, all along the narrow swath of no-man's-land from Gommecourt and Hébuterne to the River Somme, 60,000 young men lay wounded, dying, or dead, a carpet of bloodied khaki that writhed and moaned in the sullen sunlight. Optimism began to drain from a culture that had conquered a world.

In many ways, the Somme was like the Kindermord at Langemarck two years earlier. There, the men mowed down by machine guns had been student volunteers; here, they were eager recruits who had signed up with their friends at the behest of Lord Kitchener and his famous mustachioed face on the recruitment poster reading, "Your Country Needs YOU." Much of the huge British army at the Somme were Pals Battalions, civilians from a village, a workplace, a town who joined the army en masse on the condition that they could go to war together. For John Keegan, whose *Face of Battle* remains the most stimulating book of military history available to the nonspecialist, the nationwide enthusiasm for the Pals movement showed "the inarticulate elitism of an imperial power's working class."

The Pals of the Somme trained, often without so much as a rifle between them, throughout 1915 and the beginning of 1916. They were marched and drilled incessantly. Such parade-ground training would come in handy for their suicidal foray into no-man's-land; orders called for them to march in regular formations, at a slow and orderly pace, toward the German trenches. The professionals of the British army judged its citizen soldiers too dim-witted to do anything else.

The planners of the fiasco assumed that the artillery barrage prior to the attack would obliterate all opponents. The Germans survived because they had dug into the welcoming chalk of the Somme a network of subterranean shelters—in some places more than forty feet deep—and thus had sat out the seven days of deafening detonation. There was, in fact, less artillery per meter of front attacked than at the Battle of Neuve Chapelle a year earlier. This was known at headquarters, but General Rawlinson quashed all suggestions that the effects of his artillery campaign should be gauged. No one on his staff checked to see if it had, indeed, worked. Instead, Rawlinson sent tens of thousands of volunteer soldiers walking into no-man's-land. The terrible midday scene of July 1 was the outcome.

It might be thought that the wastefulness ended there, but that would be underestimating the wretched excess of 1916. Death rattles are violent, and the First World War's destruction of nineteenth-century verities would require much more than just the few bad months that lay in between the French decision of late February and the British debacle of early July. There was still the summer and autumn. It was as if tight-laced, tight-lipped imperial Europe had become a roaring lush seeking oblivion. French and German commands continued the bloodletting at Verdun, while British military leaders had the insane temerity to proclaim that progress had been made on the Somme. The "push" would therefore continue, as if the towering losses of that first day constituted a proof of victory. The magnitude of the screwup led the British brass to persevere in the hope that future achievement might erase present calamity.

Nothing of the sort occurred, of course. Generals pushed their men forward in assaults that rivaled each other as exercises in meaninglessness. "A battle fought from July to November 1916," historian Denis Winter succinctly notes in defining the Somme, "saw the British and German armies fire thirty million shells at each other and suffer a million casualties between them in an area just seven miles square." It took months for the British to reach objectives originally intended to be captured on the first day. Dominion troops—South Africans at Longueval, Canadians at Courcelette, Australians at Pozières—got sucked into the maelstrom, ordered to attack or hold flattened villages that had no other military merit than that of occupying a spot on Haig's map. According to Australian historian Peter Charlton, the senseless attacks ordered of the Aussies in the summer of 1916 brought to fruition the sentiment that had germinated at Gallipoli. Charlton, quoted in Richard Holmes's *Fatal Avenue*, writes: "If Australians wish to trace their modern suspicion and resentment of the British to a date and a place, then July–August 1916 and the ruined village of Pozières are useful points of departure. Australia was never the same again."

By the last murderous push at the end of November, the same might be said of the entire army. Ever the weather vane of future sentiment, the gifted generation of British soldier poets now celebrated squalor and decried futile suffering. No one emulated the noble sentiments of Rupert Brooke any longer. The acid acuity of Sassoon, Edmund Blunden, Isaac Rosenberg, and Wilfrid Owen became the Zeitgeist—and not just among the British. The French and the Germans, whose vicious struggle at Verdun ended in the late autumn, were just as shell-shocked and embittered. By November 1916, enthusiasm had vanished, idealism had crumbled, and mistrust prevailed. Rosenberg, a brilliant Londoner who would die in battle during the spring of 1918, captured the mood of nihilistic resignation in an arresting poem, "Break of Day in the Trenches." Gone are appeals to patriotism or high-flown ideals. Instead, the soldier talks to a rat:

> The darkness crumbles away—
> It is the same old druid Time as ever.
> Only a live thing leaps my hand—
> A queer sardonic rat—
> As I pull the parapet's poppy
> To stick behind my ear.
> Droll rat, they would shoot you if they knew
> Your cosmopolitan sympathies.
> Now you have touched this English hand
> You will do the same to a German—
> Soon, no doubt, if it be your pleasure
> To cross the sleeping green between.
> It seems you inwardly grin as you pass
> Strong eyes, fine limbs, haughty athletes
> Less chanced than you for life,
> Bonds to the whims of murder,
> Sprawled in the bowels of the earth,
> The torn fields of France.

What do you see in our eyes
At the shrieking iron and flame
Hurled through still heavens?
What quaver—what heart aghast?
Poppies whose roots are in man's veins
Drop, and are ever dropping;
But mine in my ear is safe,
Just a little white with the dust.

2. *Beaumont Hamel to Thiepval to Guillemont*

The Somme. The wind in my hair, the sun in my face, the silent fields. Hackneyed, but true. My bicycle, rented for the day from a suspicious local merchant through the intercession of Patrick and Marie-Claude, wings me north of Albert, downhill toward the River Ancre. I plan on making a great clockwise loop of the battlefield, a Tour de Somme. Throughout the furious fights of 1916, the British lines slowly bulged forward, by increments of about seventy-five yards a day, so that the swath of destruction broadened like a stain over the rolling Picard countryside. The lunar scene created by war eventually reverted to a mix of farmland and open-air exhibition of the monument maker's art.

The surroundings are varied. The Ancre flows south to meet the River Somme near Albert, the two meandering waterways having cut marshy valleys in the chalky plateaus and escarpments to the east of town. On the heights above these converging river depressions, little peekaboo pleats in the land form finger valleys, charming now, deadly then. In between occasional stands of trees, large fields of wheat alternate with sugar beet, forming what resembles a motley flag that is just settling unevenly on the ground. The biggest "crease" in this flag is a narrow crest of land, reminiscent of the ridge at Ypres, that runs southeast for a few miles from the village of Pozières to just beyond the hamlet of Guillemont. This long lozenge of high ground was the center of the battlefield, which I hope to reach before saddle sores or spells of callow inattentiveness make me turn my bike back toward Albert.

In the morning, I coast down toward the northern reaches of the 1916 Front, where the disaster of July 1 was unredeemed by any gain in ground, however minuscule. The Ancre, a lethargic little river hemmed in by reedy flats and a couple of characterless campgrounds backing out onto a railroad track, does not look the part of world-historical awfulness. A young boy and girl float by in an inflated inner tube, the picture of pacific childhood. At Hamel, a mile or so farther on, things begin to look more congruously squalid. The village, which sat on the British front line, consists of two filthy streets permeated with the essence of pig. The stench is remarkable.

I pedal harder to escape it, past the dual rows of mud-spattered red-brick houses and uphill toward the fields of no-man's-land, a few hundred yards away. Near the crest of the ridge a military bus, its gunmetal green grill smiling maliciously, appears suddenly at a blind turn and barrels down on me. A horn blares; I skedaddle sideways into the ditch and wipe out. A close call. I wrench myself around to yell out a curse but see instead a flapping banner hung on the rear window of the bus. In red letters is the slogan *Versöhnung über den Gräbern—Arbeit für den Frieden* (Reconciliation over the Tombs—Work for Peace). This juggernaut's passengers, I realize, are students who spend their summer vacation sprucing up the German graveyards of the Western Front. I wonder how many of the living they take out with their big fat bus on the tiny country lanes of France.

They have just come from a visit to one of the most remarkable battlefield sites on the entire Western Front: the Newfoundland Memorial Park. A rectangular parcel of land located between the villages of Hamel, Beaumont, and Auchonvillers (or "Ocean Villas," as it was wittily called by the British), the park has been left in its wartime state. Trenches snake across the now grassy land, and shell craters pockmark the ground. The story of the Newfoundland battalion that met its doom here on July 1, 1916, is movingly told in David Macfarlane's *Come From Away*, a masterly account of one family's experience of the First World War. Blindly ordered to try again where the initial attack had utterly failed, the 752 men of the battalion climbed out of a support trench—the communication trenches leading forward were too clogged with the dead and the wounded—and walked three hundred yards above ground toward their front line. They were alone up there—no artillery shells flew overhead to cover them, and no other units on either side of their position joined in their attack. There was no protection whatsoever. Many of the attackers never even made it to no-man's-land. Some of the German machine gunners, complacently watching the exposed advance coming closer, held their deadly fire until the Newfoundlanders bunched up to file through the gaps in their own barbed wire. Then the bullets flew fast and thick. The few who managed to get free slogged on the last three hundred yards toward the German trenches. According to one eyewitness cited by Macfarlane, "Instinctively, they tucked their chins into an advanced shoulder, as they had so often done when fighting their way home against a blizzard in some little outport in far-off Newfound-land." Some 91 percent of the men—684 of 752—were wounded or killed. It was a shocking waste, and a devastating heartbreak for a small island community. When Newfoundland became a part of Canada in 1949, the cruelest irony of all ensured that the islanders' new national holiday—July 1 is also Canada Day—coincided with the anniversary of their bleakest collective memory.

Today a statue of a caribou overlooks the scene. On the perimeter, trees and bushes native to Newfoundland have been planted. The place is not only a stranger in time but also a foreigner in space. Nothing here looks like the surrounding countryside. The visitor to this park feels like some lunatic suburban surveyor crossing a particularly misbehaved lawn, but eventually the fading scars in the ground work their quiet effect. For me, a pilgrim of the invisible, the park offers a tantalizing moment of tangibility. This is the Western Front unimagined, in its dotage, seventy or eighty years on. On either side of this plot of land, the invisible Front takes over again, a pulverized band of ditches and craters hidden under farmers' fields and village streets, stretching from the sea to the moun-tains. Here, the Front has come out into the bright light of day.

Last week it was Vimy, now it's Beaumont Hamel. It is odd that Canada specializes in caretaking these battlefields of the First World War, that a country with so much space should make a point of preserving a few forlorn acres in France. For other countries, memorials in stone suffice. Canada tries to keep its imprint in the earth itself, as if that were somehow a more durable way to glorify its dead. Yet the passage of time softens even the worst scores in the land. Deep craters grow more dimple-like, and once jagged, saw-toothed trenches become shallow, indistinct depressions. The protean earth pushes up, a great leveler in the literal sense, and the furrowed record of sorrow becomes an even plane again. The canvas is blank, the slate is clean. In the Newfoundland park, this slow leveling is well under way, the progress of the flattening inspiring an irresistible parallel to the workings of memory. The land of the Front, if left alone by farmers and custodians and others of their ilk, will even-tually forget, just as surely as we who are now alive have—and will be, in our turn—forgotten.

Beyond the park I walk across a farmer's field to look at a mine crater. The explosives underneath a German position known as the Hawthorn Ridge Redoubt were blown at 7:20 on the morning of July 1, one of the eleven mines that went up a few minutes before the 66,000 attackers in the first wave scrambled up their ladders and out of the trenches. I'm here out of televisual duty—of all the things that I have read or heard about the Great War, this explosion is the only one I've actually seen take place. It was on TV, therefore it exists. A motion picture camera caught the mine as it went up, and the image, a great shower of loose earth flying upward in the grainy light of early cinema, has become the signature documentary footage of the Somme, if not the entire war. Middle-aged men addicted to war specials on cable TV have probably seen the Hawthorn cloud of debris so often as to have absorbed it as a childhood memory.

As is usually the case with life, reality is a letdown. The once dramatic crater looks like an overgrown rookery. Shrubs and brushwood hide the lip of the pit, and careful plowing all around has made the surroundings as innocuous-looking as any farm field in France. In the nearby hollow leading to the village of Serre, an enormous graveyard attests to how far from innocuous this countryside is. The indispensable Martin Middlebrook, in his *First Day on the Somme*, cites at length one Karl Blenk, a German infantryman who was manning the trenches in front of the village at 7:30 that morning:

> When the English started advancing we were very worried; they looked as though they must overrun our trenches. We were very surprised to see them walking, we had never seen that before. I could see them everywhere; there were hundreds. The officers were in front. I noticed one of them walking calmly, carrying a walking stick. When we started firing, we just had to load and reload. They went down in their hundreds. You didn't have to aim, we just fired into them. If only they had run, they would have overwhelmed us.

The hundreds who fell were buried in the Serre Road Cemetery Number 2, which would later become improbably useful for something other than the expression of grief. During the Second World War, the cemetery's toolshed was used as a hiding place for Allied flyers who had been shot down over France and were being smuggled back to safety by the Resistance. Thirty-two airmen stopped for shelter this way, concealed by their deceased predecessors. The cemetery was, in effect, recycled and made into an underground railway station.

On my way back to the Newfoundland park, I stoop down to pluck an old bullet from between two chalk pebbles. I look carefully around me— pieces of rusted barbed wire lie innocently on the ground two furrows away. The field, freshly plowed, is yielding its usual harvest of scrap metal from the war. From the air it must exhibit the chalk scar of my imagined

no-man's-land. A few hundred yards away from where I stand the great
British humorist Hector Hugh Munro, who wrote his misanthropic little
gems under the pen name of Saki, once walked and talked in the trenches
that cut through this field. In the cold mists of the morning of November
14, 1916, as he and his men rested in a shell hole, Saki was mortally
wounded by a sniper. Seconds before that moment, his last, irritated
utterance had been "Put that bloody cigarette out."

I pocket the bullet and head back to my bike.

THE OTHER BANK of the Ancre slopes up toward the heart of the Somme
battlefield. In a large wood just above the river, I poke around tentatively
to get a look at the crazy upheaval of heavily shelled land. There is really
nothing more evocative of the war than this frozen violence. All of the
woods in this region have the same obscene, unnatural floors—no one
thought it useful, or wise, to plow under the traces of the fighting when,
immediately after the war, these copses were just random patches of
blackened stumps. Here at Thiepval Wood, the remnant of the British
front-line trench can still be clearly traced, bracken-covered and hump-
backed, swimming its way through the trees like some slow-moving sea
monster.

This countryside cannot let the past escape. Above the lane leading to
the village of Thiepval looms the massive British memorial to the Somme.
Aside from the fanciful accounts produced by historians paid to get the
British military command off the hook, this structure is the official
response to the catastrophe. It is an eye-opener. The closer you get to the
oft-glimpsed edifice, the more repulsive it becomes in its Lego-like
gigantism. One hundred and forty-one feet tall, the multiarched redbrick
structure, designed by Edwin Lutyens and inaugurated in 1934, must
have been intended as an eyesore, a Cyclopean blight on an already
blighted landscape. If not, that is definitely the purpose it serves now—
and the honesty is refreshing. From most points on the battlefield, its
profile slouches on the horizon, or rears up above the treetops, or spoils a
perspective. The mammoth block of stone and brick is an in-your-face
reminder that something hideous occurred in the vicinity. There is no
nationalism here, as at Vimy, or any of the faintly ridiculous stone lions
found padding around other British monuments. Just ungainly mass and
unforgiving volume.

As I approach the Thiepval arch over a putting-green lawn, it occurs to
me that the thing looks like a huge horseshoe magnet, held forever to the
earth by the attraction of a million skeletons. (It is now estimated that

there were 1,300,000 Allied and German casualties on the Somme in 1916.) In its central arch and numerous bays, there is the familiar sight of names upon names upon names, the ledgers of vertigo drawn up by a shamefaced establishment. Here, the stone letters spell out the names of the doomed soldiers of the British and South African armies (Australia, New Zealand, Canada, Newfoundland, and India built their own monuments to the missing) who died on the Somme in the years 1915–17 and whose bodies were never recovered or identified. There are 73,412 of them. The memorial's inscription reads, "The Missing of the Somme"; it could just as well say the sum of the missing. The magnitude of the number is too large to comprehend, just as at the Menin Gate. Like there too, the trick of absolution through accountancy is attempted — only here it works. The spectator, alone and vulnerable on the Thiepval ridge, feels oppressed by the weight of the engraved stone, as if it got there through some insensate natural force, ordained by an unkind universe rather than by the blunders of the powerful.

The first time I saw this monument, on my winter visit to the Somme, I thought these names were like cuneiform, the indecipherable scratchings of a dimly remembered civilization. Today is different. Both the detachment I felt at the fetish-house interior of Ypres's St. George's Memorial Church and the anti-imperial scorn that came over me in Ploegsteert Wood have vanished. They have been replaced by an uneasy urge to connect. I try summoning up my grandfathers, Daniel and Bartholomew, who are, in a sense, just names to me. They were the contemporaries of these names at Thiepval; perhaps they knew or soldiered alongside some of them. As was the case in front of the Madonna of Albert, the speculation leads nowhere, to a failed séance at the foot of a monument. My grandfathers are now among the missing. I return instead to Private Cadogan, my man in Flanders, a fleeting, occasional presence beside me during this past month walking down the Front. Surely he can help me understand this place. Or Musketier Leopold Aronsohn, the man from La Targette. But they too remain maddeningly out of reach. Weary and defeated, I walk out of the grounds of the memorial and set off to the crossroads outside the village.

The defeat is not total. I coast around a BMW with British plates parked by the corner and almost run into a couple snapping off a roll of pictures. In front of them is a sign that reads *Reconstruction d'un Boyau* (Trench Replica). Inside the trench their two sons play an irreverent game they call over-the-top, which, as far as I can gather, consists of pelting each other with dried sheep droppings. There don't appear to be any rules.

The woman turns toward me with an ivory grin of complicity, then holds out the camera. Her husband, recognizing a fellow Somme buff, points out the essential elements of the replica: parapet, firestep, transverse cuts, communication trench, dugout, duckboards, sandbags, and sap. On the corrugated metal sheet protecting the sap someone has chalked helpfully, for the benefit of cross-Channel visitors, WAR↓ WAR↓ WAR↓.

Inside their car sits a disgusted daughter, bored out of her wits, reading a comic book. It takes some coaxing but she's eventually persuaded out into the sunlight to pose for the family portrait. The shutter catches the five of them beaming up from the trench. I move the camera to the left. A bicycle, one wheel still slowly turning over the edge of the parapet, comes into view. With a start, I realize that this time the bicycle in no-man's-land is mine. This family and I are the levelers now, giving new meanings to old landscapes. We're like the Belgians at Bellewaerde, steamrolling an earlier generation into oblivion. The bike and the smiles are just gentler ways of doing it.

"ICI ON PISSE dehors!"

The waitress in the café near Longueval, a village on the Pozières ridge, has pointed me to the great outdoor toilet that is Picardy. "There's lots of room out there," she adds, to the delight of two farmhands standing at the counter. They echo her words to my back as I sheepishly head outside.

I look at an abandoned factory standing out in a field in the middle distance, its windows shattered, its walls buckling, at last a monumental structure that has nothing to do with the war. There are more than 250 military cemeteries and dozens of private memorials on the Somme, the great majority of them lovingly maintained. The villages of the living are a different story. The dark redbrick and black-slate houses have now settled into a permanent ugly slumber. The hamlets I've passed through since Thiepval—Pozières, Martinpuich, Bazentin, Courcelette—have been tightly shuttered, perhaps to block out the old tales told by their surroundings.

Here at Longueval, to take an example, two woods on either side of the town hold the usual dreadful secrets. The one on the highest ground, logically called High Wood, was the scene of a successful nighttime attack by the British on July 14, 1916, followed the next day by a cavalry charge that was supposed to break out into the open country behind the German lines. This, the essence of Haig's tactics, was suicide. One moment, there were lances glinting in the sunshine and magnificent caparisoned animals galloping across open country. The next, the shallow cough of the machine gun sent the thundering anachronism crashing to the earth.

The wood on the other side of town is Delville Wood, which is the property of the Republic of South Africa. From July 15 to July 20, 1916, troops from South Africa fought for every yard of ground in Delville. All but one tree, it is said, were destroyed by the blizzard of bullets — most of them were sawed off just above ground level by the streams of red-hot metal. Of the 3,150 South Africans to have gone into Delville, only 778 could reply "present" to roll call five days later.

In the village of Guillemont, I brake to look at the Celtic cross erected in front of the church. A couple of British motorcylists speed past me and take the turning back to Albert, as if showing me what to do. I decide to follow, suddenly impatient with monuments and memorials and ready, rather crassly, for a good dinner. The Guillemont road rises as it leaves town, passing yet another cemetery on its way to high ground crowned by a wood. Despite my newfound hurry, I stop and get off the bike to take in a beautiful view. I scribble a hurried description in my journal: "Let's make a movie: to the immediate right [of me], the black pointed spires of Guillemont and Longueval piercing the level of the trees. Far to the upper right, along a rolling quilt of green and yellow, the town of Bazentin, and further still, on the limit of the horizon, the hazy behemoth at Thiepval. In front, a road skirting a dark green wood pouring down the slope toward a little cemetery. To the left, fields upon fields of wheat, interrupted only by a small spur on the Montauban-Carnoy road." I set off again, determined to return the bike to Albert on time. On passing the wood, I glimpse a memorial to a rifle brigade, inscribed with the strange words "The Greatest Thing in the World." Later I will see a picture of the view I have just described — mud everywhere, not even the hint of any feature on the land. The only distinguishing characteristics are injured and dying men in a shell hole.

The road leads across the ridge to a rose-covered house in Montauban, someone's solitary attempt at beautifying the village. A further couple of miles to Carnoy, past the stretch of no-man's-land where a certain Captain Nevill handed out four soccer balls to his platoons and had them dribble their way toward the German trenches at zero hour on July 1. One platoon wrote on its ball:

> The Great European Cup
>   The Final
> East Surreys v. Bavarians
>   Kick-Off at Zero

Elsewhere on the Somme, a public schools' Pals battalion kicked a rugby ball ahead of its leading wave of attackers.

I turn at Carnoy to breeze past the villages of Mametz and Fricourt. The rising land beside the sunken road still looks as if some furious giant had ripped it apart. Soon the odd Madonna is ahead of me, silhouetted against a reddening sky.

3. Vaux to Chaulnes

Yesterday's mobility has spoiled me. Out of Albert after an early break-fast, I hope to thumb a ride to Maricourt, where the Front fords the River Somme and heads straight southward across the plain of the Santerre. But to hitch in Picardy, I conclude, is to intrude on the animal privacy of drivers in their cars. Not only do they not want to pick up a hitchhiker, they do not want him to be there at all, littering their field of vision and souring their sweet solitude. The icy glares turn the summer morning cold; the animosity is almost palpable. I check to see if I've inadvertently been brandishing a bloodstained ax or lewdly fondling a statue of Joan of Arc—how else could I have possibly offended all of these people?

One reason must be war. Not just the Great War, but every war. This fertile swath of France has known the tramp of armies since its forests were first cleared by the farmers of Gaul. The morning's route, for example, was not only the trace of the trenches—it also carried Henry IV's men to nearby Agincourt in 1415, and who knows how many other wild-eyed armies on their way to binges of the id. In this, Picardy is eminently European, a province awash in past violence and insult. Such a legacy must seep down into some murky collective well, from which people instinctively draw when confronted with the unfamiliar. Here, at the Somme, that well must be bottomless.

The other reason for the glowering faces, I know from long residence in France, is the automobile. An occasional outlet for aggression in all cultures, the car turns many French people nearly autistic in their relation to society. Anyone who has traveled French expressways and secondary roads knows this generalization to be true—it is never Dr. Jekyll at the wheel of that Peugeot, but always Mr. Hyde. The central, soul-bending pretense at the core of cultivated French behavior—feigning indifference to strangers whom you've been trained to despise—can be safely jet-tisoned once within the insulated confines of the car, and all of that stifled malevolence can at last be expended. Thus, the respectable matron on foot may become the classic snarling harpy in a car; the well-mannered, obsequious notary, a nose-picking speed demon delighted with his last road kill; and the mildly hostile shopkeeper, an Attila of the *autoroute*. If in America the car has turned into a prosthetic device in the service of mobility, in France it remains a form of therapy for the strain of moral hypocrisy. Putting a hitchhiker in front of most French drivers is like waving a red flag before an already dyspeptic bull. The wonder is that they don't swerve to hit him.

It should be apparent by now that I do not get a ride.

THE WALK DOWN to the river from the village of Vaux gives a commanding view over the Somme to the east. Land and water bleach together into one wan pastel under a milky August sky. The Somme here carves not so much a valley as a wide ravine, guarded above and below by spinneys of sentinel poplars. The road descends gradually through the trees to the marshes and pools formed by the stream's meanders. Near the grassy hamlet of Eclusier, at the bottom, scores of fishermen sit in small, fenced-off plots, not letting anyone or anything venture onto their sacred patch of shady riverbank. A few have managed to squeeze undersized camping trailers in between the fenceposts. They try to land their catch unseen, their fishing rods sticking out of the side doors of their trailers. The scene looks slightly less convivial than the cemeteries I have been visiting.

A lunch of fresh eel, no doubt caught by one of these introverted sportsmen, helps to dispel any lingering lack of pedestrian enthusiasm. I powder my feet and start up a steep incline, leaving the riverbank of compartmentalized fishermen behind me. At the top of the rise, an enclosed pasture fans out from the edge of a bluff. In a far corner, as if afraid of the commanding view, a couple of old draft horses huddle close together, their enormous brown and white backsides the only landmark I can see on what appears to be a blank, flat plain. This is the plateau of Santerre, from the Latin *sana terra*, or good land. It is so boring as to be almost painful to behold. The sun has gone in, turning everything a uniform gray. Harvested crops stretch out in unbroken monotony to the village of Dompierre-Becquincourt. I sing "Do You Know the Way to San José" to kill the time and continue to put one foot in front of the other, a speck in motion from one map coordinate to the next, a lone pedestrian in this wilderness of mechanized agriculture. The miles pass, slowly.

At Dompierre my arrival creates a stir. I suspect that anything would, given the vapor of ennui in the air. As if on cue, a buxom young woman comes out from behind a mournful gray fence to stroll aimlessly about the village square. She casts three backward glances as she walks, then rounds a corner. Gone. A group of boys on bicycles swarms about me at a respectful distance, hoping that somehow I'll amuse them. Who knows? Perhaps I'll ask for directions, or fall over, or explode. Even a few of the local pre-apéritif crowd waver in the doorway of the square's spare, echo-chamber café. The black roofs and dark red bricks, the blazon of Picard towns, do not look welcoming, so I set out across the shorn fields in the direction of Fay and Estrées, the next settlements in no-man's-land. A hint of relief to the right—a long and narrow wood standing over what was the French front line in 1916—makes this stretch of the walk more tolerable than the last.

As I cross the main highway, which leads straight as an arrow from Amiens to St. Quentin, a teeming cloud of black birds rises from the wood and heads east. I am surprised when I realize that they are ravens. If they continue their route for a few miles, past the beet sugar mill, the tacky roadside hotel, and the expressway cloverleaf, they will reach Belloy-en-Santerre, a "disputed barricade" in the Battle of the Somme. The phrase belongs to the first verse of a once-admired poem:

> I have a rendezvous with Death
> At some disputed barricade,
> When Spring comes back with rustling shade
> And apple-blossoms fill the air—
> I have a rendezvous with Death
> When Spring brings back blue days and fair.

Its author, Alan Seeger, an American in the French Foreign Legion, attacked across the fields between Estrées and Belloy on the last day of his life. By dying in battle, he posthumously captured the imagination of his countrymen as they weighed their decision to go to war. A sometime poet and full-time bohemian on graduating from Harvard in 1910, the handsome Seeger had sought a life of dash and valor that his circle of literary friends in New York's Greenwich Village could not provide. Aimless in Europe when the shots rang out in Sarajevo, Seeger marched with the first band of American volunteers through the streets of Paris in 1914. Others emulated him, the most famous being the young American pilots who formed the Lafayette Squadron of the French air force. By 1916, it was still possible for an American to be idealistic about the war, given his country's clean hands and unbloodied hearths. Seeger's rhymes roused many to clamor for an end to what they viewed as national cowardice in a time of world crisis. Taste in poetry would change once American casualty lists grew.

Seeger marked a messianistic, all-American moment—he was still writing about apple blossoms and destiny while the battle-worn Rosenberg and his peers were composing apostrophes to rats. When Seeger raced to his death across the Santerre, he came not only as the older, rasher brother of the literary Lost Generation but also as the harbinger of the new American century. It was not his fault that his successors might be more self-interested or levelheaded; Seeger set an idealistic, macho standard that would come to grief a few generations later in Southeast Asia. Unlike the soon-to-be-disabused patriots who volunteered for Vietnam, he was not "born on the Fourth of July." Alan Seeger *died* on the Fourth of July. It was in 1916, and he must have been happy.

I HAVE WALKED too far today, and see no end in sight. The land south of Estrées has been a succession of dusty villages and barking dogs. At the German and French cemeteries that punctuate this limitless battlefield, the friable soil of the flatland has whipped up and begun to eddy around the graves. Not that I care—it is nearly seven o'clock, and my feet ache. Animal discomfort can easily overwhelm the duties of the observant traveler.

I must be trudging quite tragically, for the unbelievable occurs. A man on a moto-scooter pulls over on the roadway and hollers across the field at me. At first I take him to be a tetchy farmer, then I realize that he is offering me a lift. I can't believe my luck as I move across the dry earth toward him—I have been spotted by the only person in the entire département capable of such a generous gesture. He's wearing sunglasses, a dirty brown suitcoat, a moth-eaten sweater, gray stretch slacks and red running shoes, and he hasn't shaved in at least four days. There is a crazy intensity in his eyes. He's obviously not all there. We make a good pair.

His moped is towing a little wagon open to the four winds, barely larger than a child's toy. I believe the correct name for it is a dog cart. Gratefully, I squeeze my rear end down onto the cart's platform and leave my tired legs hanging akimbo over the road. It is an enjoyable two-mile ride into central Chaulnes, a small market town in the heart of the farm country. Housewives heading home from the *boulangerie* frown in undisguised horror at the sight of us—the local eccentric putt-putting his way into town with an ungainly trophy found wandering the fields. Gallic good ole boys at café tables shout encouragement as we pass, small children burst out laughing. We arrive at the central esplanade beneath a statue of a stern Enlightenment grammarian.

My benefactor pulls me to my feet and firmly rejects my offer of a drink. "No! No! No!" he says in a gravelly voice. "When you're on the road you don't give anything! Understand?" I must not look convinced, so he continues. "If you're given something, that's okay, but you're not to give anything. Understand? Understand?"

I nod. His face creases into a toothless smile and he pats my shoulder. "Look, I won't wish you a good journey, so I'll just say *merde*. Understand?"

It's my turn to smile.

"Merde!"

With that, the Angel of Chaulnes fires up his moped and trundles off into the evening light.

4. *The Noyon Salient*

The Noyon Salient was a large bulge in the German lines, a blunted belly of destruction and menace that hung over Paris, some sixty miles to the south. The Front, as one walks down it from Flanders and Artois, turns left in this part of Picardy and heads east toward Champagne. Noyon, as befits a turning point, has the distinction of being a palindrome. Sex at Noyon taxes.

The word play is not mere whimsy—Noyon is also the birthplace of John Calvin, the man whose followers would make income a metaphysical come-on. And Calvin's unexpected appearance in Noyon, in turn, coincides nicely with Ypres's relation to Cornelius Jansen. Oddly, two great Christian reformers are associated with the two great salients of the Western Front, two catalysts of religious renewal connected to two catalysts of deicidal disbelief. It's as if St. Francis came from Antietam, twice.

All of the towns and villages within an immediate southerly radius of Noyon were deliberately destroyed in the spring of 1917, when the Germans evacuated the bulge and fell back on the *Siegfriedstellung*, or Hindenburg Line, a fortified defensive position that allowed them to shorten their trenches. The Germans laid waste to hundreds of square miles of land when they made their surprise withdrawal from the salient around Noyon. It was one of the greatest property crimes ever perpetrated on France—farmland was ravaged, towns dynamited, wells poisoned, churches and castles destroyed, and the resulting rubble booby-trapped. Until then, the Noyon Salient had been a relatively quiet sector of the Front. But quiet—especially "all quiet"—is a loaded term. In those times when no great offensives were being held, it is estimated that the French army alone lost 100,000 men a month. For end-of-the-century ears, the number sounds impossibly, unimaginably large.

My walk through this part of Picardy inspires little more than a few consecutive days of irritation. A province of France rich in cathedrals and supposedly redolent of medieval glory, Picardy south of the Santerre reveals itself to be a blanket of rural bleakness made even more disagreeable to the walker by impassable thruways and fenced-off train lines. The express from Paris to the northern city of Valenciennes once derailed in this washed-out Pissarro landscape because of a sudden track subsidence. The railbed, at the point where it crossed the Front, collapsed into an unseen and unsuspected underground hollow made by an old trench. For once history had undermined engineering, rather than the other way around.

I look at my route map. Fouquescourt, Damery, Beauvraignes, Crapeaumesnil. Lackadaisical little villages file by in the shuttered-up silence of midafternoon, their only structure of note the inevitable and usually dramatic war memorial. A maiden weeps, a soldier falls, a cock crows—all decisions made by town councilors when a postwar French government decreed the erection of a monument to the war dead a legal obligation. The eternal duet of small-town France—*mairie* vs. church—was joined by a mute third party, so that even the most insignificant collection of houses now has a memorial in its midst. It is said that the political complexion of a town after the war can be divined by its monument: sober or regretful means socialist or anticlerical, triumphalist or bloodthirsty translates as conservative or nationalist, Pietà-like or angel-filled almost always tips off a militant Catholic or right-winger. A French hamlet might not have a water tower, a baker, or even a store, but it will always have a list of the dead chiseled in stone. The Great War added a dash of lugubrious kitsch to every village of France that no amount of romanticizing about arty country living can erase. For the French, the Great War is an immutable presence, like Church and State.

The war did, however, change its name. For a while it was known as *la grande guerre* or *la der des der* (short for *la dernière des dernières*—the last of the last) until the debacle of 1940 showed it to be just another conflict in France's long inventory of inconclusive bloodletting. Now it's called, with actuarial breeziness, *la guerre de quatorze*, and is usually shrugged off as a necessary nightmare over which too much time has been spent and too much ink spilt. The expression *"C'est reparti comme en quatorze"* (roughly: It's 1914 all over again), a reference to the war hysteria that swept the country at the prospect of a rematch with the Germans (the first round was in 1870), survives in the French language to describe any activity enthusiastically taken up again. The kickoff of a soccer match between rivals, the reconciliation of a quarreling couple, even the onset of a rainstorm—all are good pretexts for dunking a sugar cube into your demitasse and uttering, knowingly, "C'est reparti comme en quatorze."

Of all the clichés and bywords related to the Great War, there are few that have lived on through to the end of the century. Most are fairly musty, but it is surprising how many linger on somewhere in the recesses of memory. Below is a short list from the lexicon of World War I commonplaces:

The powder keg of Europe	Shell shock
The Balkan tinderbox	Dogfight
The war to end all wars	Peace without victory
The war to make the world safe for democracy	*Gott strafe England*
	Hang the Kaiser!
The Fourteen Points	*On les aura!*
Trench coat	Freedom of the seas
The Western Front	*La fleur au fusil*
Tommy	Home before Christmas
Poilu	The miracle on the Marne
Doughboy	The taxis of the Marne
Feldgrau	*La Voie Sacrée*
Fritz	The Big Push
Jerry	*La Madelon*
Heine	Over there
Boche	*Wacht am Rhein*
Hun	No-man's-land
Jack Johnson	Over the top
Big Bertha	Go west
Creeping barrage	Buy the farm

Some are too obvious to explain, others not. A Tommy, for example, is a British soldier, derived from the name Thomas Atkins, the John Doe chosen during the Napoleonic Wars to show infantrymen how to fill out an army paybook. Similarly, *poilu* (hairy) is the name of a French infantry-man, taken from prewar slang for any male acquaintance. The German equivalent, *Feldgrau*, refers to his field-gray uniform. (The Germans had other words for the infantryman: *Kilometerschwein* and *Lakenpatscher*, respectively, "kilometer pig" and "puddle splasher.") The American doughboy is more of a mystery: depending on the source one consults, the word is either a corruption of "adobe" or a tribute to a dumpling. As for the words that follow it in the list, everything from Fritz to Hun counts as an anti-German slur.

Jack Johnson, the black boxer, was the undefeated world heavyweight champ from 1908 to 1915—hence the name given to a certain type of concussive shell emitting black smoke. Bertha, after whom a massive long-range gun was called, was Bertha Antoinette Krupp von Bohlen und Halbach, the heiress to the Krupp armaments empire. The expressions of hostility are more straightforward: for the Germans' famous "God Punish England," there is Prime Minister David Lloyd George's "Hang the Kaiser!", General Philippe Pétain's "*On les aura!*" ("We'll get 'em!"), and President Woodrow Wilson's "Peace without victory," his idea for a winner-take-nothing peace.

La fleur au fusil (flower in the rifle) refers to the raucous sendoff given to troops marching off to war in 1914. Old newsreel footage shows young Parisiennes rushing out and planting kisses on soldiers' cheeks as they headed to almost certain death. Whether this was staged for propaganda purposes is still debated by historians. "Home before Christmas" indicates the expected length of the war at its outset. The Allied victory at the Marne in September 1914 was transformed by myth-making publicists into a miracle—as indeed it may have been, given the blundering that had preceded it—and the taxis in question were Parisian cabs requisitioned as troop transport. *La Voie Sacrée* (the sacred road) was the thirty-three-mile route from Bar-le-Duc to Verdun that, in 1916, kept the French side of the killing ground supplied with men and munitions. The Big Push occurred in 1918, as the Allies kept attacking until the Germans gave way.

The next titles in the list could be called the Great War Greatest Hits. "Over There" is American and, naturally enough, self-assured; "*Madelon*," French and convivial; "The Rhine Watch," German and soulful. "No-man's-land," although an expression dating back to the Middle Ages, came to be almost exclusively associated with the treacherous, shell-shattered clearing between the underground armies of the Great War. "Over the top," the locution used to describe climbing out of the safety of a trench to attack, has shaken off the war and come to mean off the wall, out of bounds or, simply, beyond the reasonable. The last two in the lexicon—"go west" and "buy the farm"—are ways to express what going over the top into no-man's-land often meant: getting killed. Wordplay is not always innocent.

THE DOGS IN the Noyon Salient seem uninterested in pouncing on the dusty drifter as he passes. After all, they've seen armies go by. The war cemeteries in this stretch of the Front grow rarer—not only because it was a quiet sector in 1915–17, but also because the posthumous gardening instincts of the British have been left behind. Strictly speaking, the Western Front gives way here to *la ligne des tranchées* or *Die Westfront.* The French and the Germans preferred large national ossuaries to bury their war dead, the former out of a Jacobin urge to centralize, the latter from the necessity of taking whichever few plots of land were grudgingly allotted to them. Aside from the suspect prevalence of 1920s-era housing, the traces of war have all but disappeared in the Noyon Salient. I find myself ashamed at being annoyed at a landscape that has returned to obscurity. To belong to no one—to be no-man's-land—carries a perverse notoriety, but to belong to a nobody, to have reembraced the discretion of individual ownership, robs a countryside of cachet.

Not that the newly ahistorical province is devoid of charm. Southwest of the forgettable market town of Roye, the Picard plateau offers the first signs of relief I have seen since bidding good-bye to the sociopathic fishermen on the Somme. Ahead are the forests of the Noyonnais, a region of small hills that stretches east along the line of the Front. Beet fields are replaced by orchards, swirling dirt by swarms of flies. In Lassigny, a cheerful red-roofed town just within the département of the Oise, beauty returns to the world. At Thiescourt, Lassigny's neighbor along the line of the Front, there is even a handsome, reconstructed Gothic church standing alone on a rise, looking like a postcard for liturgical bliss. I have become so accustomed to sad villages that I fear I've somehow wandered off course, to a place unaffected by the gore of the Great War. It's only on seeing a French tricolor float behind the church above a farmer's field—always a telltale marker of many soldiers' graves—that I realize the Front is still with me, beneath my boots as I tread the black pavement.

On the way out of Thiescourt, a boy of about seven on a bicycle keeps pace with me on the opposite side of the road. He glances over warily. I smile in what I hope is an avuncular manner. The rider and his bike sidle ever closer. Curiosity finally wins the day.

"Monsieur, where are you going?"

"To Ribécourt."

"Are you going to walk there?"

"Yes."

"You're going to have sore feet, Monsieur."

5. Ribécourt to Nampcel to Soissons

A slope leads down toward the industrial town of Ribécourt on the River Oise. Behind me, on the crest of the hill, stands a domesticated forest. Every hundred feet or so some zealous souls have posted signs, *Défense d'Entrer—Chasse Gardée*, to underscore the private nature of their private property. This is someone's land. Between the trees near the roadway, the owners of the different swaths of the forest have seen fit to string barbed wire, so that no stray animals can get in or out without injury, and no army of picnickers or fornicators can wreak havoc in the undergrowth. There are no stiles here for scaling fences, no hiking paths for the cross-country wanderer, and no visible hints that humans are welcome any-where in the vicinity. This is not the wilderness—and has not been for a long time. The local government has already put signs up for next year's celebration of the founding of the French national monarchy: *Oise 987–1987, il y a mille ans, la naissance de la France!* (A thousand years ago, France was born here!) Oise, appropriately enough, is pronounced "was."

I cross the river and leave Ribécourt's industries behind me. A long row of houses follows the trace of what was the French front line toward a town called Bailly. Family men stand in their plot of no-man's-land, washing their cars in the driveways of model homes that resemble oversized shoe boxes topped with steep circumflex accents. The men momentarily stop what they're doing and look up hopefully at the passing pedestrian. I sense that if I were a nubile young woman, unwanted conversations might be struck up or unpleasant gestures with the garden hose might be made. As it is, yeti-like canines come gamboling over lawns toward me, unrestrained by either a leash or a reluctance to drool. It is Sunday morning and this is purgatory.

Relief comes from yet another woodland. The sylvan stretch ahead is an outgrowth of the much larger acreage of greenery known as the Forest of Compiègne. The city of the same name is a few miles to the south, but my path leads me away from it, away from the clearing where the armistice was signed on November 11, 1918. The Front lies due east through the forest towns of Ollencourt and Tracy-le-Val. At the latter I stop in for a quick coffee, only to remember that Sunday morning is the congregating time for country drunks throughout France. This place is no exception. Rheumy eyes peer through the cumulus of cigarette smoke as beers are knocked back and last night's lottery drawing is debated in numbing detail. At café counters such as this, the French language is less enunciated than gulped, usually in brief glottal intakes that would give most other people the hiccups. Occasionally, one of the debaters lets loose a great hacking gob of a cough that hushes his fellows until the final gurgles of angry phlegm have trickled off into silence.

My footsteps hasten, as I try to shake off the dog-loving car-washers and tubercular tipplers that inhabit this section of the Front. In an access of sudden scenic prettiness, the road winds between two bosky hillocks before heading up and out onto an utterly treeless plateau that stretches for a few miles. The French countryside, a succession of microcosms that make the continental features of North America seem inhuman in their scale, never ceases to surprise. I had thought myself locked into a day or two of sourly fenced-off shadiness; instead, I am on an exposed upland with little more than the sky as companion. A succession of wildflowers —Queen Anne's lace, morning glories, thistles, poppies—leads me into a long low field of sheared wheat. The road tapers off into a dirt track, then a cowpath, then trampled weeds. A gust of wind ushers a human-sized swirl of white dust across a neighboring meadow. I begin to sing, from the sheer joy of solitude. The only bump on the horizon is a large manor farm, placed squarely on a gray crossroads a couple of miles away. I think of Private Cadogan, the dead youth in Flanders, and how today, right now, there can be no eulogy for him save the wind and the clouds. There is no Western Front here, just the wide embrace of emptiness. There is no trace of it in the soil, or the sky. I am walking a *tabula rasa*.

The plateau, called the Toutvent (Every wind), just happens to conceal its secrets well. After an hour or so of brisk hiking, the land suddenly dips, as if at the top of an intermediate ski slope. The cavity deepens and the grassy walls of a natural depression rise higher on either side. Two large German cemeteries of Great War dead, lost amid mature trees the tops of which are invisible from the plateau, lead even farther down toward the gulley floor. Inevitably, for this is France, a village has been built in this topographical vulva, a banged-up Brigadoon that war, if nothing else, has managed to find. The road sign reads, "Nampcel." I check my map, see that I have wandered behind German lines—hence the cemeteries—and that I should be close to something called *L'Abri du Kronprinz* (The Crown Prince's Dugout). A woman in the village waves an irritated hand in one direction when I ask her where it is. Up a small track, over a rusty gate, and suddenly I see, hidden by the undergrowth like some Mayan monument, a three-story concrete structure built into the side of the gulley wall.

I pick my way around in the cool semidarkness. The same barely breathable dankness that I came across in Vimy permeates the lower floor. It is the smell of damp earth, cold stone, and old fear, the clammy musk of the Great War. The structure may not have been built for the Kaiser's nephew—German fortifications tend to get inflated in importance in local legend—but it certainly could have housed an entire general's staff. Square, spacious rooms lead off a central corridor on three levels. Where once heels clicked, confiscated local wine flowed, and telephone operators barked orders to poor subalterns stuck in the open country at such places as Tracy and Ollencourt, there is now only a bit of lonely graffiti from a later time. The place is a delinquent's dream—the litter of beer bottles and charred campfire remains shows its current vocation. Outside once again, I can see the cleverness of its location: tucked as it is into the south side of the Nampcel depression, no French artillery shell could ever have had the boomerang trajectory necessary to hit the place. For those inside the capacious hideout, the war must have been all sound and fury—and not much else.

Back on the plateau above Nampcel the sky opens. This is my first truly bad moment of the walk. I am caught in wide-open country as a summer thunderstorm comes dancing over the plain. I hurry on, aware of the inviting electrons coursing through me. I wonder if being short makes me less appetizing as a spark plug, or if I can find another nook like Nampcel before the business end of the clouds passes overhead. A motorist approaches, sees my plight, drives on. My Francophilia touches bottom. I let loose a long stream of curses—until I feel the hairs rise on the nape of my neck. Then the world goes blindingly white. There is a tremendous clap of thunder.

I sit on the ground. I am too frightened to feel foolish. "War Buff Found Toasted." "Western Front Strikes Again." "Historical Hiker a Thing of the Past." I work up headlines for imaginary obits, which takes my mind off the obvious question: Why did I ever leave the safety of the bunker? The first pellets of hail go bouncing off the road surface and are soon biting into the canvas expanse of the backpack now perched atop my head. They are followed by a torrent of hailstones, a sustained burst of icy shrapnel. The air goes white as another electrical discharge crackles over the land. The noise of the falling hail is smothered under a deafening blanket of thunder. The temperature drops, the rain teems down. I watch as puddles form around me. They are soon muddy ponds. I can feel the rain through my sodden sweatshirt. The poor poilus.

A car honks its horn. Dutch license plates. I get up—I'm going where they're going.

QUI A CASSÉ la vase de Soissons? (Who shattered the Soissons vase?) This is, in French folklore, the unanswerable, rhetorical question par excellence. It refers to a story of misplaced loot and capricious decapitation in Merovingian times—nobody knows the name of the anonymous soldier who defied his king Clovis and broke the vase, but the conundrum has survived to the present day. A more descriptive question, given the depredations of the nineteenth and twentieth centuries, would be, "*Qui a cassé Soissons?*" for the town, once the capital of the Gauls and an important ecclesiastical see, is now a sorry mess. The cathedral is disfigured, halfheartedly restored, its statuary smashed, its walls covered in an obscene acne of shell and bullet holes. Another large church in Soissons, belonging to a once thriving monastery, was dismantled in a moment of post-Revolutionary zeal, leaving only twin Gothic towers to loom over the town as a reminder of former glory. In the other main church, an exhibition entitled "150 Years of Restoration in Picardy" serves as a nice counterpoint for any sightseer who happens to be marooned here. There is so much to restore because so much has been wrecked.

As if to underscore the waste, a military parade is being held this drizzly Monday morning. Soissons marks the beginning of a region of soldiering. All around the town there are military bases and artillery firing ranges, some of them placed smack in the middle of the Western Front. Thus, an armed-to-the-teeth march can be summoned up at the drop of a kepi. The reason for today's spectacle, as far as I can tell, seems to be the commissioning of a new commanding officer for some outlying contingent. Tanks rumble past, and troops too old to be conscripts stride down the main street as if they own it. The morning shoppers look on impassively, apparently accustomed to such inane muscle-flexing in the middle of modern Europe. It is strange to see such martial pride in a town that has been robbed of interest and of its heritage by the destruction of war and the collapse of armies sent to defend it.

6. Home Leave

Soissons gets on my nerves so much that I give myself a furlough. I go on home leave in mid-August, to get away from the Front and the army. Although most Parisians have their toes in the Med at this time of the year, many of my acquaintances from the magazine business have already returned to the city. It is the moment to begin churning out hype-filled articles on what to expect in September when Paris comes to life again.

This is especially true of *Paris Passion*, an English-language monthly run on a shoestring and written for a pittance. In the summer of my walk, it is still an enthusiastic post-collegiate enterprise staffed by people of unbending principle who just happen to sleep together a lot. I write about bars and restaurants for the magazine—thus I spend a couple of evenings in both types of places explaining what I've been doing on my summer vacation. Eyes invariably glaze over, until I produce the bullets and barbed wire picked up along the way. The reactions are varied.

"You mean this shit is just *lying* out there?"

"You could make earrings out of the bullets. Start a line of no-future jewelry."

"What about the pesticides? Don't you end up covered in pesticide every day?"

"I'd be depressed. I can't stand farms."

"See any skulls?"

"At least it's not crowded."

"Where'd you say this place was again?"

The home front is, as always, difficult to understand. A middle-aged French friend shakes her head and says sorrowfully, "*La boue, la boue, la boue*"—as if repeating the word "mud" like a mantra sufficed. It reminds me of the pitch for the war porn place near the Menin Road.

Perhaps my going out to the Front is an exercise in doomed voyeurism. Might it not be possible that there is nothing to see? That you can't go back to where you've never been? That it would be better to stay here, in my Paris apartment, digesting a dozen snails and expectorating the word "mud" over a cognac? I think of the amusement park at Ypres, the diesel fumes at Loos, the hollow sky of the Santerre, the hailstones of Nampcel. I think of becoming a deserter. Pilgrims, unlike soldiers, need to believe in something.

THE NEXT MORNING I reluctantly pick through the mail that has accumulated over the past few weeks. Bills, bank statements. The usual, except for a small envelope with an Irish stamp. The postmark reads Baile Átha Cliath, which is the Celtically correct way of saying "town of the hurdle ford," or Dublin. Someone has used India ink to address the envelope; old-fashioned penmanship gives tails to many of the letters and leaves the p's unclosed so that they look like umbrella handles. I recognize the handwriting from childhood, when our grandmother used to send harp and shamrock badges for her Canadian grandsons to wear on St. Patrick's Day.

Inside the envelope is a small card, slightly bigger than a business card. There is no salutation, no accompanying note, no signature, just the words "Thomas Conlon. Guillemont Road Cemetery," written in the same decorous hand. I look at the card in bewilderment. I know a Thomas Conlon—he is Uncle Tommy, my mother's bachelor brother, a quiet, witty Dubliner to whom I owe my middle name, Thomas. There is obviously a connection here that I am missing.

The place name looks familiar as well. I consult my guidebooks, peruse the hiker's journal I've been keeping. My jaw drops open. I reread what I had written: "Let's make a movie: to the immediate right, the black pointed spires of Guillemont and Longueval piercing the level of the trees . . ." Of course! The cemetery near "The Greatest Thing in the World." Of the scores of cemeteries passed and ignored, the roads not taken, the fields left untrod, could I have stumbled unknowingly into the sole graveyard on the Western Front that bears some connection to my family? For I did visit a graveyard on the Guillemont Road—that is where I was sitting when I wrote the entry in the journal. The bucolic loveliness of the view made me stop my frantic pedaling. I then remember seeing a Celtic cross in the village. Could that have something to do with my uncle Tommy's namesake?

No one in Ireland is answering his phone. It's too early to call Canada. The train for Amiens, with a connection to Albert, leaves the Gare du Nord at noon. My watch shows eleven o'clock. It's a half-hour metro ride to the train station. My backpack is hurriedly refilled, my walking boots are laced up, and my urge to desert is, well, *history*. I'm going back to the Front.

THE 2,255 GRAVES of the Guillemont Road Cemetery stand pallid in the failing light of the day. Were it not for old photographs, it would be impossible to imagine the surrounding countryside as a battlefield. Yet it was obviously a savage place in 1916, for fully two-thirds of the graves here contain unidentifiable bodies. A picture taken in September of that year shows a couple of trucks, their canvas coverings emblazoned with shamrocks, carting the wounded from an advanced dressing station, itself nothing more than a couple of shell craters in a limitless lunar mudscape. The trucks, juddering down the pitted surface of the Guillemont Road back to Albert, must have caused agony to the wounded men stretched out in their vans.

Those who couldn't make the journey are buried here. The land in front of the village of Guillemont had been the scene of pointless attacks since midsummer. One of the dead was Raymond Asquith, the thirty-seven-

year-old son of British Prime Minister Herbert Asquith. It is said that
Guillemont broke the older man and allowed the allies of David Lloyd
George to take control of the government that much sooner. The younger
Asquith's grave in the Guillemont cemetery reads: "Small time but in that
small most greatly lived this star of England." Like Rudyard Kipling,
Herbert Asquith began to question the wisdom of sending so many young
men to die once he had lost a son. In Kipling's case, the disappearance of
his eighteen-year-old son near Loos brought forth a bitter couplet: "If any
question why we died / Tell them, because our fathers lied."

A few rows over from Asquith, between the graves of a Captain G. M.
Shufflebothan and a Private Gilham, I find my man. The inscription is
simple:

23914 Private
T. Conlon
Royal Dublin Fusiliers
6th September 1916 Age 20

My great-uncle Tommy? I look around: I am standing no more than
ten paces from the spot where I sat down to write in my journal during
my Tour de Somme. A coincidental near-miss becomes an uncanny
reunion. The entry in the cemetery registrar, with the name of my great-
grandfather the farmer printed on the yellowing page, seals the encounter: "Son of Richard Conlon, of Duleek, Co. Meath." I have read so
many names—at Thiepval, the Menin Gate, Notre Dame de Lorette, La
Targette—yet here the force of the forgotten assumes a shape I can begin
to see. A twenty-year-old Tommy Conlon, the younger brother of my
grandfather Bartholomew, running down this slope with rifle aloft and
fear in his heart, in pursuit of a meaningless objective during a miscon-
ceived campaign of a needless war. A shellburst, then blackness. The life
of one young Irishman gone, barely begun. Fresh out of school at
Drogheda, fed the usual lies, obliterated. One family's anti-militarism
was born in this field and passed down to their descendants, who would
share it across time and oceans.

I stand in front of the Commonwealth-issue headstone, smoking a
cigarette in the twilight, the first member of Tommy Conlon's family to
have come to France and visited his grave since his death in 1916. He's
like a grown-up cousin that one meets for the first time at a wedding. I
don't know what to do, what to say—so I invite him along. Henceforth,
Private Cadogan and Musketier Aronsohn will have company as we walk
the Front.

The downlands in front of Albert darken and the stars start to come out. It will take me a good two and half hours to walk back to my hotel in town. I set out on the Guillemont Road, this time unconcerned about hailing a ride. There is no one out on these country roads on this summer night.

Tommy Conlon was not the only Tommy or indeed the only Thomas to die in Guillemont. One of the commanding officers of the Royal Dublin Fusiliers was Tom Kettle, a beloved orator, Irish nationalist politician, essayist, and poet. He is said to have served James Joyce as a model for the character Hughes in *Stephen Hero*. Kettle was shot and killed between Guillemont and Ginchy on September 9, 1916, and his body was never identified for burial. Doubtless his is one of the nameless tombstones in the Guillemont Road Cemetery. Kettle, shortly before he joined Tommy Conlon, Raymond Asquith, and two thousand others underground, wrote at length about the legacy of the Great War. He is quoted in Tim Cross's invaluable *The Lost Voices of World War I*:

> When the time comes to write down in every country a plain record of it [the war], with its wounds and weariness and flesh stabbing and bone pulverizing and lunacies and rats and lice and maggots, and all the crawling festerment of battlefields, two landmarks in human progress will be revealed. The world will for the first time understand the nobility, beyond all phrase, of the soldiers, and it will understand also the foulness, beyond all phrase, of those who compel them into war.

It's difficult to say whether Kettle, or any other soldier on the Somme, would be shocked about how low his war has sunk on the horizon of general consciousness. How it has truly gone "beyond all phrase" and turned into mute monument and unread indignation. What was all-consuming, in the literal as well as the figurative sense, is now the stuff of solitary musing on a long walk through a starry night. The battlefields are silent; my footfalls don't awaken any presences. Voltaire, of all people, once admonished: "We owe respect to the living; but to the dead we owe nothing but the truth."

Home leave is over. The walk east must resume.

7. *Soupir*

The early-morning mist accompanies me along the right bank of the River Aisne. Soissons and its grimy streets, which I reached via an intercity bus ride across Picardy, fade into memory. My route out of town follows that taken by Joan of Arc when she was dragging the ineffectual Dauphin to

Reims to be crowned King Charles VII. Sesquicentennial plaques mark the way, done in the Art Deco style popular in 1929. The commemorative signposts were no doubt a sop to historic decency thrown by a French state and army that, through gross incompetence, had caused massacres and mutinies along this stretch of the Front only a decade or so earlier. What better way to forget the criminal behavior of the immediate past than by harking back to a halcyon time of martial, mystic grandeur?

The banks of the Aisne are covered with lush, impenetrable shrubs and vines that bar access to the river to any nonresident bather. The fog has dulled the flowering bushes along the roadside into vegetable monotony, which is a shame, for the locals here seem to take great pride in competing to see who can create the most colorful rock garden. At Vailly-sur-Aisne, a picturesquely situated place framed between blackwater river to the south and wooded height to the north, the sun eventually burns off the lingering mist, revealing an artfully rebuilt town that does not betray its past as the site of furious fighting in 1914, 1917, and 1918. On the outskirts of Vailly, where ramparts must once have stood, midway rides have been set up. The carnies, in their mobile homes, are gathered around their television sets, awaiting the opening of the fair and the coming of customers. Tomorrow is the Assumption holiday, yet another anomalous religious festival on the official calendar of agnostic France. That day—August 15—marks the moment when, impossibly, the glacial pace of country life slows down even further. Traditionally the hottest day of the summer, it is also the absolute zero of social and business activity. As if rehearsing for the big sleep on the morrow, the main market street of Vailly is devoid of life at ten o'clock this morning.

I continue eastward through the stillness. Even the cars must be snoozing in the building heat; the traffic is nonexistent. At the village of Chavonne, I pass French and British military cemeteries on my way to a crossroads pointing to a place called Soupir. I'm attracted to the name, for *soupir* is the French word for "sigh." In yet another instance of toponymic irony like that at La Targette, the countryside around Soupir is a landscape of sighs, a place of cosmopolitan bereavement. Near the tombs of the French and the British are German and Italian war graves, all casualties of the last two years of the war. Beyond them and the village itself, another casualty awaits. The wrought-iron gates to the Chateau de Soupir swing open, leading into a field empty of any construction save a triumphal arch standing improbably alone, bereft of the large mansion to which it once belonged. The Picard bishop and man of letters, François de Fénelon, is supposed to have stayed here several centuries ago, when this arch looked out onto a formal French garden with its rational mastery of space and perspective. Now the remnant of the Chateau de Soupir looks forlorn and faintly ridiculous in its neat field of hay, like an arch of defeat.

Unlike Shelley's Ozymandias, Soupir is an instant ruin, divorced from the Romantic ideal of ruination that required deliquescence over centuries. This chateau or others like it inhabited the world and the imaginations of our grandparents and great-grandparents, those with whom we might have been contemporaries for a few short years. It disappeared overnight. The ruination was what Lutyens partly conveyed with his Thiepval memorial—an evocation of defeat and disappearance. I know that across the road, in the wooded hills called Mont de Sapins and Les Gouttes d'Or, the ground is scored with the usual awful undulations of the Great War, yet here the violence is done through absence, by what is suddenly missing and gone forever. Alone in its field, the shattered manor has become a gnomon in a large sundial, the shadow of the freestanding wall turning endlessly on itself with the passage of each day. It is in and out of time, a grandfather clock in a forgotten room. In Soupir I have found my monument for the Western Front, my link to Tommy and Cadogan and Aronsohn and Daniel and Bartholomew and all our grandfathers. The wind in the grass sighs.

I am not alone. The grandfathers of the Great War have come back to haunt contemporary writing long after my afternoon in Soupir. Sebastian Faulks's *Birdsong,* Jean Rouaud's *Les Champs d'Honneur* (*Fields of Glory*) —both are novels in which people of the present era seek out truth about their grandfathers' experience of World War I. Geoff Dyer's smart nonfiction *Missing of the Somme* begins thus, "When I was a boy my grandfather took me to the Museum of Natural History," and soon thereafter goes into the old man's war history. Pat Barker, whose superb Great War fiction trilogy—*Regeneration, The Eye in the Door,* and *The Ghost Road*— has no such reminiscing from the modern day to the past, nonetheless cannot escape the lure of the grandfather clause. In *The Ghost Road,* her ambivalent, bisexual hero Billy Prior goes back to the trenches for a third tour of duty. He meets a young officer there who has come to the hell of the Front for the first time. The imagery is inescapable:

> Ghosts everywhere. Even the living were only ghosts in the making. You learned to ration your commitment to them. This moment in this tent already had the quality of *remembered* experience. Or perhaps he was simply getting old. But then, after all, in trench time he *was* old. A generation lasted six months, less than that on the Somme, barely twelve weeks. He was this boy's great-grandfather.

CHAPTER
5

Champagne

1. Cerny-en-Laonnois to Craonne to Berry-au-Bac

THE DRY, HOT Assumption holiday under a leaden August sun begins in Picardy and finishes in Champagne. There is an end to the summer in sight, as the blue line of the Vosges grows closer with every step I take. I shall walk out of the last of the scarred Picard woods today and into the great chalky Champenois dust bowl that stretches out from the sacred city of Reims to the dark hills of the Argonne. The agony of the Front continued on beyond Champagne, into Lorraine and Alsace, but perhaps nowhere was the sting of incompetence as sharp as right here, along the Chemin des Dames.

The attack launched here in the spring of 1917 showed French military planners to be a band of blinkered dilettantes, like so many rubes hopelessly outplayed and outpositioned in a game of skill. For *dames* is also the French word for checkers, and on this crimson landscape the German generals knew every move of their opponents in advance and countered devastatingly. Tens of thousands of ordinary soldiers were killed, swept off the checkerboard thanks to the impossible tasks set for them. The sheer magnitude of the rout at the Chemin des Dames called for the enforcement of willed amnesia. The French army—any army, in fact—is a natural enemy of truth. Alliances shift, but the opposition between the logic of military obedience and that of informed criticism will always remain. Arguably, covering up its blunders and cruelties is what the French army has done best in the twentieth century.

It waited until 1995, for example, before one of its official spokesmen begrudgingly allowed that Alfred Dreyfus had been wronged one hundred years previously. Similarly, its behavior during the war of Algerian

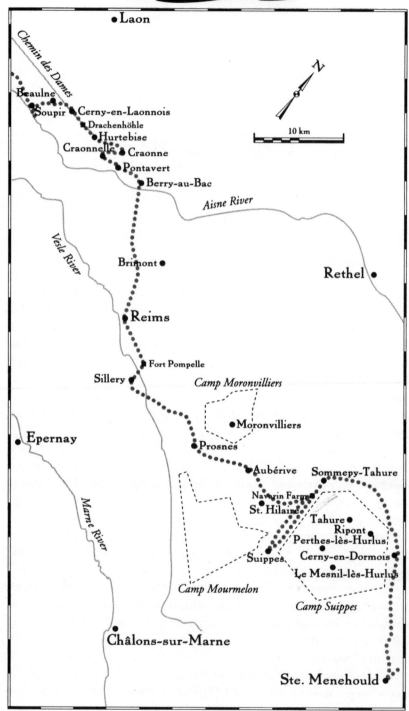

CHAMPAGNE

Laon

Chemin des Dames

Beaulne
Soupir   Cerny-en-Laonnois
          Drachenhöhle
          Hurtebise
Craonnelle   Craonne
          Pontavert
          Berry-au-Bac

Aisne River

Vesle River

Brimont   Rethel

Reims

Fort Pompelle
Sillery   Camp Moronvilliers

                        Moronvilliers

Epernay   Prosnes

                        Aubérive   Sommepy-Tahure

Marne River   Navarin Farm
                        St. Hilaire
                                   Tahure
                                   Ripont
                                   Perthes-lès-Hurlus
                        Suippes   Cerny-en-Dormois
                                   Le Mesnil-lès-Hurlus

Camp Mourmelon

                        Camp Suippes

Châlons-sur-Marne

Ste. Menehould

••••• author's route

independence in the 1950s and 1960s, during which thousands were tortured and killed by French officers, remains a taboo subject in French military and political circles. The smothering of the Chemin des Dames debacle and its aftermath followed the same implacable need for mendacity. In a well-known instance of the long hand of military censorship reaching across time, Stanley Kubrick's *Paths of Glory*—a film made in 1957—was successfully kept off French movie screens until well into the 1970s. Its depiction of the unfair courts-martial of poilus for insubordination in a futile Great War offensive was considered too biased for the impressionable minds of French moviegoers.

The graduates of French military academies after World War I would learn precisely the wrong lessons from the Chemin des Dames fiasco. They poured all their efforts during the interwar period into building a useless fortification, the Maginot Line, as a means of thwarting any other Schlieffen-like German attack on France. The decision to build the Line—it failed miserably in 1940—rivals the plan of attack along the Chemin des Dames as an illustration of awe-inspiring incompetence. As I write these words in the 1990s, the current generation of bemedaled French strategists is exploding nuclear bombs under a Pacific atoll in anticipation, perhaps, of some future aquatic threat. History will judge whether these fellows are any cleverer than their predecessors.

Such judgment goes by the name of hindsight, a backward-looking, second-guessing perspective that I have often used in recounting the events at the Front. Professional historians find hindsight unjust, even distasteful; I believe it to be a necessary weapon to fight against the apologists of mayhem. Scholars quite rightly point out the exaggerations of popular rumor and the paranoid imaginings of the mistreated—no, hundreds of men were not shot as a result of the Chemin des Dames mutinies, as was once commonly believed. But as these overblown bubbles of oral transmission get punctured, sometimes the emphasis gets shifted. The hunt for inaccuracy becomes paramount, and in redressing a minor libel the original enormity gets lost. No, Haig did not bungle everything, completely, all the time, but—lest we forget—he did send hundreds of thousands unnecessarily to their deaths on two occasions. The men who routinely referred to him as "the Butcher" are all dead and gone now, yet his statue still stands in London's Whitehall. Haig and Joffre and Falkenhayn and their ilk died not on some hopeless, hellish battlefield but of old age, in their beds, and their memory, while fading, is still honored in some quarters. We have forgotten how heinous a lesson about the military mind they inadvertently taught the world. The twentieth century's opening event, the murder of millions through incompetence, has become unacknowledged, and the perpetrators unpunished in our vision of the past. A little less intellectual charity toward them is in order, even if that means using the disreputable narrative tool of hindsight. The reluctance to put one's life in the hands of the military, an ancestral reflex made universal by the Great War, should never be allowed to weaken.

THE CHEMIN DES Dames cries out for hindsight. It is hard to imagine a stupider place to order an attack. Seeing is disbelieving. In the valley below Passchendaele, I had to picture the mud, reconstruct the horror from accounts I was reading; to the uninformed eye, the notorious spot looks like an unprepossessing village in an unremarkable landscape, but not much else. The Somme, too, looked innocuous, or, at least, like a place where the attacker in a war was not automatically doomed to failure. It was command error on a colossal scale rather than the nature of the terrain that had led to the mass British suicides in 1916.

Not so the Chemin des Dames. The landscape is such that no casual hiker with a knowledge of the past can fail to pity the poor poilus ordered to assault the German lines here. When I leave Soupir to head northward, the road starts to ascend and will not stop its ascent for a couple of miles. North of the River Aisne between Soissons and Reims the land resembles a tall escarpment. The incline is steep in parts. On either side of my route outcroppings of the plateau summit, some three hundred feet above the floor of the Aisne valley, jut out from the body of the incline. Imagine an oak leaf a hundred yards thick—its lateral lobes are these jutting cliffs, from which machine-gunners had a field day mowing down the men slogging up the gentler slopes to the flat land at the top. To attack here was insane.

My walk continues in the building heat. The floors of the reforested parts of the slopes show the customary egg-carton craziness of Great War carnage; the plowed farmer's fields, the usual collection of dud shells and rusted bullets. Near a village called Beaulne, I quickly pass some old bones piled up against a fencepost. This time the toponymic coincidence does not charm. I am eager to finish the ascent.

The top is the location of the *chemin* of the Chemin des Dames, a road used by the daughters of Louis XV whenever they visited a noblewoman of the district. These *grandes dames* enjoyed the road—the midrib of our oak leaf—because it provided such dominating views to both north and south. The distant spires of Laon and Reims could be glimpsed on very fine days. What provided agreeable scenery from a jolting eighteenth-century carriage also made an admirable firing range for twentieth-century gunners looking downhill. To worsen matters for the French attacker, geology favored the defenders too. The rock of the plateau is porous—indeed, the great cathedrals of the region had been built from the stone quarried here—and the land was already a maze of tunnels and subterranean chambers long before the engineers of the German army dug shelters deep into the ground. The moles who built the redoubtable blockhouse into the gulley wall of Nampcel would use all the advantages of malleable stone here. At the easternmost point of the Chemin des Dames, where the upland is called the California Plateau, a series of underground tunnels was so extensive that it could comfortably hold 8,000 men. The German soldiers, never at a loss for Sturm und Drang modifiers, named the feature *die Drachenhöhle*, the Dragon Hole.

The French plan of attack was simple. Thousands of troops, less than six months after escaping from the slaughter of Verdun, were to proceed uphill, between machine-gun-infested cliffs, in full view of an impregnable enemy, with no attempt to use the element of surprise. How could the French command have done this to its soldiers? Good question. What's even more puzzling is how the civilian authors of a major French two-volume compendium, *La première guerre mondiale*, could write as late as 1968: "Strategically, the attack sector was judiciously chosen because, as long as the breakthrough occurred in the first twenty-four or forty-eight hours, the entire center of the German line would collapse. Unfortunately for the French, no ground was ever better suited to the defensive." Love of the dialectic—or at least its first two contradictory statements—must have afflicted the writers. If the terrain was so formidable, how could the sector have been "judiciously" chosen? The slope up toward the Chemin des Dames is an infantryman's graveyard. And when did great French breakthroughs *ever* occur in the First World War? Passages such as these litter books on the war, as if military historians never visited battlefields or realized that the men in the fanciest uniforms frequently have a lot of unfurnished rooms upstairs. To understand the Chemin des Dames, it is not necessary to find lame excuses; it is far better to understand 1917.

OR, RATHER, THE result of 1916. Between them, the strategists of the French, British, and German general staffs had managed to kill more than one million men in nine months—and the Front had not budged. Small wonder that political leaders began to question the abilities of their generals. The near-loss of Verdun had led to Joffre's being promoted beyond the reach of the levers of command. The man responsible for the most horrendous casualties in French history—hundreds of thousands of his countrymen killed in incessant, repetitive attacks in Lorraine during the debacle of 1914—was raised to the rank of field marshal. Ever the dullard in tactics, he initially did not realize that this meant he would lose effective control of the armies.

Perhaps Joffre thought he would be treated as gently as the British treated their commander. Douglas Haig—the man who made July 1, 1916, the worst day in all of British martial history—was also elevated to the heights of field marshaldom, but he was not relieved of command. His protector and patron, King George V, wanted to show some overt support for his friend and reward him for standing up to the assaults of the new prime minister, David Lloyd George. The king rightly saw that Haig was in danger of deserved demotion. Lloyd George, just as rightly, viewed the new field marshal as a plodding old soldier with too little imagination and talent to be left in charge of so many British lives. The Somme had sickened Lloyd George—he wanted to see anyone but Haig conduct the battles of 1917. The prime minister, unable to fire the well-connected bumbler, would henceforth look to circumvent his military commander.

Unfortunately for the poilus of 1917, Lloyd George and other politicians fell under the spell of the French general Robert Georges Nivelle, a heretofore obscure officer who had scored a few high-profile victories in the closing days of the Verdun battles. Much of the ground he won back had already been evacuated by the Germans, but the symbolic purpose of regaining lost territory did not escape the notice of a French press desperate for good news after the horrible losses of the year. Nivelle, perhaps the most canny manipulator of opinion of the entire war, was soon considered by almost everyone as a man with a plan, a bold new tactician who would somehow outsmart the stubborn realities of trench warfare. What had actually happened in his Verdun successes—a short, intense artillery barrage on a very small front, followed by an advance over ground that was in the process of being surrendered—got lost in the enthusiasm for Nivelle's messianistic military message: I can win the war. I have the secret. Everything is under control.

He was saying it in English, too. Nivelle, whose mother came from Britain, was an urbane man who could knock back port with the best of his cross-Channel colleagues and speak English fluently and persuasively. Nivelle's cozy parleys with Lloyd George clinched his appointment as military supremo. He was believed in both languages, because people in power hoped that the searingly murderous mistakes of the past could somehow be halted. This new general exuded self-assurance; he had, after all, won battles in the world's most awful battlefield. Nivelle was charming, cultivated, and convincing. The French populace, and, more important, the French army, took him at his word and dared to hope that the end of the war was just around the corner. Not since 1914 had there been such optimism afoot. To be fair to Nivelle, he believed his own hype.

Once made de facto commander-in-chief of the Allied effort, Nivelle worked only minor modifications to Joffre's plan for 1917, but they were crucial nonetheless. The British would attack near Arras, the French at the Chemin des Dames. This way, the new commander hoped, the Noyon Salient, that weak, quiet sector of the line, would be cruelly pinched, and the Germans would have to waste their reserves in shoring up their defenses.

Trouble came to Nivelle's paradise when the Germans retreated from the Noyon Salient in March 1917 and hunkered down along the Hindenburg Line. There was no Salient left to pinch—the Germans had shortened their lines by forty miles and thus freed valuable divisions to use as a reserve in case of Allied attack. Such a defensive coup might have given other commanders pause, but not Nivelle. A collective suspension of disbelief reigned at headquarters, despite a few rumblings from rivals he had beaten for the top job. These criticisms were discounted as sour grapes from also-rans, even though detailed plans were known to have been captured by German raiding parties. Nivelle's own loquaciousness around the press ensured that the coming attack counted as the worst-kept secret of the war. As March became April, disaster drew nearer.

That winter and spring of 1917 were, in many ways, as momentous as the summer of 1914. The changes latent since Princip fired his bullet finally took place, and the nineteenth century expired. In December 1916, Franz Josef, the decrepit Austro-Hungarian emperor who had let his ministers issue Serbia the unanswerable ultimatum thirty months earlier, died unhappy in Vienna, to be succeeded by a twenty-nine-year-old eager for peace. The glue that had held Mitteleuropa together quickly began to come unstuck. In Germany, a failure of the potato crop turned the winter into a nightmare of watery turnip soup and starving children. Hurt by the British-enforced shipping embargo, the German government felt compelled to return the favor and cut Britain off from its vital supplies. On January 31, 1917, the Germans announced that they would

begin unrestricted submarine warfare—that is, they would sink any ship
on the high seas, whether belligerent or neutral in its national origin. The
Americans were naturally appalled; three days later the American cargo
ship *Housatonic* was sunk by a U-boat in the north Atlantic. It was the
first of many that spring.

The American century began in 1917. The U-boats ushered it in, with
the help of the new German foreign minister, Dr. Alfred von Zimmermann, and the strange, unsolicited telegram he sent to the Mexican
government. Zimmermann promised lavish German support, in the
event of an American entry into the war, should Mexico wish to wrest the
southwestern states of the union back from their Yankee usurpers. Bribes
were paid, and the telegram was deciphered, translated, and leaked to the
press. Five weeks later, on April 6, 1917, the United States Congress
declared war on Germany. President Wilson, elected the previous
autumn on the slogan "He Kept Us out of the War," couched the
American action in the terms of unalloyed idealism. He was a new pope
launching a new crusade. He might also have added that American
business could not afford to let France and Britain renege on their
mountainous debts, and that the Allies' credit line was exhausted.
Someone had to make sure that they won the war—or everyone would
go broke.

At the same time, ice was breaking in Russia. Two weeks after incensed
Americans read about the Zimmermann telegram in their newspapers,
Czar Nicholas II was forced to abdicate by his rebellious army. The
bloodbath on the Eastern Front had been too great, the suffering too
harsh, the incompetence too patent. The creaking, 303-year-old oligarchy
of the Romanovs came to an ignominious end on March 15, 1917. Russia
remained a belligerent nation at grips with the Central Powers, but it was
now teetering on the brink of neutrality. The German government
gambled that it could get Russia out of the war altogether before the
Americans arrived in force. In April, it allowed a closed train with
Vladimir Ulyanov Lenin as a passenger to cross its territory and shunt
home to Russia. The newly empowered democrats of Petrograd intended
to continue the fight alongside the Allies. The Bolsheviks, on the other
hand, promised to have no truck with the imperialist powers of either
side.

Thus in April 1917, a new era dawned, one in which the old powers of
Europe would eventually have to share the world stage with an inter-
nationalist America and a turbulent Russia. Fittingly, for a senescent
civilization that had placed millions of its youths in two long parallel

ditches, spring refused to come in 1917. The weather over the Front was execrable, a filthy, unseasonable mix of cold sleet and chilling winds. On April 6, the shivering Allied troops were warmed by America's declaration of war. Three days later, the British launched their attacks near Arras as part of the Nivelle offensive. The Canadians took Vimy Ridge in a snowstorm, but elsewhere the usual failures occurred with the usual horrific human cost. A week after that, on April 16, Lenin arrived at the Finland Station of Petrograd, ready for his rendezvous with destiny. The same day, in northern France, the weather was a howling mess as a cold deluge of sleet and snow swirled out of lowering gray clouds. In the murky darkness of 6:00 A.M., the French army stepped out of its trenches and headed uphill toward the Chemin des Dames.

I HAVE REACHED the fertile desolation of the plateau. A straight road leads east through the wavering kinks of scorched air. Unlike many rural routes in France, the wayside is devoid of shade trees. There is nothing to block the prospect or deflect the wind. The fields have been harvested, leaving the baked brown earth a cracked labyrinth of tractor treadmarks and flattened furrows. A few skeletal hayracks stand out against the blue sky, their supporting beams bleached by the sun. By the shoulder of the road, a small *borne* informs me that I'm on the Chemin des Dames. No one is in sight. My stride quickens, and soon several miles have passed and the inventory of the hours lengthens: a huge graveyard, a flagpole, a private memorial; a chapel built in the late 1950s and visited in 1962 by German Chancellor Konrad Adenauer and French President Charles de Gaulle; a rebuilt village, Cerny-en-Laonnois, snoozing at a crossroads; then more empty fields with distant ricks sweltering in the afternoon glare. Off to my right I catch occasional glimpses of the Aisne valley. In places it still bears the puckers of seventy-year-old detonations.

The morning of April 16, 1917, was a massacre. As one lieutenant later told a French parliamentary committee investigating the fiasco: "At six in the morning, the battle began; by seven, it was lost." Regiments disappeared in a withering hail of bullets and shellfire. Nivelle, whose plan had called for an intense artillery barrage, made precisely the same mistakes as the British had on the Somme. There was a ten-day artillery campaign before the sixteenth, which robbed the attack of any possible surprise, and the wrong guns were used. Less than a third of his artillery was of the heavy caliber needed to entomb the defenders in their cavernous shelters. Worse, of the 392 German gun batteries trained on the advancing troops, only 53 had been spotted by reconnaissance aircraft in the run-up to the fatal day. The French thus climbed up an inclined no-man's-land rocking with deadly explosions. Worse still, the stormy weather had prevented most airplanes from flying in the days imme-diately preceding the battle—thus no one detected the fresh divisions the Germans had moved into the sector. The French attackers were meant to follow a creeping barrage in the manner of the Canadians at Vimy. They were meant to effect a war-winning breakthrough, to advance seven miles in a few hours. By day's end, those still alive were five hundred yards at most from their starting point, hugging the ground as the wind swept snow into their faces. The next day, Nivelle sent thousands more to their deaths.

I arrive at the Dragon Hole, scene of some of the fiercest fighting of 1917. The land to the south becomes clifflike; there are shell craters in the meadow far below. Inside, a pompous little man leads a group of war tourists around the dankness, extolling the courage of the doomed army in a spiel of florid French that never once shrinks from cliché. Nothing is said about the wisdom of attacking the spot or about the subsequent mutinies. The guide sells us a version of 1917 with a shrill nationalist pitch, like a paraplegic celebrating the car crash that disabled him. We look at fading displays under glass. Once back out into the air, everyone breathes easier. A bottle blonde in high heels clicks across the parking lot in pursuit of her hyperactive son; an old man soothes a crying youngster who has fallen off a cannon; an Assumption Day picnic on a crater lip degenerates into a family quarrel. The view and my mood suddenly improve—at a feature of the Chemin des Dames called the Isthmus of Hurtebise, the land drops away on both sides, and the prospects to the north and south stretch to rivers and ridges that lie outside this crude swath of the Front. Undamaged France beckons. Champagne has been reached.

The time line falters as well. At Hurtebise I have stumbled onto a Napoleonic battlefield. On March 7, 1814, Bonaparte's men clashed on this picturesque height with the Russians of the Grand Alliance sent to crush the French Emperor. Napoleon, as usual, won, but the victory was Pyrrhic at best: for the 5,000 Cossacks killed on the battlefield, there were 7,000 French dead. A monument marks the spot at Hurtebise Farm. A poilu holds a tattered flag with a *Marie-Louise*, the name given to the conscripts of 1814. The casualty total a century later would show the progress of technology and the regression of generalship. Nivelle lost 275,000 soldiers on the Chemin des Dames. Napoleon would have been dumbfounded by Nivelle's mulish wastefulness, and by the result—in mid-May, the descendants of his Grande Armée began talking back to their officers. The soldiers heading up to the line bleated like sheep, derisively, in an open admission of loss of faith in their leaders.

From Hurtebise, I walk to the easternmost, wooded end of the Chemin and the villages of Craonne and Craonnelle. This is the so-called California Plateau, named by a nineteenth-century entrepreneur who thought the gold rush association would attract quarrymen to his outdoor dancehall. It became the most dreaded part of the battlefield. By May 1917, it was known to the entire French army, thanks to a song that smacked of the now-rampant defeatism. The *Madelon* was forgotten. I quote from René Courtois's monograph, *Le Chemin des Dames*:

> *Adieu la vie, adieu l'amour*
> *Adieu toutes les femmes*
> *C'est bien fini, c'est pour toujours*
> *De cette guerre infâme*
> *C'est à Craonne, sur le plateau*
> *Qu'on doit laisser sa peau,*
> *Car nous sommes tous condamnés*
> *Nous sommes les sacrifiés.*

> (Goodbye to life, goodbye to love
> Goodbye to all women
> It's all over now, finished for good,
> This awful war.
> At Craonne, on the plateau
> That's where we'll lose our lives
> Because we are all doomed
> We are sacrificed.)

Mutiny and sedition got started among those about to be rotated back to such places as Craonne and Cerny-en-Laonnois. In early May, a regiment that had been taken out of the line and promised leave stayed in their billets drinking wine and playing cards when the order came that they were to return to the Chemin des Dames. The poilus elected representatives, who politely told their officers that there was no way they were returning to the Front. When the officers insisted, the men said they would shoot them first.

The revolt spread with astonishing speed. Before long, more than two-thirds of the units of the French army were affected by insubordination, or worse. Some units agreed to man the trenches, but not to attack. For the first time on the Western Front, men got together as a mass and denounced the madness. It was the war's finest moment. Tens of thousands of poilus refused to go back to the Front. They wanted the whole sorry slaughter to be history. Now. Immediately.

Ordinary soldiers took over towns behind the Front—martial Soissons is still trying to live down the shame—and commandeered troop trains. There was talk of taking Paris, of overthrowing the government, of going home. The offensive on the heights of the Chemin des Dames petered out into inertia. Henceforth, it would be "the sanatorium" of the Front, the place to send the shell-shocked and those too weary to fight.

Something remarkable happened in May 1917. A shared wave of common sense and common dignity swept over multitudes of mistreated men. The message implicit in their mass disobedience was clear: No longer could their lives be squandered in pointless slaughter. They were men before they were soldiers, individuals before being Frenchmen. The mutineers of the Chemin des Dames are the Front's only true heroes. It is their statues that should have pride of place in the capitals of Europe instead of those of their executioners. The mutineers, by their actions, resisted the industrialization of murder. Had their example been followed more often during the twentieth century, there might be less reluctance to look back at history. The men of the Chemin des Dames tried to save their skins and, in so doing, save the past from the obloquy of forever being an example of the grotesque. Instead, the skeleton of Soupir's chateau stands alone in its field, unknown and unneeded.

THE SUMMER AND fall of 1917 saw the tumult on the Western Front return to its more normal medium. Pieces of steel, rather than ideas, were exchanged. Nivelle was dispatched to an obscure command in North Africa after being found blameless by an indulgent board of inquiry. His replacement was Henri-Philippe Benoni Omer Joseph Pétain, a saturnine but humane general who would disgrace himself in old age as head of France's collaborationist Vichy regime. Pétain quelled the mutinies in the army by promising to call off suicidal offensives, institute more frequent home leave, and improve the food. That was the carrot. The stick was the series of courts-martial conducted by an army hierarchy terrified of its brush with total collapse: 23,385 men were convicted of mutinous actions, 432 were condemned to death, and 50 were shot. Henri Barbusse, according to historian A. J. P. Taylor, claimed that 250 men were purposely obliterated by their own artillery. The soldiers whose death sentences had been commuted were sent instead to penal servitude in the tropics. It is a complaisant commonplace in French histories of the war to state that these figures prove that the army showed leniency toward its mutinous men. To make such a statement is to be a stooge. Leniency was shown to Nivelle, not to the four hundred or so lives that were ruined for standing up to the lunacy of 1917. Even Pétain realized this. Henceforth, the strategy of the French army would be to sit and wait for the Americans.

The British thought otherwise. Haig might have blood on his hands, but Lloyd George had egg on his face. The prime minister's previous support of Nivelle now looked foolhardy, proof of the politician's misapprehension of all things military. Haig, claiming that the French generals wanted him to launch a major offensive to keep the German invader away from their convalescing army, argued for a huge new campaign in Flanders. The French, in fact, had asked the British simply to keep the Germans occupied with diversionary attacks, but with the mood of I-told-you-so reigning in the war councils of London, Haig was hard to resist. When the mines were blown under the Messines Ridge in June, signaling the first painless British advance since the heady opening day of Neuve Chapelle in 1915, the momentum for the Flanders campaign became unstoppable. There was no gainsaying Haig; he would have his Third Battle of Ypres. It began on July 31, 1917. Another slaughter commenced. On August 29, nineteen-year-old Private E. R. Cadogan died near the Ramscapelle Road outside of Nieuport. Eleven days earlier, Musketier Leopold Aronsohn perished in Artois.

The Ypres campaign ended in the ghastly slime of Passchendaele. Now that so much of the Front and the war is behind us, perhaps the true scale of the crime can be better understood. Field-Marshal Haig advocated frontal assaults, devoid of surprise, in the rain and the mud of the Salient, and even spoke of his cavalry breaking through into open country. He promoted these tactics after the Chemin des Dames, after Verdun, after the Somme, after Loos, after Neuve Chapelle, after the Kindermord at Langemarck. It is astonishing that his name did not become a verb meaning "to learn nothing." At war's end Haig received a lump sum gift of £100,000 and was made a peer. Leniency was shown once again.

THE WALK DOWN from Craonnelle into the plain of Champagne has me limping in the lengthening shadows. I pass the first vineyard of my journey—quite an accomplishment for someone who has spent several weeks hiking through the French countryside. It's as if I'd driven across America without glimpsing a Wal-Mart. This vineyard overlooks the lowlands near the Aisne; next to it on the slope is a large military graveyard, its headstones perversely planted in the same arrangement as the grapevines. The effect is eerie, as if the cemetery were a desiccated vineyard and its crosses oversized stakes deserted by the vine. In contrast to the greenery of the growing grapes, the burnt brown grass of the cemetery seems sad and neglected.

At Pontavert, a village that grew up around a canal lock, I am picked up by a vanful of tipsy country boys. They give me a lift, at hair-raising speed, to the main road leading to Reims. On the way there we pass a sign pointing to Julius Caesar's encampment. Yet another battle was fought around here, this one in 57 B.C. There is no record of mutinies or of fallen Cossacks in that battle.

I am deposited at a road junction opposite the village Berry-au-Bac. On one side of the main road are tanks and a war monument, placed in memory of a tank cemetery that formed here during the Nivelle offensive. Signs point off to craters where hundreds were killed by exploding mines. Farther up, there's a farm called Le Choléra.

I look around—cholera, tanks, and craters. In the distance, on the plain of Champagne, the towers of the Reims cathedral stand out in the deepening gloom. The decision is not too difficult. I stick out my thumb and start walking toward town.

2. Reims

Hundreds of starlings are swooping around the façade of the Reims cathedral this evening. They dip and dive as one, controlled by some unseen puppeteer in the scarlet sky above. In the plaza several groups of hang-together tourists wheel about in a sluggish variation of the birds' aerial dance. The clicking of shutters accompanies the white exclamation of flashes. Automatic light meters adjust to the failing day.

The crowd grows denser on the square—no one wants to go into the sanctuary as long as the birds continue to career around the towers, dart between the statues, twist and turn about the spire. The spectacle makes the eye giddy. It's as if the mass of sculpted stone were suddenly lighter than air, ready to be drawn aloft by the skittering flock. The pale cathedral has at last awakened to the throngs of men and women staring at it with uplifted faces. That's when I spot her.

Joan. In armor and on horseback. She rides off to one side of the square. This used to be her town and her show. At the moment she's half-hidden behind a sanitation truck. Someone has managed to climb her tall pedestal to get a better view of the birds. Of the two great medieval presences in this city, the cathedral and Joan of Arc, one is faring much better tonight.

They used to work as a team, particularly when the Front was just a few short miles to the north of the city. Reims, with its cathedral and its armored virgin, became the poster child of the Great War. Although other towns suffered greatly, this prosperous city became the *ville martyre* known throughout the world. When Woodrow Wilson was taken on a tour of its devastated streets after the war, the proponents of clemency toward Germany cried foul. Reims had become too emotional an object. The Kaiser's artillerymen had pounded much of the city into rubble— surely Wilson's much-lauded equanimity would be shaken by the sight of the devastation. Besides, Reims's worst moment of the war, when 20,000 shells rained down from the skies, occurred on April 6, 1917, the same day that the U.S.A. went to war with Germany. It was unfair to upset the American president as he prepared to negotiate.

For the better part of four years, the German army had been dug into the heights near Berry-au-Bac and Brimont, training their cannon on the city. Like the tourists turning their cameras on the starlings, all they had to do was point and shoot. The cathedral was first hit in September 1914. Stupefaction greeted this bombardment. Until then, no one thought such vandalism possible. The Germans shrugged off international criticism by claiming that the church was being used as a lookout by French artillery spotters, which it probably was. When the building's roof caught fire after one well-aimed round of shelling and the magnificent medieval timbers came crashing down into the nave, talk turned to the barbarism of the German soul. This event, along with the burning of the university library of Louvain, Belgium, counted as the greatest aesthetic crime of the war. The fate of Reims and its cathedral would henceforth galvanize world attention as French propagandists used the city's predicament to full effect. Stories were told of schoolchildren taught in the champagne cellars of the city, of local priests and politicians holed up for months on end as the shells exploded overhead, of apparitions of Joan of Arc during nights made ghostly by the flares above the trenches.

It is difficult to imagine today the spell cast by the image of heroic Reims. People once avidly read news of the place. The educated of the world followed the sandbagging of the cathedral in 1915. The mayor's name, Langlet, and the cardinal's, Luçon, were known to every phi- lanthropist itchy to write a check. The town became a magnet for self- promoters. To be a prominent Parisian and not to have visited Reims was an unpardonable lapse, an insult to the notion of patriotic chic. Well- connected tourists flocked to the place—actresses, industrialists, and politicians made sure to have their pilgrimages to this Front-line fortress

followed in loving detail by the popular press. A totteringly old Sarah
Bernhardt showed up in September 1916 to pose with the statue of Joan
of Arc on the cathedral esplanade and to film a short scene in some now-
forgotten movie. An eyewitness recounts that the actress, dressed as a Red
Cross nurse, held a handsome actor-soldier in her arms and then uttered
the line, "Oh! An airplane!"—after which cast and crew dashed back
to the safety of Paris. Other performers came to declaim patriotic verse
in the cathedral doorway as proof of their courage and as filler for the
new medium of newsreel. The procession of self-serving pilgrims did not
escape the notice of satirists. One political cartoon published in 1915
showed the silhouettes of several well-fed grandees picking their way
through the rubble-strewn city. Looking on, an older man confides to the
youngster on his shoulders: "That's a cabinet minister, my boy. He's
come to inaugurate our ruins."

I TAKE A closer look at the statue of Joan the next morning. She looks
mannish, with a small head. She was moved from her place of honor in
front of the cathedral sometime after the Second World War. Originally
placed there by a national subscription in the 1890s, Joan was first
unveiled by President Félix Faure, the French statesman whose most
famous act was to die in the embrace of his mistress. At the time Faure
inaugurated the equestrian statue, much of French nationalist discourse
was tied up with the lost lands of Alsace and Lorraine. Champagne was
thus a border province of France. Joan, a mystic from the Lorraine town
of Domrémy, had shone in Reims; hence, placing her here would show
the dastardly Prussians that turn-of-the-century France meant business.
Joan would soon get around to taking back what was hers.

At the same time as the local and national notables used Joan for their
own ends, the French church went to bat for her at the Vatican. In the
nineteenth century, a rash of Virgin Mary sightings by young girls had
become a mainstay of European popular religion. With Joan, France
could have it both ways—a visionary and a virgin rolled into one. As her
five hundredth birthday approached in 1912, the pressure mounted to
have her made a saint. A first step was taken in 1909, when she was
beatified. It would not be until 1920, however, after the war and the
shelling of "her" cathedral at Reims had made its mark, that Joan would
be canonized. The gesture was a metaphysical sedative for a country still
in shock.

The psychic pain inflicted by the Great War on the French needed
soothing. Just as the grieving English reached for an Arthurian shrub at

Ypres and celestial bowmen from Agincourt at Mons, the French embraced the myth of Joan of Arc. The war had been too incomprehensibly cruel to fit any rational scheme for most people, and Joan met too many needs. She had repelled the invader, given up her young life, founded the very idea of France. What better representative of the four war years? A few things might not match—it was the English, not the Germans, who had burned her—but that did not matter. Her presence would disguise the squalor and despair of postwar France. Her image began appearing on postcards, on sentimental engravings; her voice was heard at the many séances held by bereaved families throughout the country. She kept in touch. The First World War made Joan a modern, and the Reims cathedral sacred once again. The team worked its magic. When the Nazi capitulation ending the Second World War in Europe was signed in Reims under Joan's watchful eyes, the duo's symbolic power peaked.

Nowadays Joan has faded into the background, as has the cathedral as a spiritual force. A more agnostic country than France is difficult to find. Those who venerate Joan tend to come from the same political family as those who celebrate Pétain's achievements in both world wars. Every May 1, thousands of right-wingers march through the streets of Paris to honor Joan of Arc and wax xenophobic about her role in history. The idea of expelling foreigners is irresistible to these proponents of old-style French nationalism. Not surprisingly, some of the same crowd end up at far-right rallies in Dixmude at midsummer. On November 11, they assemble at Verdun to honor Pétain—except in 1995, when they weirdly gathered in the southern French town of Carpentras. They rallied there to demand an apology for being wrongly accused of desecrating a Jewish cemetery in the town four years earlier. Posing as aggrieved victims of reverse discrimination, the French neofascists used the Great War commemoration as a cover. However insulting and absurd the entire exercise, no one was really surprised at their exploitation of November 11, just as no one balks at their appropriation of Joan. The Great War and Joan have become wed, for better or worse, to modern France's merchants of hate. No wonder the starlings are trying to get the cathedral away from the two of them.

3. Sillery to St. Hilaire

I'm at a french-fry truck outside the village of Sillery. Traffic whizzes by on the main road, kicking up the white dust on the shoulder. I've just come from the Fort de la Pompelle, a Great War ruin on a chalky hump of land southeast of Reims. Pompelle was bombed, shelled, strafed, attacked, overrun, smashed, stormed, and defended for four straight years. Now it's a war buff museum in white, the exploits of its former occupants celebrated in a depressing succession of nationalistic exhortations. I flee the place.

"Got any salt?"

"But of course!"

The french fries are sprinkled with the stuff and the steaming packet is eventually handed over. A few bees take a halfhearted interest in the proceedings.

"You sell any drinks?"

"What?"

A Fruehauf-flapping truck passes to deafen us.

"I said: Got anything to drink?"

"Just champagne and Coca-Cola."

"Champagne?!"

"Brut or demi-sec?"

This is definitely like no other french-fry truck I have ever seen. The man pours me some of the local vintage, and I sit at a plastic picnic table. If only the Front always came this close to the region's vineyards. A few miles to the south, the green, vine-covered slopes of the Montagne de Reims can be seen rising up on the horizon. Even from this distance, the villages look postcard pretty with their windmills and red roofs.

The Front, however, lies to the east, away from the vineyards and the charming villages and across the wide, treeless plain of Champagne where fields of cereal crops stretch for miles in the spring and early summer. At this time of August, everything has been taken in and the land looks like an enormous empty lot. I can hardly believe I'm going to walk across it. I feel as if I've joined the Donner Party, those California-bound settlers who took a wrong turn in the desert and ended up eating each other. Then I remember I'm alone, so I have nothing to worry about.

Instead, I walk and think, as the chalk pebbles stretch on forever over the tilled brown earth. The countryside is the acme of trench warfare landscape, the place where photographs were taken of white ditches snaking across a gently rolling, featureless plain. There was fierce fighting here in every year of war except for 1916. In 1915, Joffre ordered two calamitous offensives that budged the lines a few hundred yards and kept the grave diggers busy. The land is so wide open that the French army had bought large plots of it in 1857 to practice for campaigns of complex maneuver that would never happen. The stationary Front came to lie across these staging grounds for a war of movement, as if purposely ironical in its positioning. The villages that had prospered near these grounds—Moronvilliers, Perthes-lès-Hurlus, Le Mesnil-lès-Hurlus, Tahure, Ripont—were pulverized into nothingness during the war and never rebuilt afterward. The army obligingly extended its holdings, perhaps to disguise the damage, so that now the bases of Mourmelon, Suippes, and Moronvilliers sprawl over large sections of the Front. These are no-go zones, fenced off and accessible only to career soldiers stuck here in this French Canaan. I will have to zigzag through this swath of no-man's-land, since the army now owns so much of it. It must be a point of honor for them.

THE SIZE OF the emptiness here is impressive. No other spot on the Western Front contains such a broad cinematic sweep, which is why many war films were once made in this countryside. Most of these are quite rightly forgotten, like the war itself, but the genre remains an interesting footnote to movie history. The most accomplished, with the exception of Jean Renoir's *La Grande Illusion*, were filmed in the dozen or so years following the war, either in Hollywood or on the unearthly terrain of the Front in Champagne. To view them today is to step out of time.

Aside from the obscure propaganda films that flourished in the war years, there were perhaps only two movies shot during the conflict that were worthy of the wide attention they received. Charlie Chaplin's *Shoulder Arms* is a bravely satirical piece filmed in 1918, in which the calvary of trench life is successfully sent up by the genial comedian. The film's most famous scene had Chaplin and his unfortunate fellow soldiers trying to sleep underwater in a flooded dugout. In an entirely different register was Abel Gance's *J'Accuse*, an effort supported by the French army's film office despite the implicit pacifist message of its closing sequences. It premiered just days after the Armistice and, as cultural historian Jay Winter points out in *Sites of Memory, Sites of Mourning*, many of the soldiers who had been given leave in 1917 to play the resurrected dead in the film's final scene were doubtless *actually* dead by the time the movie was released. Their scene, a nightmare moment in which an enormous field of graves suddenly becomes thronged with the animated cadavers of its occupants, meshed well with the apocalyptic imaginings common in postwar thought. *J'Accuse* also chilled audiences for whom the dead were still a recent, palpable presence in the homes

they had left. It is a memorable sequence. Historian Winter quotes
Gance, never the shrinking violet, saying of his film:

> Since the great Red Tragedy has not had its Homer and its Rouget de Lisle
> [composer of "La Marseillaise"], since the tears, the blood, the widespread
> suffering, the gestures of the heroes and the starry eyes of the dead have not
> yet found their sculptors and their painters, we have tried humbly to create
> a lyricism of the eye and to make the images sing.

"We" might well include Blaise Cendrars, the co-writer of the film and
one of its on-screen contingent of the living dead. It is hard to get
Cendrars out of my mind today, since the empty fields I traverse near
Prosnes and Moronvilliers is near the area in which he lost his arm.

The apocalypse had been such a close call that many conventional
European filmmakers preferred not to touch on the topic of the war once
it was over. Even during the years of stalemate at the Front there had been
a reaction to the war's invasiveness of all thought and speech. Hollywood,
however, refused to observe any moratorium on the subject, sensing it to
be a boundless source of tear-jerking drama. In 1921, director Rex
Ingram's *The Four Horsemen of the Apocalypse* tried with some success to
romanticize the war for the first time since 1914. The attempt was
overshadowed by the appearance of a new star, Rudolph Valentino, as a
Franco-Argentinian playboy who finds moral salvation in the sacrifice of
the trenches. People flocked to the film to see Valentino dance the tango,
not hold a rifle. It was not until four years later and King Vidor's *Grand
Parade*, one of the most influential silent films made, that the Great War
became a staple of the box office. The story, that of yet another playboy
who finds meaning in the noble squalor of the Front, matters less than the
film's many imitators. They set the stage for the great talkie war movies of
the early 1930s.

The year 1930 saw the release of two remarkable anti-war films, G. W.
Pabst's *Westfront 1918*, an adaptation of Ernst Johanssen's pacifist novel
Vier von der Infanterie (*Four in the Infantry*), and Lewis Milestone's *All
Quiet on the Western Front*, a faithful screen version of Erich Maria
Remarque's best-selling work. Two years later the French director Ray-
mond Bernard made the French equivalent of these German and Ameri-
can efforts: *Les Croix de Bois* (*The Wooden Crosses*), an adaptation of
Roland Dorgelès's novel. The three films, although stylistically different,
tell the same story. A closely knit group of friends faces the horror of the
Front and becomes increasingly callous as their number gets reduced by
the constant toll of death in combat. The pacifist message of these films

was supposed to have been self-evident, yet many audiences leapt to their
feet and cheered on "their" side in the well-orchestrated battle sequences.
In the French film, the terrifying charges across a Champenois no-man's-
land had Paris crowds applauding wildly. In writing of such anti-war war
movies, the writer Marcel Aymé remarked:

> To do something truly pacifistic we should offer the spectacle of life, rather
> than death, in the trenches. The genuine film of pacifist propaganda would
> show men stupefied with boredom and fatigue duty, masturbating in the
> dug-outs, killing their lice, scraping the mud off their uniforms and looking
> over the top at some desolate plain where nothing happens. The success
> would be perfect if the audience went to sleep in their seats. But nobody
> would have the courage to go and see such a film.

These movies, then, were diversely appreciated. In America, *All Quiet*
won the Oscar for best film; in Germany, the same film was banned for
years. Pabst's overtly pacifist movie was disliked at home but widely
applauded in other convalescing European countries. *Les Croix de Bois*
regularly provoked jostling in front of movie theaters between white-hot
nationalists and long-suffering pacifists. Its title, a reference to the
makeshift wooden crosses of battlefield cemeteries, was known to everyone because of a sardonic marching song intoned by the disgruntled
French army of 1917 and 1918. The gallows humor of doomed soldiers
had become a national ditty:

Oui, tu l'auras ta croix, ta croix,
Si c'est pas la croix de guerre,
C'est qu'ça s'ra la croix d'bois!

(Yes, you will win your cross, your cross,
But if it's not the Military Cross
Then it'll be the wooden cross!)

The gentle slope down from the army's "Keep Out" signs at the
Moronvilliers camp stretches on endlessly. The white farm track on
which I walk is embedded with rusty strands of barbed wire. My boot
strikes something hard. It is the nose of a crusty old shell, unexploded and
no doubt unstable. I'll leave it for the farmer—he, like all his fellows
along the Front, must have a steel shield between himself and his plow. If
I am to reach Alsace and the end of the Front, I will need both feet.

At a place called Aubérive I wolf down two pâté and pickle sandwiches
at the village's sole café. The bread tastes as if it dates from the Great War,

but I don't care. I've had nothing to eat since my fries and champagne breakfast, having been unpleasantly surprised in several places today by the absence of any businesses. The car has killed the Champagne village as effectively as any cannon. People zoom to hypermarkets in the suburbs of the city, then return to their village homes for a blue evening of TV behind well-fastened shutters. The French call it the "desertification of the country." Here in this flat drivers' paradise, the process seems unstoppable. Not since leaving Belgium have I seen sadder villages.

I make a long detour south of Aubérive to visit a Russian cemetery. There are men from both world wars buried here. An ornate onion-domed chapel stands in the midst of the graves, although some of the tombs read "Soviet." I suspect that these are not the soldiers who took part in a Soviet-style mutiny in Champagne during the closing stages of the Great War. Some Russian émigrés who had been fighting alongside the French in their own battalions revolted against their officers and began espousing the newly triumphant Bolshevik truths after Lenin and his fellows had taken power in the homeland. The French command, terrified of a new wave of disobedience in its army, diverted a division to surround the would-be revolutionaries' units and eliminate them. Comrades-in-arms could not also be comrades.

THERE IS AN impeccably dressed young lady swirling around and around in the white dust of midday. Her partner is a youthful soldier, clad in formal red, lips pursed from the effort of leading the dance.

I lose the thought . . .

The stars are bright in the night sky. A moon just off the horizon illuminates the white chalk of the soil. Nightfall has caught me in a field to the east of Aubérive and St. Hilaire, following the trace of the Front as it uncoils to the east. My map says that I also have been following the line of an old Roman road, but somehow I doubt it. This arrow-straight dirt track looks as if it was made by John Deere, not Julius Caesar. Still, on a night like this I could easily convince myself that the distant tramp of the legions can be faintly heard.

A shooting star crosses the vault of the heavens. I'm lying on my back, looking up at the tendrils of the Milky Way. Tired legs and the warm night air conspire to make further walking in the darkness seem pointless. My backpack is my pillow, the constellations my canvas.

Fade to white. The scene is a British army camp in northern India at the turn of the century. The men and officers are in drill formation on a parade ground in the blazing heat of the day. They are rehearsing for an official occasion. The regimental band goes through its repertoire. The day grows hotter. A bead of sweat trickles beneath a stiff collar . . .

This memory is my grandfather's. As a youngster, Daniel O'Shea enlisted with the Duke of Wellington regiment of the British army and was sent to what was called the Northwest Frontier. It was the heyday of the Raj, Britain's colonial empire on the subcontinent. Just a few short years after that hot afternoon in India, the same regiment took him to the Western Front, where he would lose an eye and receive a shrapnel wound in the leg.

My father, as a young man in the big city, used to go visit Daniel whenever the pain of his war wound landed him up at the Leopardstown veterans' hospital in Dublin. The ex-soldier talked of everything and anything except the cause of his distress. When *All Quiet on the Western Front* came to Ireland and caused a sensation in the deeply Catholic countryside, he refused to see the film. He wanted nothing to do with it. Perhaps he, like Marcel Aymé, thought that anti-war films encouraged war, or that talking about the war romanticized it. He probably would have disapproved of this book. Whatever the reason, a veil was drawn over that part of his past.

Not that he was ashamed to have been in the army. When, in the early 1920s, the thugs of a Black and Tan death squad descended on a neighbor's house to haul away a man suspected of IRA sympathies, Daniel raced next door and pulled rank on their British army commander. He saved the man by using his sergeant-major bluster. He could become the old soldier whenever circumstances called for it. Another family tale concerns two itinerant Indian cloth salesmen entering my grandfather's tailor shop in Tralee in the 1930s. They stayed for a week. To everyone's astonishment, including theirs, this small-town, one-eyed Irish tailor spoke their language fluently. They traded tales and shared drinks like old friends.

But these are all memories about him. They are not his, just as this Front I walk is not actually the Front, but a landscape that remembers the Front. Daniel's memories are all gone now, except for one that has seeped through the cracks of time down to me, ninety years later. Fortunately, this is a cinematic countryside and the lights have dimmed:

The regimental band strikes up a waltz. Its first notes drift over the treetops that sway beyond the compound fence. The tune is familiar, Franz Lehár's "Merry Widow Waltz."

A woman absently comes out onto the porch of the colonel's bungalow. It is his young wife, just arrived in India from England. She toys with her parasol, then sets it down against the rail. The bandmaster glances over at her.

She emerges into the sunshine, her long pale dress just clearing the fine white dust of the yard. Her clear eyes survey the ranks, her head sways in time to the music. She makes her choice.

"Would you like to dance?"

The young Irishman stammers a reply. He steps forward, takes her in his arms, and they're off. They swirl through the whiteness, followed everywhere by the music. Around the red and gold of the band, beyond the ranks of massed men, in front of the barracks, behind the bungalow, alongside the compound wall, back though the stark light of the parade ground. His youthful legs are strong and his eyes are dark. Her eyes are closed, her dress twirls in the dust. There is no one in the yard except them. They dance together as if that's all they've ever done.

The music stops. They are in front of the bungalow. The colonel looks on with a bemused smile.

"Thank you for the dance, sir."

"Thank you, madam."

The young man crosses the silent yard and regains his place in the rank. Glances are stolen, the moment is held. All is quiet . . .

All is quiet indeed. It's supposed to be, in this part of the world. I close my eyes to the stars over the Front. They were his stars, too.

Good night, Grandfather. I hope you don't mind me borrowing the memory. What else do men think about when they're stuck out in a field?

Sleep comes quickly.

4. Suippes to Ste. Menehould

Army towns seem to fit a pattern no matter where they're placed. Once you're in one, it's easy to hitch a ride, buy a beer, or start a fight. I've arrived in the town of Suippes dusty and hungry after a night outdoors and a morning's detour to the Navarin Farm monument out at the Front. There I saw more names upon names, testament to the offensives of 1915.

North of Navarin was the *Tranchée des Tantes* (Aunts' Trench), a German defensive position that the French infantry took on September 25, 1915, as part of a massive attack along the Front between Aubérive and the Argonne. The generals, inured to failure in Champagne, refused to believe reports stating that the Aunts' Trench had been taken by their men. They resisted pleas to resight the artillery accordingly and stop shelling the trench. No fewer than ten French reconnaissance planes flew from Suippes over the position and reported that yes, indeed, the Aunts' Trench was held by French units. For three days headquarters refused to believe them, having no faith in the newfangled technology of aviation. By the time a survivor had managed to crawl back and convince the doubting staff officers, it was too late. Yet another chapter in the annals of Great War generalship had been written.

"CRAZY FUCKIN' BASTARDS, whadda they want now?" My note-taking about Navarin in a Suippes lunch room has been interrupted by what sounds like a Yankees fan.

"Crazy fuckin' bastards!"

I look up, fearful that I'm about to be involved in some NATO head-butting tournament. I expect to see some demented G.I. on hangover leave from his home base in Germany.

Instead, the speaker is the café's owner, an elderly gent with whom I had spoken French on my way to this table. He is immensely pleased with his deception.

"Bastards, whadda they want now?"

The inflection is perfect, even if the meaning of it all has become cryptic. He pulls up a chair and explains in his native French that he says his crazy bastards line to any American he encounters. He introduces himself as Roger.

He's up and out of the chair again, dashing past the cash register to pour a few beers for the crewcuts at the bar. He returns with a badge.

Roger turns out to be the honorary police chief of Lackawanna, New York. Do I know it? Of course, I must. He owes this position to a Second World War acquaintance with whom he has long corresponded. He does not take the distinction lightly—I am asked to examine the badge several times, which I do. It is not certain that the people of Lackawanna need a police chief whose knowledge of the English language stops at one flawless phrase. But Roger intends to find out. Once he gets tired of Suippes, he's going to retire to Lackawanna. I don't ask when this is going to occur: Roger is in his late seventies.

MY LAST DAY in Champagne continues at random. I decide to travel around the outside perimeter of the forbidden Suippes miltary base. Roger arranges a ride for me to the village of Sommepy-Tahure. Today I'll give up the animal acquaintance with the land that walking confers for some speed.

My ride, a wiry middle-aged fellow, cheerfully informs me that there is a killer on the loose in the area of Mourmelon and Suippes. Several young conscripts have been found molested and murdered by the side of deserted country roads like the one we're traveling. He says that these murders are not only a criminal offense, but also, technically, a destruction of army property. If you pick up a soldier hitching and get into an accident, you're held liable by the army. The same must be true of murder.

He asks me, creepily, what I think.

I say that I'm going to visit my uncle. He doesn't believe me, but neither of us cares.

MY GREAT-UNCLE Tommy is a no-show today, as are all my other ghosts from the Great War. Walking cross-country to the distant village of Cernay-en-Dormois, I realize that it is time to get out of this landscape of fenced-off military bases. Even though the scenery has improved— wooded hillocks and fields of dairy cows have taken over from yesterday's vacuum—I prefer my armies and my murderers to be stashed safely in the past.

Within minutes of arriving in Cernay, I am on the back of a motorcycle screaming southward. I asked some lawn chair loungers for the quickest way to get to Ville-sur-Tourbe, a Front-line town, so that I could spend the night there. You can't stay there, they protested, you must go to Saint Minoo.

Saint Minoo? Before I can unfold my map a youth named Thierry has already wheeled his bike out of a garage.

Now he is talking to me from the front of his motorcycle as we tear through the country air.

"*Yah ka oo eh ohn ohoh vachement eee. Oo eh eh ohrss eh oo moto?*"

"*Oui,*" I reply.

SAINT MINOO, LIKE the entire day, turns out to be full of surprises. Ste. Menehould, as it is spelled but not pronounced, lay far enough behind the Front to have preserved some of its older neighborhoods. It sits in a defile carved by the River Aisne through the forested hills that mark the transition between Champagne and the Argonne. A statue of its most beloved son, Dom Perignon, the clever monk who first put the bubbles in champagne, stands at the western entrance of the town. The sculptor has put a sly, cackling smile on his face, as if the old vintner were half-Voltaire, half-Mephistopheles. Perhaps he just knows the town's odd secret.

It takes me a while, too. I first assume that the highlight of tourism in Ste. Menehould is its local government building, erected in 1730 and fairly frequently remodeled ever since. Then I think civic pride must be linked to the elegant, eighteenth-century square dominating the eastern end of the town. Wrong again. In the main market street leading from the square, I come across a series of establishments exclusively devoted to the study, sale, consumption, and veneration of pigs' feet. The lowly trotter, not Dom Perignon or civic architecture, is Ste. Menehould's claim to fame.

The Soleil d'Or seems to be the trotter temple. Garish flashing lights adorn the restaurant's exterior, attracting the eye to the large trophy window that gives out onto the street. Yet the trophies here are not just for the biggest pig foot feast of the year; some commemorate the owner's exploits with pedal-operated sailboats. The largest cup marks his prowess in being the first to cross the English Channel in one such contraption. Two small station wagons parked in front of the restaurant are painted with the French word *Pédalovoile* (pedal-sailing), proof that the man's obsession is full blown. I cannot resist going in. A long-distance hiker walks into the establishment of a pedal maniac to dine on a plate of feet—perhaps I have joined the Donner Party after all.

The interior is an antiquarian's dream. Tables, chairs, and cooking utensils from the eighteenth century and earlier occupy a low-ceilinged back room. It is here where the trotters are served breaded, roasted, baked, stuffed, stewed, or any of a number of ingenious ways listed on the menu to disguise the revolting combination of gristle, fat, grease, blood, and bone that constitute the delicacy. The only other diners in the room are the two fattest people I have seen since moving to Europe. How fat are they? It is a wonder their arms can reach the table. They are so big that the hefty pile of trotters in front of them look like the legs from an underfed quail. When my sole breaded pig's foot is placed before me, it looks monstrously large, like a football without the laces. I poke at it gingerly with my fork, then notice the two wet-chinned mountains at the next table smiling at my squeamishness. I promise myself never to come back to Saint Minoo.

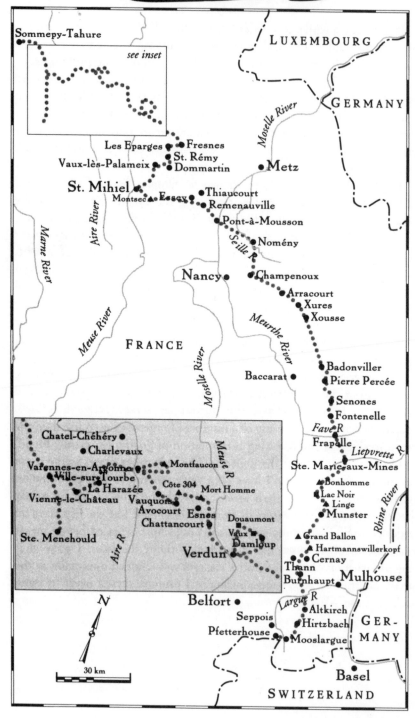

ALSACE-LORRAINE

LUXEMBOURG

GERMANY

Moselle River

Sommepy-Tahure

see inset

Les Eparges • Fresnes
St. Rémy
Vaux-lès-Palameix • Dommartin

St. Mihiel
Montsec ▲ Essey • Thiaucourt
Remenauville
Pont-à-Mousson

Metz

Aire River
Marne River
Meuse River

Nomény

Nancy • Champenoux
Arracourt
Xures
Xousse

FRANCE

Seille R.
Meurthe River

Moselle River

Baccarat

Badonviller
Pierre Percée

Senones
Fontenelle
Fave R.
Frapelle
Liepvrette R.
Ste. Marie-aux-Mines

Chatel-Chéhéry •
Charlevaux

Varennes-en-Argonne
Ville-sur-Tourbe
La Harazée
Vienne-le-Château
Ste. Menehould

▲ Montfaucon
Côte 304 ▲ Mort Homme
Vauquois
Avocourt Esnes
Chattancourt
Douaumont
Vaux
Damloup

Verdun

Meuse R.

Aire R.

N

Rhine River

Bonhomme
Lac Noir
Linge
Munster

▲ Grand Ballon
▲ Hartmannswillerkopf
Cernay
Thann
Burnhaupt
Mulhouse

Belfort
Largue R.
Seppois
Pfetterhouse
Altkirch
Hirtzbach
Mooslargue

GER-
MANY

Basel

SWITZERLAND

30 km

••••• author's route

CHAPTER
6

Lorraine/Alsace

1. The Argonne

BUSHWHACK: TO MAKE one's way through thick woods by cutting away bushes and branches.

Today is the first day of the rest of my walk. The Argonne, a forest that is a lozenge-shaped patch of dense greenery between Champagne and Lorraine, must be crossed before reaching Verdun. It was once well known in both French and American folklore as a place where tremendous sacrifices had been made. To say "Argonne" to an American of the 1930s was like saying "Normandy" to his counterpart in the 1950s. The word meant France, the war, the battlefield, abroad. For the French, of course, the Argonne was simply another bloody episode in a sanguinary pageant.

Ignoring the dark clouds scudding in from the east, I head along a track out of Ville-sur-Tourbe toward Hardemont Wood. My passage causes a lot of bovine discussion among the reclining occupants of the fields, but no animal bothers to stroll over and include me in the debate. The wind begins to whip up and a few droplets come singing down, although not so many as to cause alarm. To my right another village lies nestled in the embrace of a broad and gentle ridge. A large black mass moves in, draining the red rooftops and steeple of their color in the darkening shadow. To my left, about four hundred yards distant, a tall spinney of poplars sways in a snapping breeze that drives yet another black cloud forward over the land. Above this windbreak three hawks hover motionless, enjoying a small Wagnerian moment. Miraculously my stretch of moist cowpath is spared the rain clouds. I reach the forest edge, pause, then enter.

In moments, my boots are covered in mud, and my progress is like that of an astronaut on a damp planet, one foot squelching in front of the other. My path goes through two dark canyons of trees before bordering on a stagnant watercourse. It is there that the insect attacks begin— mosquitoes, bees, and two very large and stupid flies that keep buzzing directly at my right eyeball. After swatting ineffectually for a time, I begin spitting at them, presenting the edifying spectacle of a bowed and muddied backpacker seething with obscenities and spittle. I step over what looks to be a dead dog and arrive, at last, at a clearing. Only it isn't—every square inch of cleared land is taken up by sunflowers. Beautiful. Even the path is gone. I feel as if I'm intruding on a crowd of rush-hour commuters.

Unwilling to turn back, I scrape my way along the edge of the field. As it is a dull overcast day, the flowers have nothing to look at but me. A strange sort of self-consciousness sets in as I walk past these vegetal voyeurs, but it is quickly banished when the drone of my accompanying insects reaches symphonic proportions. I begin yelling in rage, only to wake a pondful of ducks at some unseen haven one or two hundred yards to my left. They set up a raucous, laughing chorus of derision at my yelps and shouts. Chastened but still muttering, I continue picking my way around the wall of sunflowers. I was never a Boy Scout.

A large open field appears on my right, newly plowed and free of insect-harboring weeds. I run toward it, almost tumbling headfirst into a hitherto unnoticed drainage ditch separating field from forest. I clamber down and up the ditch, treading with a squirt on the tonguelike orange slugs that trail their slime over the moist leaves. I won't be eating escargots for many years. At last I am in the field, a muddy but open space that rises slightly toward the east. All is now peace and tranquillity as a village appears on a rise a mile away. Calculating that I should head toward the woods opposite the village, I set a lively pace to make up for lost time. A dip in the field reveals a red Massey-Ferguson tractor sitting idly in a hollow a stone's throw away. The muddy furrows give way to burnt hay stubble covered with millions of ladybugs.

I walk on, content to be out in the open, until I happen to glance once more over to the left to take in the bucolic village scene. It is no longer visible. A thick black curtain of rain is advancing rapidly toward me. I look over at the distant woods, their shades of dull green now a dark mass of indistinguishable shapes. The rain begins sweeping horizontally across the field, making any further advance an exercise in melodrama. Just the two of us out here, me and the tractor. The tractor! I squint to see if it's worth the trouble. Yes, it has a cab. I begin running over the ladybugs and damp cinders to shelter. Soaking, I climb into the cab and listen to the wind rock the machine in its muddy moorings.

The worst of the squall passes and I step down into the morass left by the rain. I move toward the woods in the insistent drizzle, knowing that ahead of me, at least, there will be a fairly dry forest floor. The last fifty yards I cover like a swamp creature, sodden and mud-caked and foul-tempered. I slide into the forest, only to find that the track I've taken abruptly ends in a thicket of brush and thorns. Outside the rain and mud, inside the brush and—trenches! They are here, camouflaged under a cover of wet leaves but unmistakably Great War pits, sinuously twisting beneath the obstacles on the forest floor. I climb down into one that's going my way—east—and begin to walk in what might pass for a war buff's dream. Thus far, I had only scratched the surface of the Western Front. Now I am in it.

I pick my way carefully down the trench, conscious that the leafy carpet below and the canopy of undergrowth above might conceal twisted metal, live ammunition, or worse. The twists and turns go on for a few hundred yards before I reach an impasse formed, unexpectedly, of treetops. The trench has unhelpfully led to the top of a cliff, out of which tall oaks are growing. Seeing the impassable steepness of the slope, I clamber out of the snaking main trench and look around for another route. I see a straight communication trench leading south and decide to give it a try. Within minutes, I come face-to-face with a young deer, staring with indignant fright at my twig-snapping approach. It bounds out of the trench and leaves me alone again. A quarter of an hour later, I am in a shaved wheatfield, in sight of a lovely sylvan village. The trenches have gotten me out of trouble.

Mud-covered and flushed, I enter the lone café of Vienne-le-Château. Conversation pauses for a moment, then resumes. I order a hot chocolate and listen to the regulars complaining about this spell of March weather in August. The bartender insists I have some hot food. I munch a few proffered fried potatoes and gaze hopefully at a map that is supposed to show me the way through the heart of the Argonne.

THE WHOLE PROBLEM with this forest is its denseness. In 1914 and 1915 both the French and the Germans found it impossible to take in its entirety. Indeed, in eight months of deadly skirmishes in this tiny Front-line part of the Argonne—an area only seven miles wide by two miles deep—150,000 men were killed. In 1918 the Americans advanced through it, at a similar human cost. The latter Argonne operation was more chaotic and haphazard than any offensive of the entire war—thousands fell as massive traffic jams on narrow roads slowed the delivery of needed ammunition and supplies to the troops doing battle. Not that they had set out with a paucity of means. The American army began here its budget-busting twentieth-century tradition of overkill in firepower and funding. The initial bombardment of September 26, 1918, on the German positions expended more explosives in three hours than had been used in all of the American Civil War. One historian, John Toland, calculated the cost of this murderous sound and light show to be $1 million a minute.

The Meuse-Argonne offensive, as it is known in military histories, gave rise to two now obscure American legends of the Great War. One of the stories concerns the so-called Lost Battalion, a group of 550 men who were surrounded at Charlevaux, a wooded vale located about six miles north of where I am currently eating my midday potatoes. Commanded by Charles Whittlesey, a storklike Wall Street lawyer known for his imperturbable demeanor, the encircled battalion held out for three days and nights of repeated, merciless attacks from all sides. In fact, mercy was shown on one occasion: a German squad, led by an officer who had learned English selling tungsten for six years in Seattle, pleaded with Whittlesey's men to surrender. They refused. A subsequent attempt by the main American force to take the pressure off the embattled soldiers backfired badly when the artillery started shelling the precise spot where the Lost Battalion was holding its ground. Dozens of men died in the first moments of this "friendly fire," and it looked as if most of the unit was going to be annihilated. A courier pigeon named Cher Ami—which was later stuffed and given to the Smithsonian—eventually got through to the gunners with a message to point their cannons somewhere else. When the Lost Battalion was finally rescued on October 7, 1918, only 194 men were healthy enough to walk away from the most famous death trap of the American war effort. Whittlesey had survived, but not for long. In November 1921, he boarded an ocean liner bound for Havana, had a drink at the bar, then went out on deck and threw himself overboard.

The other war story shows the hero in a better light. It occurred the day after the Lost Battalion was found and relieved, in the nearby village of Chatel-Chéhéry. There, Alvin York of Tennessee, a hard-drinking hell-raiser turned born-again teetotaler, would perform a barely credible stunt that would eventually make him the most decorated American soldier of the Great War. During an American attack that was clearly a fiasco in the making, York crept away from his decimated platoon and surreptitiously made his way to a hiding place near the enemy lines. A backwoods marksman, York began picking off German machine-gunners without giving away his position. One gunner would fall, another would take his place, York would fire again, that gunner would fall, another would take his place, York would fire again, and so on. Soon the yokel's unerring aim had spooked scores of Germans into surrendering to what they thought was a far superior force. Incredibly, Alvin York had single-handedly killed 28 German soldiers and captured 132 others.

Ferdinand Foch, the Allied commander-in-chief in 1918, although no fan of the awkward Goliath that was the American army, called the Tennessean's act "the greatest single feat of arms accomplished in this war." York is reported to have remarked, "It weren't no trouble nohow for me to hit them big army targets. They were so much bigger than turkeys' heads." The story of this Hun-killing hick had so charmed Americans that when the time came to convince the country to go to war again, the Alvin York saga exploit was dusted off and given an anti-isolationist edge. Gary Cooper played the title role in the 1941 film, *Sergeant York.* Its bellicist tone matched the mood of the time. The Howard Hawks film won the Academy Award for best actor, an ironic turnaround from ten years earlier when *All Quiet on the Western Front* had won the top honor.

In the autumn of 1918, however, the WASP Whittlesey and the cracker York came to symbolize the American offensive in the Argonne. Recriminations would come later, once hindsight practitioners took a close look at John Joseph Pershing, the man who brought the Americans to slaughter. Crushed by the death of his wife and three daughters in a fire in 1915, Pershing was reputed to be a dour taskmaster, mistrustful of his European counterparts and mule-headed in repeating their mistakes. Commended for keeping the American troops away from the profligate French and British commanders clamoring for more men, Pershing nonetheless threw many American lives away by organizing overambitious offensives with untrained troops and sending men walking into machine-gun fire. Whatever the verdict of history, the millions of doughboys clinched the victory on the Western Front, a bald fact that French and British histories continue to begrudge their junior partner. Even when totting up casualties, these European history books always underline that more American soldiers died of influenza than in battle. I've even done it just now, and I have no ax to grind.

Feeling sufficiently dry and warm to brave the rest of the Argonne, I take
the road out of Vienne-le-Château to La Harazée. Two young women on
my way out of town look at me as if I were the Antichrist. I really should
buy a hairbrush.

Soon I am once again alone, on a snail-smothered pathway that fords a
tiny stream, skirts a trout pond, and crosses a couple of marshy meadows.
At La Harazée a couple of moss-covered manor farmhouses stand in a
clearing with a chapel and a large French military cemetery. I consult my
map and take the track leading from the cemetery into the woods. The
darkness closes around me.

The muddy path is, in fact, the parapet of an old Great War trench.
The earthwork of the ditch's lip has been shored up over the years, so that
any walker through this stretch of the woods is, in fact, "over the top."
The parapet path eventually becomes a logging road, until that in turn
narrows into waterlogged tire tracks. Finally I head into the thicket beside
the road, where the ground seems marginally drier. Two hours of bush-
whacking ensues as I struggle cross-country. Fortunately the sun has
come out overhead, giving the foliage a friendly speckled look that helps
allay my natural tendency to panic. I have read too many war books about
men getting sucked into the mud, or being blown up by old shells. I don't
like being lost in the Argonne.

I eventually emerge into a clearing. Scarcely thirty yards away from me
is a small stela in honor of the 150 R.I. (*Régiment d'Infanterie*) and a
French tricolor fluttering on a flagstaff, proof that my wandering has kept
me near the Front. The rest of the huge clearing, which is perhaps half a
mile wide and about two long, contains nothing. The trees have been cut
and hauled away. The brush has been burned in smudge fires—a few
large piles of sticks smolder in the distance. This is the heart of the Bois de
la Gruerie, the scene of horrendous French losses in 1915. My map shows
the emplacement of the monument, but also hiking trails and logging
roads that are nowhere to be seen. I venture into the vast openness,
peering at the forest edge for the sign of a break, or a path. Two deer lazily
walk out of the woods and pay me no heed. I steady my compass, look at
the map, then at the deer, then back at the compass—and decide to go to
the right. Ahead of me now is a stand of pines, looking dark and
impenetrable even in the hot afternoon sunshine. Once past the first
screen of undergrowth, I am relieved by what I see on the forest floor. The
trenches once again, heading east. If there is no path or road, then I shall
follow the scars of the Front. They once led all the way to Switzerland; for
my purposes, I just want them to get me out of the woods.

Back and forth, zigzagging across the land, the trenches lead on like a terrier straining at the leash. I stay above the ditches this time, for water has collected in their hollows and the poilus' duckboards have rotted into the earth generations ago. There is no panic now, just an odd sense of a journey shared. Whatever else the trenches represented—the futility of war, the failure of a civilization, the birth of the modern—for me they have become a companion, often glimpsed on this long hike from the shores of the North Sea. This realization embarrasses as much as enlightens, because the trenches should be more a mark of shame than a sign of fellowship. The silent ghosts I carry with me should suffice for company.

The afternoon wears on in idle daydream until finally a landmark is reached. At a place where the trenches cross a dirt road an elderly man in a white golf shirt and shorts appears from behind a bush, like Death on holiday. When I hail him to ask for directions, he skulks away behind a blind of greenery and soon I hear some muttering in a language I cannot identify. Expecting to come across some tabloid horror, I advance cautiously around the bush and catch one last glimpse of him vanishing into a bunker with what looks like his twin brother. My appearance must have frightened them. I look at my map and realize that I have reached another *Abri du Kronprinz* (Crown Prince's Dugout), the name given on my map to a fortified complex near the edge of the forest. Having no wish to play hide-and-seek with the timorous old fellows, I backtrack onto the dirt road and walk the last few hundred yards out onto a highway. A sign greets me—"Mushroom Collecting Strictly Regulated"—showing that rule-crazy, Jacobin French civilization cannot be far away.

The road describes a gentle arc and soon I am out of the woods and into the copper light of early evening. A wheatfield lies in the foreground, the pimples of Vauquois and Montfaucon stand on the horizon. In the middle distance is the town of Varennes-en-Argonne, my destination for the evening. I quicken my pace, passing the large monument south of town that commemorates the doughboys of Pennsylvania who fought near here. A glimpse at my notebook tells me that George Patton and Harry Truman also saw action around this lovely little town on the River Aire. Varennes's biggest claim to fame, however, lies not in the Great War but in the French Revolution. A plaque on its eighteenth-century clock tower tells the story, for it was at this building, on June 22, 1791, that Louis XVI, Marie Antoinette, and their children were arrested as they tried to flee France. The king had been on his way to rally monarchical Europe to crush the fledgling revolution. When news of this treachery got back to Paris, support for the deposed Bourbons evaporated. It was a courageous republican innkeeper in Ste. Menehould who had recognized the family and outdistanced the king's carriage through the Argonne to organize the fateful arrest in Varennes. This small act in a far-flung provincial village, the tourist brochure in my hotel room tells me, changed the course of History.

I sink down at the writing table and look out the window. Young boys are fishing with long poles outstretched over the Aire, a needlelike steeple rises from a mansarded church, the apéritif hour has commingled *boule* players and pastis drinkers on the village square. This is France as it should be, a postcard of present-day peace and turmoil past. I have stumbled across a Frenchman's dream for his own country, the one exploited by salesmen and politicians, the picture of a *douce France* made up of simple village life on a gentle summer night. The nightmare, Verdun, lies a dozen miles to the east.

2. *Montfaucon*

> Basket case: an armless and legless casualty
> Cat stabber: a bayonet
> Cognac-eyed: drunk
> Dishy billy: *déshabillé* (undressed)
> Frog's paradise: Paris
> Jenny's pa: *je ne sais pas* (I don't know)
> Pants rabbits: lice
> Sandbag Mary Ann: *ça ne fait rien* (it doesn't matter)
> Soldier's supper: anything nonexistent
> Suicide ditch: front-line trench
> Toot and scramble: *tout ensemble* (all together)
> Zeppelins in a cloud: sausage in mashed potatoes

The inventiveness of the doughboys' slang can still tickle the cornball in me. Their fractured French lived on in grade-school humor, especially in English-Canadian classrooms where the study of French became the temporary anchor for a drifting sense of national identity. When we apprentice wags at recess exchanged "mercy bucket," "silver plate," and the like, we did so in ignorance of the long pedigree of putting the French language through the wringer, a tradition that the Great War amplified and brought momentarily to Middle America. Similarly, when we used such words as "scrounge," "wangle," "lousy," and "chat" (to chat meant to delouse), we would never have guessed their origin in a distant war. At age eleven, I was told by a doctor that I had contracted "trench mouth." My mother, mortified, ordered me to tell no one of my affliction. The link between the blisters in the lining of my cheeks and the infantryman of the Great War would have hardly occurred to me.

TODAY I'VE TAKEN it easy and made a small detour northward from Varennes to pay a visit to the American hill of the Argonne. Here at Montfaucon a pseudoclassical American memorial overlooks the battle-field of the 1918 offensive and, in the distance to the southeast, that of the 1916 Franco-German slaughter at Verdun. The memorial column, a 180-foot-tall Goliath of stern republican virtue, shows by its very size that the war loomed large on the American horizon. The Doric column, made of Italian granite, is the largest U.S. war memorial in Europe.

As I sit on the lawn munching a sandwich and staring up at the memorial, it occurs to me that Montfaucon may also stand as a testament to a change in mentality. Two and a half million Americans came to France in 1917 and 1918, and some of them liked what they saw—at least those who ventured away from the Front. "How ya gonna keep 'em down on the farm," went the song, "after they've seen Paree?" In some ways the Great War was the Grand Tour gone haywire, the harbinger of American Express and backpackers like myself. In 1918, while those on the home front in America were girding their souls for Prohibition and the struggle against sin, the people in the lands near the Western Front were getting ready to celebrate the passing of the plague of war. Without the Great War, it is doubtful whether Jazz Age Paris would have attracted the heavenly homeless, those artists and writers whose café antics in the 1920s have kept generations of tourists glued to overpriced seats in Mont-parnasse ever since. Without the war, the French capital might not have attracted young and talented Americans long after it had been eclipsed by other places as a center of creativity. Without the war, France might not have existed as a place, much less a destination, in the world-view of ordinary Americans. The erotic charge of France, the notion of it as the homeland of transgression, the sheer *irresponsibility* it implied—all were received ideas reinforced and disseminated by the passage of millions of young men who happened to get in on the tail end of a war.

What was true for all American soldiers was especially so for African-American men in uniform. The discriminatory practices of the U.S. army during the war scandalized many Europeans. According to white army orthodoxy, the black doughboy divisions, 200,000 soldiers in all, were thought suitable only for menial jobs behind the Front. Even an American daredevil black ace flying with the French was grounded for the duration of the war when, in 1917, his squadron of volunteer airmen was switched from French to American command. In the Breton city of St. Malo, an American army general lodged an official complaint with French authorities when he had to deal with a local administrator who was a black man from the West Indies. These and other similar incidents of individual and institutional racism multiplied as formerly segregated Americans rubbed elbows in France.

It was mainly through the intervention of the French that African-Americans saw combat. Black units were transferred to French command, thereby sparing white American units from having to go to war alongside them. The Germans, true to the itinerary that would make them within a generation the most noxiously racist nation to have ever lived, protested over having to fight black American troops on the Front. The Kaiser's propagandists accused the French of sinking to new depths of uncivilized behavior—a rather breathtaking claim to make after three and a half years of abominably uncivilized warfare. The color distinction did not bother the French, or the African-Americans for that matter. Thanks to the Great War, an unlikely alliance was struck up between black America and France that continued for generations. Memoirs speak of black doughboys' delight in being treated as equals in the streets of Paris, of French villagers in the Vosges "walking the dog" when the all-black army band of Jimmy Europe played its jazzy, syncopated repertoire, and of a whole spate of incidents in which French restaurant owners sided with black American patrons when white American customers insisted that their countrymen leave or go eat in the kitchen.

The Montfaucon memorial speaks of this unofficial, unexpected off-shoot of the Great War, this link between the Harlem Renaissance and the Western Front, even if it speaks very softly now, and fewer and fewer people sit at its base to listen. Although the American forces were most conspicuously not "toot and scramble" (*tout ensemble*) on the Western Front, this old, unvisited column on a French hill can make one think otherwise. I decide that I'm becoming sentimental, so I head back to Varennes and the Front of 1916.

3. Varennes-en-Argonne to Verdun

At eight in the morning I have the town to myself. My route leads along the riverbank, then up a long and gradual slope to the east. The walk is enlivened by a few inevitable dogs, a foggy dew, and a head emptied of all thought. At the crest of the rise I turn around and see a little postcard of Varennes below me, wrapped in the wreaths of morning mist and backed by the black hills of the Argonne. I bid good-bye to pigs' feet and antiroyalist snitches, then resume my walk eastward into the enveloping greenness of the Meuse highlands.

Green everywhere. Lime green on the grassy swards, gunmetal green in the dark woods, pale green in the pastures. Hills and buttes stick up at random, small ravines and ridges succeed each other as if in a hurry. Each field is a microcosm, a miniature of the larger landscape. Warped by war, the parcels of fenced-off farmland present humps and hollows, creases and folds to bewilder the eye accustomed to the ordered, tailored fields to be found elsewhere in France. Land such as this should be photographed, written about, but not guarded against trespassers.

A farmer by the roadside turns into a generous giver of directions, his French sounding as if he has a beach ball permanently lodged in his mouth. If you think this land is bad, he tells me without uttering a consonant, wait till you get to Vauquois. There, things really begin to look strange. He's right—for once, a local oddity lives up to its billing. The wooded hill of Vauquois was the westernmost point of the vast Verdun battlefield, and from a distance it does look the part of guard-house. At the foot of the prominence, I peer up under the foliage like a mischievous little boy craning to get a view up a skirt. I see Paris, I see France, I see Vauquois's underpants. It is not an edifying sight. The hillside resembles a slice of Gruyère cheese or a pox-ridden thigh, with gaping holes gouged out of its slopes, the ugly work of mines set off during a vicious fight for the summit in 1914 and 1915.

I pass Avocourt, a huddle of barnlike houses standing in a muddy hollow. A field near the middle of town seems to sprout old concrete pillboxes more successfully than it does rows of corn. The deafening drone of military helicopters overhead renders the next stretch of road, which leads to the Front-line village of Esnes, even more unpleasant than it need be. Aerial maneuvers must be occurring in this proving ground of French military honor. The roadway skirts a slope that leads upward to the summit of Côte 304 (Hill 304), a famous site of the 1916 battle. I head cross-country in the hope of getting away from the copters and back into the woods.

My path turns into a snarl of brush and weeds after scarcely two hundred yards. On either side of it stand multistranded barbed-wire fences. There is no way else to advance but to squirm belly-first under the lowest rung of rusted wire. Once past the barrier I continue up a sloping pasture, which in turn ends abruptly in another nasty fence. Beyond it, beckoning the hiker, is a wide-waled path leading through a field of weeds to the woods farther uphill. To get there I have to crawl once again under the barbed wire and encounter for the first time the problem of a strategically placed meadow muffin. The cows of Lorraine, I soon learn with dismay, have conspired with the farmers to thwart the harmless pastime of long-distance hiking. Any stretch of fence admitting of easy access is rendered impassable by bovine carpet bombing. Only those parts of a fence sporting a prickly wreath of thornbushes are left free for the traveler; the rest is a festival of dung. Naming a cheese "The Laughing Cow" no longer seems so far-fetched. I head for a thorn bush and start weeding.

THE TRAIL BEYOND the fence leads directly into an enormous pine grove. I am now in what remains of the *Zone Rouge*, the swath of devastation that the French government designated as being dangerous for resettlement after the war. The physical destruction of the *guerre de quatorze* in France was appalling: 319,269 houses obliterated; 313,675 houses seriously damaged; 1,699 villages annihilated; 707 villages three-quarters destroyed; 1,656 villages half-destroyed; 20,603 factories leveled; 31,650 miles of road wrecked; 4,875 bridges blown; 4,297,800 acres of farmland and 2,060,000 acres of uncultivated land poisoned, dug up, shelled, mined, befouled, littered, and stained with a toxic, soupy mix of decaying corpses and rotting horse flesh. It was said that a cut in the Zone Rouge would fester faster than elsewhere in France, that children should always be kept away from the place, that crops would never grow there again.

Nonetheless people came back, to pick their way through the rubble and putrefaction and to rebuild their lives. German POWs were put to work cleaning up the place. The Zone Rouge shrank in the 1920s as the Front became overlaid with a palimpsest of new villages and farms and as time began to level the peaks of suffering. Ypres, Armentières, Béthune, Lens, Arras, Noyon, Roye, Soissons, Reims, and other cities arose from their ruination, some more artfully than others, as did many of the lesser towns. Miraculously, the Front began to breathe again, and the zone went from red to orange to green. The polders of Passchendaele were drained, the valleys of the Somme replanted. Even at the Chemin des Dames, farmers took to the sloping fields again, and highway engineers rebuilt the vanished roadway.

In only one place was it found impossible to perform cosmetic surgery on the scar of the Front: the hills north of Verdun. Here the Zone Rouge would remain red. The villages, or rather the powdery traces of them, were washed away forever in the spring runoff of 1919. Intrepid farmers lured to the zone for its rock-bottom prices could only do so much with the fields. Places like Avocourt and Esnes were rebuilt, as frontier towns at the fault line of two centuries. Tractor drivers plowed as far up the hill as they dared, harvesting hundreds of dead with every new turning of the soil. Explosives went off, maiming and killing men and their livestock. Classrooms around the area carried posters—some still do, in fact—warning children not to play with shells that they found in the schoolyard.

In the 1930s, Verdun's Zone Rouge was planted with hundreds of thousands of Austrian pines on both banks of the river Meuse. Parts of the zone became a firing range for the French army's artillery teams. A few thousand shells every year would hardly matter to a landscape where millions of tons of metal had fallen. To the contemporary hiker, the presence of pine trees is the giveaway. What is a slightly scarred but nonetheless pastoral area of mixed farmland suddenly gives way to acre upon acre of evergreen forest—a highly un-French note of wildness on the landscape. It is this area, the unrecoverable Front, that I have just entered.

I look ahead of me into the woods. The lower limbs of the pines have perished from the lack of sun. The light that does filter through is soft and makes the gray and wispy dead branches look like a network of warm cobwebs hanging above the reddish-brown undulations of the forest floor. Carpeted in pine needles, the floor is scarred with trenches and battered by shell craters. Within minutes of entering this soundless place, I see rusted rifles, helmets, and shells lying about in abundance. I walk through the eerie quietness for about a half hour before coming out onto a road and the final slope up to the summit of Hill 304.

It is well marked. A few picnic tables stand unused under the trees— who would want to eat here?—and a signboard explains trilingually the importance of this hill in the defense of Verdun. It was shelled almost continuously in the spring of 1916 after the German attacks to the east, on the right bank of the Meuse, failed to advance any closer to the city. There were repeated attempts, which the French repulsed, to capture the cratered hill. Thousands died. The poilus were told by the commander of the region, a certain General de Bazelaire, that any able-bodied man found retreating down the slope to Esnes would be taken to the rear of the lines and executed by a firing squad.

The forestation of the hills north of Verdun, the signboard explains, has been done to expedite the work of nature, which would have taken three to four centuries to make the area look vaguely terrestial. A nature trail has been cleared through the woods, which I take to spare myself the bother of consulting the map at every change in contour.

Here, on the path rising slowly to the summit, the landscape becomes truly cataclysmic, as unearthly as anything I have ever seen. What had been glimpsed in the copses of the Somme is now all around me, as far as the eye can see, a heaving sea of mortified land. Not one square yard of the forest floor is level—the place is madness come to ground. A few grave markers and private memorials rise and fall from sight in the shell-scarred bedlam as I continue upward. There is none of the perverse sense of companionship I felt for the trenches that led me out of the Argonne. It is all too obvious that this forest was a charnel house. This is the still-bleeding scar of the Great War, that which I had only divined in the cold December twilight east of Albert. I feel almost nauseated as the full ugliness of what I have been walking these past few weeks comes home to me. Small wonder that Bartholomew never spoke of the war or of his brother Tommy's death; small wonder that Daniel preferred a dance in the parade ground to tales of the trenches. The shock wave has been transmitted, even if the memory is now gone.

The monument at the top of the hill is a simple, tall monolith to the "10,000 dead whose blood impregnates this soil." When the Germans finally took the hill in 1916, the front-line troops asked for their tobacco ration to be doubled, because the stench was so strong. Small signs, written in three languages, are posted at several points on the clearing's perimeter:

> This land has been the cross of the soldier, each patch bears the stamp of its stations. Passerby, the respect of thousands of dead men demands the utmost silence.

As I copy this down, two combat helicopters come screaming over the treetops of the glade, shattering the "utmost silence." The air rings after their departure.

Hill 304 descends toward the east and a vale cut by a brook. The hill opposite is Mort Homme, a prewar name that became only too apt in the spring of 1916. Like 304, the prominence was pounded day and night by artillery. I stand by the stream between the two hills, away from the nature trail now and glad to be free of the leg-breaking landscape of shell craters, if only momentarily. My map shows a place to ford the rushing water of the brook. A few moss-covered yards to the north, I find the bridge and continue my trek to the lower slopes of Mort Homme. I pass through an unkempt field of tall grass, worm my way under a fence, and sit for a moment under a shade tree. Beside me are two old hand grenades, one of the "pineapple" variety, the other a German "potato masher," a wooden stick with a can-shaped appendage on its end. Despite my native caution I decide to pick one up. As I reach for the German grenade, I hear a low hiss, then a viscera-shaking roar. A fighter aircraft has thundered less than a hundred yards overhead, threading the needle between Hill 304 and Mort Homme and almost causing me to slough my bowels. I am furious when a second jet catches me unawares a few seconds later. I decide to head for the woods. I get up and make for the fence that surrounds this paddock-like pasture. In my ill temper, I don't notice until it is almost too late that an equally upset bull is galumphing over in my direction. There is no time to be squeamish about scraping my way through a meadow muffin to get under the fence.

After washing myself off in the stream, I tackle the slope of the Mort Homme. The hill is a mirror image of 304, its surface an obscene sea of shrapnel litter. At the top stands a statue representing a skeleton holding a flowing French flag and standing on a pedestal inscribed with the words: *Ils n'ont pas passé* (They did not pass). As I am contemplating this remarkable piece of kitsch, a lone German BMW cruises slowly along the summit's laneways, the tinted window on its passenger side lowering so that a woman's hand can point a camera at some unseen vista. The window quickly closes again. The car picks up speed and heads back downhill, leaving me alone with the grinning skeleton. I should be going too.

NEAR THE HAMLET of Chattancourt, on the road to Verdun from the Mort Homme, I gratefully stumble across Le Village Gaulois, a neo-rustic restaurant with a miniature golf course. I order an Asterix-burger and a beer and settle down on the patio to watch a young guy of about twenty-five putt his way around the course with the seriousness of a PGA professional. The exertions of the morning and afternoon are forgotten in this mesmerizing moment of triviality. The past falls away, as does any sense of incongruity, leaving only a callow backpacker with sore feet.

The golfer turns out to be a youthful businessman indulging a hobby. He drives a burgundy Alfa Romeo and gives me a lift into town. As we reach the River Meuse, the road broadens into a highway. It looks as if we're approaching a major city. I ask him what there is to do in Verdun.

"I wouldn't go out at night in Verdun," he says. "If I were you, I'd grab a quick dinner somewhere about seven, then rush back to my hotel. You can get stabbed in the streets of Verdun."

"Is that because of the army base?" I ask with knee-jerk antimilitarism. "It's dangerous because there are so many soldiers on the loose?"

"No, no, no! There's a constant war between the teens of Verdun and the soldiers. But the soldiers are okay. It's the local teens who start all the crap. I know—I was one of them once."

"So you like the army?"

"Not at all! The army's filled with dumbos. I did my military service so I can tell you what bullshit it is. The career officers have got absolutely nothing between their ears."

"So the teens of Verdun are rotten and the soldiers are stupid."

"You got it," he says with a laugh. We zoom through the city's industrial park, which, for reasons unfathomable, is called Chicago. "You got it," he repeats. "No one ever said this was a great town."

We pass a war memorial. The inscription is almost gleeful in describing Verdun's woes: ". . . besieged, destroyed or damaged in 450, 485, 984, 1047, 1246, 1338, 1562, 1790, 1870, and 1916–18." Like Canadians who boast with masochistic pride about month-long blizzards, the Verdunois city fathers seem to take delight in their own misfortunes. I have a sneaking suspicion that my driver's pessimistic prologue to the city may have been accurate. No one ever said that this was a great town.

4. Verdun

Verdun is an odd, unsightly town, which somehow does not live up to its world-historical significance. It is the place where France and Germany broke themselves and Europe in a futile exchange of steel, where the fruits of fascism were first seeded, and, finally, where the two countries agreed to bury the hatchet. When French President François Mitterrand and German Chancellor Helmut Kohl stood hand in hand at a military cemetery in the Verdun battlefield in 1984, the symbolism could not have been better chosen—even down to the doctoring of the resulting photograph to make the Frenchman seem less dwarfed by his German counterpart. Verdun was the most Pyrrhic victory of this most Pyrrhic of wars.

The garrison town sprawls over a humped-back hill on the right bank of the River Meuse. Of the 2,407 buildings of the town before the war, 2,305 were completely destroyed. Directly to the north of Verdun, where most of the fighting took place, the dark bluffs of Belleville loom on the horizon. The pine forests of desolation begin shortly thereafter, on the slopes that make up the Heights of the Meuse. Other than this touch of the extreme, the city seems devoid of any dignified drama or coherence, as if the Great War had taken away its life once and for all. At the turn of the first millennium Verdun was known throughout Europe for the production and resale of eunuchs. A thousand years later it is famous for its mass graves.

To anyone familiar with the First World War it is difficult to stay for very long in this city and not feel one's gorge begin to rise. Unlike Britain's apologists, who portrayed the war as an inhuman catastrophe visited upon the British by the abstract forces of history, France's shills made the conflict into a nationalist victory. The impulse is understandable—after all it is through France, not Britain or Germany or the U.S.A., that the Front meandered for most of its murderous length. In 1914 millions of men came marching over France's frontiers; in 1918 they, or their successors, went walking back home. Seen in these simple terms, the Great War was a Gallic victory and Verdun, France's finest hour. The postwar urge to *cocorico* (cock-a-doodle-do), the French term for jingoistic patriotism, proved irresistible to the myth- and monument-makers commissioned to commemorate the dead and whitewash the men responsible for the carnage.

The leaders of the French army, especially, needed what would now be called spin doctors. The notion of Verdun the victorious was used to erase from the collective memory of the war their record of disastrous decisions and wrongheaded policies: *attaque à outrance*, the Plan XVII, the repeated offensives in Artois, the repeated offensives in Champagne, the Chemin des Dames, the near-rout of 1918. All of these sanguinary items have been forgotten, the defense of Verdun retained. Were it not for modern Europe's recent descent into tribalism in the Balkans, Verdun could be viewed as a harmless museum piece. Instead, its triumphalism seems dangerous. The shops peddling war porn and the brochures singing the praises of the French army spread like a contagion. Statues of French generals abound near the city ramparts, as a sort of provocation to historical decency. Only the city's own monument—a poilu Abu Simbel with five ordinary soldiers emerging from a granite wall—puts some proper perspective on exactly who should be remembered in war memorials.

The main national war monument at Verdun is another matter. It occupies a large terraced lot off the main shopping street of the city and

looks as if it would be out of place no matter where it was set down. A
towering plug of stone that represents the eternally vigilant Frankish
warrior ready to defend his Dark Ages turf, the memorial may be the only
Merovingian phallic symbol in Europe. On either side of the structure
stand two artillery pieces, their snouts reared up in a pose of aggression.
The thing is one of the tacky wonders of the Front, a schoolyard bully's
idea of macho posturing. The stone Frank narrows his eyes at the unseen
Goth, ready to cleave any comers in two: Make my day, Germanicus. It is
a depressing sight and a terrible thing to have in the middle of a town,
even a town called Verdun. Graceful little Joan in Reims, the arch at
Thiepval, or, if one must erect towers, the Doric American column at
Montfaucon, the Canadian tuning fork at Vimy—everything except the
Flemish nightstick at Dixmude is more tasteful than this awkward
attempt at making myth. Giant Merovingians did not stop the Germans
in the hills north of town; poor unfortunate men did, by being placed by
the hundreds of thousands in the way of a curtain of whizzing steel and
high-explosive shells.

I DECIDE TO leave Verdun as soon as I can. No one ever said that this was
a great town, but neither did anyone warn me that the worst of cocorico
was waiting around every corner. A brief visit to the citadel of Verdun, the
grandest of Vauban's creations, leaves me shaking my head at the skewed
sense of narrative of those in charge of this attraction. An enormous
underground city that was almost autarchic in its functioning, the citadel
could easily house 7,000 men, including generals and their staffs in the
style to which they were accustomed. Instead of being told about the
functioning of this marvelous wartime warren, the spectator is invited to
scurry along through dank hallways dripping with groundwater in order
to catch up with the recorded patriotic spiel and martial music coming
out of hidden speakers. We pause before a Madame Tussaud–like
reconstruction of the moment in 1920 when the casket containing the
Unknown Soldier was chosen for inhumation underneath the Arc de
Triomphe. The commentary describing this unique occasion seems too
brief, especially when compared to the painfully detailed part of the
recording that lists the long-deposed monarchs and long-dead statesmen
who have bestowed medals and honors on the city of Verdun for being
such an exemplary victim. Clearly, someone is immensely proud of his
badges and baubles.

My last stop of the day takes me across the canals near the city center to
Verdun's tourist office. I ask at the desk for a pamphlet listing the visiting

hours of the forts and battlefield parks to the north of the city. I am told by a young woman that all that information can be found in a book on sale in the display case. Yes, but I don't want the book, I just want the information.

We look at each other. She is pretty. Her male colleague leans over and says it's all in the book, and that's all there is to it. I look around the office — not a brochure, a leaflet, or even the kind of approximate placemat map that fast-food places offer in tourist destinations. Nothing. The city of Verdun wants visitors to spend the equivalent of seven dollars to buy a book that they do not want. Is it just vultures that feed on the dead?

"Thieves!" says my hotelkeeper over dinner later that night to placate me. "The place has always been crawling with them."

He points out the heterogeneous elements in his dining room. An Empire console, a gilt mirror, a swath of red velvet curtain — all of them scavenged, he explains, when people started drifting back to town in 1919 and 1920. It was a very confused time, he says with a smile. He's a very large man, sitting serenely behind his cash register.

His grandparents had been among the first to return to Verdun after the war. Many of the rooms are furnished with "found" objects.

"The Zone Rouge was a place for people to do business. All kinds of business. Even you're doing business — what else is this book you're going to write?"

I open my mouth to protest, but the sage of Verdun is already laughing at me.

5. Douaumont to Vaux

Fort Douaumont is in the heart of the battlefields of the right bank. It is the Western Front's hinge of desolation, like the vale at Passchendaele and the plateau at Craonne. The forests surrounding it give way to great clearings of tortured ground and landscaped mass graveyards. It is the Frenchman's postcard image of *la guerre de quatorze*.

I stand atop the fort on a morning so gray that no distinction can be made between ground and sky. Even the earth and heavens have deserted the prominence of Douaumont today, preferring to leave the place in some intermediate limbo. Nearby is a neatly kept graveyard with 15,000 headstones stretching off beyond the mist. Beside that, a lighthouse sticks up into the grayness, its top lopped off by low-hanging clouds. At the base of the beacon is an ossuary containing the remains of 150,000 soldiers whose blasted skeletons were found scattered around the vicinity after the war. You can walk around inside the base, peering through windows at the heaps of bones piled high. Femurs go with femurs, tibias with tibias, skulls with skulls, and so on. Off in the woods, wild boars dig up unrecovered skeletal parts and make a meal.

I remember the British war buff couple in Albert who told me that this place was impressive. The Douaumont Ossuary impresses so much as to render numb, which must have been the intent of its builders. The great Art Deco monstrosity looks strange in the middle of these obscene forests, and the visitor feels strange in the presence of all these collarbones and pelvises. Unlike the monuments in the city of Verdun, Douaumont goes beyond good or bad taste. For all its immodesty with human remains, Douaumont is and always will be shame. Not a shame, but shame itself. It is the embers of the bonfire—the bonefire—that consumed our grandfathers' world. More than shame, Douaumont is folly.

Between Douaumont and Thiaumont stands the Trench of the Bayonets. Legend has it that an entire company of the 137th French Infantry Regiment was buried alive in an explosion that caved in a trench on June 12, 1916. Only their bayonets remained sticking above ground. While that is a spooky story, many historians think it more likely that the men were hurriedly interred, perhaps by their opponents, and their bayonets were stuck in the ground to mark the spot. Whatever the truth about the trench, a wealthy American, George F. Rand, liked the story so much that he paid for a memorial shelter to be erected in order to protect the bayonets from theft by souvenir hunters. The supposedly immovable bayonets were dug up and replanted in more level ground to ease construction of the memorial. Yet the tale does not end there. As Jay Winter deconstructs it in his *Sites of Memory, Sites of Mourning*: "Immediately after conferring with [French Premier] Clemenceau and confirming the gift, Rand was killed in a plane crash. The monument therefore had a double meaning: to remember the giver as well as the event he wished to commemorate."

The Trench of the Bayonets and the Douaumont Ossuary are the macabre movie stars of the Western Front. Surrounding the bald and beaten hillock that Fort Douaumont occupies there stretches an enormous pocked and pitted dump of rusted metal, bleached bones, and ruined villages, only partly concealed by the forest plantings. Verdun's hinterland, historian Alastair Horne remarks in *The Price of Glory*, his matchless account of the battle, is "the nearest thing to a desert in Europe." It took ten months to tear every trace of topsoil from a rolling, fertile farmland and wipe away all mark of man the builder and cultivator.

The battle began on February 21, 1916. The offensive, as planned by German commander Erich von Falkenhayn, was designed to kill as many poilus as possible through the use of heavy artillery. Falkenhayn cynically understood that the French command would not surrender a symbol as important as Verdun, even if that meant sacrificing an entire generation of Frenchmen. He guessed correctly that the leaders of the French army were that inept. In setting the trap, the Prussian planner hoped to break the back of France as a fighting nation. It worked, but it did not win the war. The German forces, spurred on by their own propaganda and by Crown Prince Wilhelm's ambition to try to take Verdun, eventually lost as many men as the French—which defeated the whole purpose of the operation. A sorcerer's apprentice, Falkenhayn had let his slaughterhouse get out of control.

After the war the story of the defense of Verdun quickly became overgrown by a thicket of nationalist mumbo jumbo. The Douaumont charnel house was regularly besieged by torch-bearing concelebrants, seeking some transcendent message in this testament to high-level profligacy with human lives. What is certain is that the battlefield, for a few awful months in the late spring and early summer of 1916, became a metaphor of national manhood for both sides. The killing was savage.

In brief, the first half of the battle consisted of several massive German attacks over these hills, and over Hill 304 and Mort Homme on the left bank of the Meuse. The countryside was bristling with French forts that had been stripped of their guns to feed the offensives in Champagne and Artois a year earlier. After each successive incursion, which brought them closer and closer to Verdun, the Germans would pause—always, it seems, at a time when total victory was within grasp. The second half of the battle was the reverse. The French decided, for reasons too criminal to contemplate, that every inch of surrendered territory must be retaken, even the forts now made lethal by months of German occupation and refitting.

The stories of Verdun were once well known. The most amazing concerns a certain Sergeant Kunze. In a coup that rivals Alvin York's for audacity, Kunze and a half-dozen men of a Brandenburger Regiment single-handedly took Fort Douaumont. Through an incredible series of command blunders, four days into the battle the French still had only a small garrison in this, the most modern and well-protected of forts in all of Europe. Everyone in the French military hierarchy assumed that someone else had reinforced the fortress.

Sergeant Kunze decided to go and have a look. Despite orders to stay away from the deadly construction, the sergeant carefully picked his way through the barbed wire and forests of spikes, only to be blown into the moat by the shock wave from one of the massive Big Bertha shells that the German artillery had been lobbing on Douaumont. He ordered his men down into the moat with him and, like German tourists on a Costa del Sol beach, they formed a human pyramid. Kunze scrambled up their backs and wormed his way into an unoccupied gun casemate. Once inside, he and his men rounded up the shocked French garrison, who had been firing off the Douaumont's long-range cannons unaware that the enemy was anywhere near the fort.

It was a stunning feat, akin in magnitude to an Iraqi shepherd of today bringing down a Stealth bomber with a rifle. Both the French and the Germans were agog. A Prussian lieutenant named Brandis, the man who stole the credit for the action by lying about who got there first, became a national hero. The acutely embarrassed French command decided that their honor could be salved only by retaking the fort once circumstances permitted. A French staff officer estimated that 100,000 French lives were lost because of the fall of Douaumont.

When I follow a tour of the fort seventy years after the fighting has stopped, the guide ignores the miraculous German capture of the fort—one of the strangest incidents of the entire war—to dwell exclusively on the successful, albeit conventional French attack on it in the fall of 1916. The usual patriotic nonsense spews out of the young fellow's mouth, as if an embrace of the truth might somehow belittle his country. Perhaps he, and the other custodians of Verdun, do not realize that repeating old lies makes their nationalism look that much more silly.

I walk away from Douaumont and its graveyards dispiritedly, surprised at the disappointment I feel in hearing bombast and rationalization at a memorial for such an important battle. What else did I expect? Perhaps the starkly unintelligent Gaul statue in Verdun is the proper monument for this benighted corner of Europe. Yet the caretakers of this spot do not need to resort to mystification—individual examples of courage abound and are not diminished by the ultimate worthlessness of the larger battle. At Souville I pass the place where the French line held and would not let the Crown Prince's men gain one more inch of ground. Soon the smashed fort at Vaux appears out of the gray curtain of pines and craters. The story here is mind-boggling. For more than one hundred days the German army was within three hundred yards of the structure, dug into the metal-laden forest I've just crossed. During that time, 10,000 high-explosive shells fell on the fort *every day*. By June 1 the place was surrounded. Then the attackers got onto its roof, started pumping flames and gas into the vents. A wall was breached, and gruesome hand-to-hand combat went on for days in a darkened corridor. The French commander, Sylvain-Eugène Raynal, ordered most of his men to make a break for it. Twenty-nine scampered across no-man's-land in the dead of night. Raynal sent his last courier pigeon out on June 4, begging for relief. A French attack was launched to break through to Raynal, but it ended in the customary slaughter of machine-gun and artillery fire. Finally, on June 6, the exhausted Raynal surrendered. His men came out of the cadaver-strewn Fort Vaux on their hands and knees, licking at the puddles of water on the ground. The commander followed, walking tall and holding his pet cocker spaniel. Even the Germans treated him as a hero.

A fine mist begins to close in on the forests east of Vaux. The rusty shrapnel on the ground all around me begins to glisten with the damp. The crack of a branch resounds through the silent wood. Then another crack. And another. I peer through the dim light, half fearful that some haggard men in uniform will appear out of the mists, marching toward me. What will their faces look like? Ghastly grinning skulls. I stumble down a slope, see a road, and break into an awkward run over the shell craters. For the first time since leaving Nieuport, I am spooked. If it is not ghosts in these woods, then it must be something or someone else. Someone I do not want to meet. What kind of person would want to walk through these forests of death on such an awful day?

I arrive in the village of Damloup. This time I do not need my hotelkeeper to laugh at myself. I'm the kind of person who would walk through those woods.

6. *Fresnes to St. Mihiel*

"The people here never go out much. They keep to themselves. You have no idea how bad it is. They're an awful bunch."

I'm sitting in a kitchen, having a coffee with a man in his late sixties. There is a blinding yellow oilcloth on the table.

"I used to go out. Go to dances. But not now. Not with these people. They're my wife's kin."

He invited me inside his home after he saw me rapping at the door of the village café. A woman came to the window, wide-eyed, then shook her head. She wagged her forefinger at me.

My host explains that although the lady owns the café she serves only locals. She never opens it to strangers because she has no license. Who knows? I might be a spy for the inland revenue service.

"Besides, no one else around here would ever invite you inside. Not like where I come from. People in my country have *le sens de la fête*. They know how to have a good time."

I ask the inevitable question.

"Where do you come from?"

He takes a pull on his corn-paper cigarette. "Les Eparges."

I look at him in surprise. His "country" is a couple of hills away. I just walked through that village two hours ago.

There is no smile on his face. He obviously considers himself an expatriate.

A car door closes outside the kitchen window with a tinny slam. A look of alarm crosses the man's face. He puts the lid back on the sugar bowl. His wife, a strong-looking woman in her mid-sixties, comes in carrying a clutch of plastic grocery bags. She sees me, then looks at her husband in dismay. She must disapprove of his habit of inviting in strangers and telling them what deadbeats her people are. The bags land on the linoleum with a thud. She stalks off to some other room of the house.

"See what I mean?" the old man says.

I AM NOW in a type of countryside that the French fondly call *la France profonde*, a region far from the cities and towns that pay attention to their century. These are the sticks, where old people still think that a change in contour means a change in culture and where superstitions about hexes and witchcraft have never died out. It is a place marked by emptiness, as most of the young have left. The woman who served me breakfast in the market town of Fresnes-en-Woëvre shyly asked me if distant Paris was "as crowded as they say it is."

This part of la France profonde is crossed by the Front. As it leaves Verdun the Western Front goes east for a few miles before turning sharply southwest and forming what was once known as the St. Mihiel Salient. The trenches traversed the plain of the Woëvre, a low flatland that is mercifully free of the nightmarish craters and hollows of Verdun. The scars from the war all seem to be concentrated on a large hillock near Les Eparges, the fun-loving village from which marriage had plucked the homesick old man who gave me a cup of coffee. The Eparges prominence, like Vauquois near the Argonne, was the scene of a grotesque battle of mines and countermines during 1915. The French command sacrificed men in unimaginable quantity in trying to gain a piece of the summit that they had not bothered defending in 1914. One local action, in the spring of 1915, killed 250 Frenchmen to one German. It was repeated the next day.

The countryside becomes lovely as I head back into the highlands near the Meuse. This is what the region of Douaumont and Vaux would have looked like if German and French artillery had not smashed it into its molecular components. Through the villages of St. Rémy-la-Calonne and Dommartin-la-Montagne, small fields alternate with stands of conifers, this time concealing nothing more than the occasional bike path. The area makes up part of the Regional Natural Park of Lorraine, with expansive vistas stretching out to the east. Shadows of clouds race across the deep green plain that stretches beyond the River Moselle and leads to Alsace. In the summer of 1914 the French army tried to emulate those shadows. A wall of death awaited. Great masses of young men loped across these fields, their bright red pants and dark blue coats the relic of an earlier age, in the hope of winning glory for their regiments and redeeming the martial honor of France lost in 1870. The fiasco of infantrymen charging machine guns was enacted time and time again until several hundred thousand lay inert in the farmland of Lorraine.

I think of the beginning of the war as I near the end of my walk, simply because this part of the Front saw the wholesale destruction of a French idealism akin to the spirit animating the doomed Wandervogel youths of Germany. Near the hamlet of Vaux-lès-Palameix the writer Alain-Fournier vanished forever during a risky attack in the surrounding woods on September 22, 1914. A survivor of that fatal foray maintained that he saw the twenty-eight-year-old novelist fall to the ground after taking a bullet wound to the head. The image—the brain of a young artist blown away by the war—would be revived regularly by mourners of the generation of 1914. One postwar commentator wrote: "We are still suffering from that head wound . . . The brain of the world [i.e., France] has undergone a kind of trepanning." *Le front*, in a nice lexical coincidence, means both the front and the forehead.

The notion of an irretrievably lost capital of creative talent took hold as the casualty lists from that horrendous first year of senseless attaques à outrance grew longer. Alain-Fournier, whose real name was Henri Alban Fournier, had written his masterpiece *Le Grand Meaulnes* (*The Wanderer*) about one young man's attempt to recover a lost world. News of his passing was treated as emblematic of this literary theme. An imaginative world was indeed being lost. By the end of the first year of the war, 133 French writers had been killed in the fighting. Ernest Psichari, the prewar darling of the zealous new generation of French nationalists enamored of exalted Catholicism and mystical patriotism, was among those whose reputation ballooned into myth through death on the battlefield.

Psichari's posthumous influence, however, paled beside that of Charles Péguy, a forty-one-year-old polemicist, poet, and essayist whose death on September 4, 1914, during the first day of the Battle of Marne, ensured him a place in the French pantheon within shouting distance of Joan of Arc, one of his favorite subjects for epic treatment. Péguy achieved a sort of apotheosis in death that made him an inspirational figure for combatants in both world wars.

As I set off through the sun-touched woods on the road to St. Mihiel, I feel that I am beginning to leave the war behind me. There is something irresistibly valedictory about this moment spent near the unlocated grave of Alain-Fournier. His hero, Meaulnes, is the type of fellow who would understand the sad beauty in the ruins of Soupir. Indeed, for much of the novel, Meaulnes endeavors to reconstruct a world that he never experienced. His motivation is love, set in the late afternoon of vanishing youth. I decide that somewhere in my ephemeral constitution of lapsed amnesiac, accidental historian, and incompetent hiker, there is a touch of Alain-Fournier's Meaulnes. The past must not be relinquished without a small sense of moment.

ON MAY 2, 1991, Alain-Fournier's body was at last found in the woods near Palameix. I learned of the discovery by pure chance. At the time I was working on a fashion magazine whose offices floated high above Broadway and West 50th Street in New York City. I was working late, on deadline, filling column inches with a couple of other staff writers. I went to the empty art room to procrastinate. A French glossy had been left lying around, so I idly flipped through it for want of anything better to do. The item about the discovery of Alain-Fournier was minute, but it didn't escape me. There was a blurred photograph of the author taken in 1913.

I looked out the window at the lights of a Manhattan midnight. There was no one to tell how I felt, even if I had wanted to. The sun and the sadness came rushing back. I saw Tommy Conlon's grave on the Somme, heard the strains of the *Merry Widow Waltz*, felt the hot breath of traffic on the Menin Road.

Perhaps this was memory, then.

When I returned to my desk, the others were waiting for me. We still had an hour or two of stylish, kicky copy to produce. Unconsciously I began humming "Papa Don't Preach."

The fashion editor looked at me incredulously. "Stephen, do you mind?" she said. "Madonna's history."

Her assistant seconded her. "Yeah, get a life."

7. Montsec

The grim little logging town of St. Mihiel hosts an impromptu Great War seminar, as a gay English couple and I speak in hushed tones of Siegfried Sassoon and Wilfred Owen in the dining room of our hotel. They are en route to Luxembourg, but want to spend all day tomorrow inspecting the battlefields of Verdun. They wonder if I know anywhere to stay outside the city, which they heard was "dreadful." I ask them if they like pig's trotters.

The two are literary war buffs, the most distinguished branch of a family that includes souvenir hunters, gore aficionados, munitions freaks, destruction junkies, army bores, inverted pacifists, medal collectors, mutilation perverts, macho memoirists, armchair Napoleons, misogynist camp-followers, closet Attilas, frustrated murderers, and myself. My erudite dinner companions think of the Great War exclusively as a literary event. One of them downs the last of his brandy and, to my astonishment, proposes to recite from memory the entirety of Owen's "Dulce et Decorum Est." Owen, Britain's most beloved war poet, was killed in action just one week before the Armistice of 1918.

The poem's title, I am told by way of a throat-clearing introduction, refers to a line from Horace, "How sweet and noble it is to die for one's country," which every public schoolboy in 1914 Britain would have known in its Latin original. Owen sets his famous parable on the Front as a group of soldiers leave the trenches for a rest in the rear. "Five-Nines" are shells:

> Bent double, like old beggars under sacks,
> Knock-kneed, coughing like hags, we cursed through sludge,
> Till on the haunting flares we turned our backs
> And towards our distant rest began to trudge.
> Men marched asleep. Many had lost their boots
> But limped on, blood-shod. All went lame; all blind;
> Drunk with fatigue; deaf even to the hoots
> Of tired, outstripped Five-Nines that dropped behind.
>
> Gas! GAS! Quick, boys! — An ecstasy of fumbling,
> Fitting the clumsy helmets just in time;
> But someone was still yelling out and stumbling,
> And flound'ring like a man in fire or lime . . .
> Dim, through the misty panes and thick green light,
> As under a green sea, I saw him drowning.
>
> In all my dreams, before my helpless sight,
> He plunges at me, guttering, choking, drowning.
>
> If in some smothering dreams you too could pace
> Behind the wagon that we flung him in,

And watch the white eyes writhing in his face,
His hanging face, like a devil's sick of sin;
If you could hear, at every jolt, the blood
Come gargling from the froth-corrupted lungs,
Obscene as cancer, bitter as the cud
Of vile, incurable sores on innocent tongues, —
My friend, you would not tell with such high zest
To children ardent for some desperate glory,
The old Lie: Dulce et decorum est
Pro patria mori.

The waiter looks askance at us as we sit in silence, brooding in a bath of anachronism. I eventually ask the reciter where he learned to declaim Great War poetry so movingly.

"I didn't 'learn' it," comes the reply. "I wrote it. I *am* Wilfred Owen."

The laughter arrives a split second too late, and the would-have-been poet has a fixed look in his eye. I find an excuse to leave shortly afterward. They're delighted when I turn and salute at the door.

THE LANDSCAPE EAST of St. Mihiel looks as literary as last night's dinner companions. A green plain stretches out to the east, its perspective pleasantly broken up by great stands of tall birches and swaying poplars. In the background, a sudden hill stands alone, crowned with a classical peristyle. Large puffs of cloud float over it, weightless portents in a blue sky. Birds wheel about. The view is Byronic, Romantic, as much an incitement to reverie as is the natural rhythm of walking. I half expect the classical building to be an ivy-covered ruin, or to see a riderless white charger rearing on the summit. I feel the need for a cloak, or a headful of Greek. The bucolic Olympus draws nearer.

The spell is broken as two fighter jets thunder in from the north to bank sharply over the monument. The apprentice top guns of France obviously have a favorite flight path that takes them hedge-hopping at earsplitting speed over the Mort Homme, Les Eparges, and then this hill, Montsec. The effect is unpleasant in the extreme. What was a peaceful setting becomes a disturbed chop of raw sound. A third jet rends the air above the hill. For once the Western Front had disguised itself as something other than a killing field, and these French flyboys have to go and ruin it. Petulant and proprietary, I begin the ascent of the hill.

For all my Romantic maunderings, the circular colonnade atop Montsec is a war monument. It commemorates an American attack of September 1918, just like the pillar at Montfaucon. The St. Mihiel offensive, as it came to be known, was the first U.S.-commanded military action on European soil and preceded the Meuse-Argonne effort by a couple of weeks. It raised the curtain on a new era of Old World acquiescence in leadership from abroad. The American army was a fledgling then, not the bloated beast of today that eats away at Washington's financial health. Montsec, in a way, is the birthplace of the Pentagon.

Given that dubious distinction, the view from its summit might be expected to be overpriced, or at least classified. Neither is the case. Montsec's vista stretches from the hills near the Meuse across a quilt of farmlands to the heights of the Moselle. It was here on September 12, 1918, that Pershing's men closed the giant German salient of St. Mihiel, through a combination of luck and overwhelming superiority in men and matériel. The luck came from the German decision to retreat just as the battle was about to begin. In some places, the American infantry had to go chasing after their prey, looking for someone to fight. In others, artillery obliterated the German lines. The battle, unlike Meuse-Argonne, was a swift American victory.

From Montsec the distant American and German cemeteries at Thiaucourt can be made out far to the east. Closer by is the village of Essey, where the youthful Douglas MacArthur and George Patton were supposed to have engaged in an ostentatious game of chicken by walking out in the open as German shells flew. My sole companion during my stay atop Montsec is a gray cat that slinks around the monumental columns in a private slalom. When it suddenly stiffens, I guess the reason. An instant later, yet another Mirage jet flashes in front of the sun, screaming its message about the tiresome grandeur of French firepower.

Back on the plain, after an hour or two of walking, I come across a more prosaic reminder of that firepower. A suspicious-looking copse turns out to be the ruins of Remenauville, a village destroyed in the Great War. Its flattened neighbors were rebuilt, but no one returned here, at least to live. A large sign in Remenauville's rubble warns the visitor:

Ne Ramassez Aucun Objet Métallique
Evitez Nos Fôrets en Période de Chasse

(Do Not Pick up Metal Objects
Stay away from Our Woods in Hunting Season)

The shooting never stops around here.

8. *Pont-à-Mousson to Badonviller to Ste. Marie-aux-Mines*

The long days of summer are drawing to a close. At sunset now, the slanting light in the sky betrays that Pont-à-Mousson lies closer to the pole than to the equator. Its latitude is the same as that of the uppermost tip of Lake Superior. The town sits on the left bank of the Moselle, midway between the two major urban centers of Lorraine. Upstream is Nancy, the baise-beige gem of eastern France; downstream, Metz, the region's battered industrial and religious center. Pont-à-Mousson, although small, is famous throughout the country. On any given day thousands of people in French cities look down to see whether their shoes are still clean and glimpse the words "Pont-à-Mousson" stamped on manholes and sewer covers. It may not spell glory, but it is recognition.

On crossing the Moselle, the warrior Western Front is almost over; indeed, many histories do not consider the Franco-German face-off that took place from this point to the border of Switzerland as trench warfare in the traditional murderous sense. Their maps of the Front stop at St. Mihiel. Yet there were trenches in most places, even if the warfare was limited. After the lemming-like attacks of Plan XVII in the summer and fall of 1914, the remaining Lorraine segment of the Front became a fairly somnolent sector, loosely held and leisurely in its rhythms. The vagaries of terrain and inadequate transport links ruled out offensives of the gruesome magnitude of the Somme or Verdun. One story of these lackadaisical trenches tells of a French reserve unit in the front line firing off its ammunition harmlessly in the air at the same hour and day every week. The German troops opposite would then do likewise, after which everyone went back to playing cards and skittles with their friends. In rugged Alsace, a few savage battles took place in 1914 and 1915 until the generals who ordered them realized, presumably, that they were looking at large-scale maps of remote mountaintops lost in a sea of conifers. All was then quiet in most of Alsace and Lorraine, an ironical wartime fate for the regions that had been peacetime bones of contention.

Thus the last part of the journey must hasten over a Western Front that is little more than a dotted line. Hunting season approaches, and as I struggle up the slopes of Vosges I do not want some schnapps-sipping rifleman to mistake me for an oddly foulmouthed deer. Dispatches will suffice as I race not to the sea but to Switzerland. The Front is ending, as are the summer and the warm weather. So too is the war. Nineteen-eighteen is upon us.

THE MOMENTOUS EVENTS of 1917 spelled both trouble and triumph for the Allies. The Americans had finally plumped for war, but they were not about to let their ever-increasing contingent of men in France be placed under the authority of the likes of Haig and Nivelle. The sorry slaughters of the Chemin des Dames and Passchendaele had given proof of command incompetence, and army morale now rarely rose above the parapet of the muddy trenches. Unlike the volunteers in the first half of the war, most new conscripts at the Front in 1918 knew that they were cannon fodder in a questionable cause.

The Western Front was one of the few fronts that remained a stalemate in the world at war of 1918. In the Ottoman lands of the Middle East, the work of British armies and agents had done what the ineffective landing at Gallipoli had failed to do three years earlier. The Ottoman Empire teetered on the brink of collapse. Arab nationalists, aided by T. E. Lawrence, one of the few dashing figures of the entire conflict, had cast their lot in with the Allies and fought effectively against the Turks. In its desire to lay its hands on Ottoman possessions, London spoke of nationhood to all who could help in the struggle. Not only were Arabs promised autonomy, but so were European Zionists. The Balfour Declaration of 1917 recognized the principle of a Jewish national homeland in Palestine. When the British army took Jerusalem just before Christmas, 1917, much was made in the press about this being the first time since the Crusader era that Westerners had controlled the sacred city. Less was made of the British determination to keep the place. To the embarrassment of British and French governments paying lip service to Woodrow Wilson's idealism, the newly empowered Bolsheviks of Russia published the secret treaties that had been signed among Allies with an aim to divvying up the Ottoman Empire. The British and French now looked as rapacious as their worst caricatures of the Germans.

Embarrassment, however, was the least of the worries to emerge from Russia. Under Lenin and Trotsky, the Bolsheviks had yanked Russia out of the war—or rather they had recognized that in the long-suffering Russian army there was no real will to fight any longer. Combat stopped on November 29, 1917. As good revolutionaries, the Bolshevik delegation to the peace talks at the Polish town of Brest-Litovsk refused at first to negotiate with the German representatives. How could heralds of a new world order deal with the lackeys of an imperial power? In response, the German armies advanced farther and farther into Russia until Petrograd itself was menaced. Trotsky changed his mind and on March 3, 1918, signed a peace treaty. The gigantic Eastern Front ceased to exist. The Germans could do what they hadn't done since the summer of 1914: concentrate all their strength in the West. The Americans hadn't yet arrived, and the British and French had exhausted themselves the year before. For a warlord like Erich Ludendorff, who along with Hindenburg now commanded the war effort, the moment was propitious to renew the attack. Visions of winning the war once again swam in front of Prussian monocles.

THE ROUTE FROM Pont-à-Mousson to the next Front town of Nomény may be the Platonic Form of a French roadway. Magnificent poplars line both shoulders, giving a rustling, silken shade to the walker as he looks out at the golden fields rolling to the horizon. The three *b*'s of Francophilia—beret, baguette, and bicycle—would not look out of place here, especially if the first were worn by a wrinkled peasant taking the second home from town on the third. Some say that the French originally started planting these roadside trees so that their armies could march in the shade. Others maintain that it's done to halt erosion and provide windbreaks. Still others claim that they are placed there because they look good. Whatever the case, it is a pleasant way to start my several days of forced march southeast toward the Vosges.

The Front turns at Nomény to head south along the valley formed by the River Seille. After a few hours' walking through its villages, I am convinced that it should be renamed the River Dog. Woofers bound out of yards, from behind fences, seemingly out of trees. A particularly friendly one slobbers on an unproffered trouser leg. I press on, past the vale of Champenoux, an important site of the battle for Nancy in 1914, and a lonely French military cemetery on a rise outside of town. There is not one signature in the visitors' register. Long days go by serenely as the Front snakes through windswept farmland east to Arracourt, then southeast past the villages of Xures, Xousse, and finally to Badonviller, at the edge of the forests of the Vosges. The landscape thus far has been untortured, but unlovely too, the village churches always a variation of reinforced concrete and stern slate roofs. Mud from tractors scores the roadways and leaves telltale marks in front of the large slatted doors that serve as entrances to the farmhouses. People in Lorraine used to sleep with their livestock; now it appears they cohabit with their farm machinery.

Badonviller is a town that once was to pottery what the nearby city of Baccarat is to crystal. The works have all closed, and the place is a somber snapshot of rural France, the crows in its main square sharing a bench with an aging curé in a black soutane. Beyond is the leading edge of pine trees and an abrupt ridge that I cross at a gap called Chapelotte. Bunkers and pillboxes can be seen sticking out of the forest floor, and a hiking trail has been laid out to titillate the war buff. I follow it over well-marked trenches and a carpet of needles to end up in a small outdoorsy tourist outpost named Pierre Percée. The ruin of a pink sandstone castle overlooks a placid lake mottled with wind-surfers. This is too beautiful to be the Front. A man in a wet suit gives me a ride in his four-wheel drive through the forests to the town of Senones. He never realized that the guerre de quatorze came anywhere near his sylvan paradise.

IN ITS CLOSING stages, it didn't. By the spring of 1918, Ludendorff was ready to launch his final offensives all the way back up in Flanders and Picardy. Unlike their French and British counterparts, the planners on the German general staff had learned from years of static warfare. They might have been undemocratic, class-conscious, heinous Junker autocrats, but they were open to new ideas. These were supplied by a certain Captain Geyer, one of the shrewdest tacticians of the war. He saw that the Allies' adoption of the German defense-in-depth system—whereby the first trench was lightly manned and the main fighting force kept in different positions well away from no-man's-land—spelled failure for the offensive tactic that had been adopted by both sides since the time of Verdun. The defenders could always counterattack.

It is important to linger for a moment here on tactics, because Geyer had found the way to end trench warfare. He eliminated the static Front. Henceforth, the war would be one of movement, the type of moving mayhem that generals had been seeking since the failure of the Schlieffen Plan. Geyer's tactics called for an intelligent use of surprise, precision artillery, and specially trained *Sturmtruppen*, or storm troopers.

Sturmtruppen were the key. These elite troops probed the lines right behind the creeping barrage of artillery until they found a gap in the defenses. They then ran through, rifles slung over their shoulders, throwing grenades and reaching the enemy's second or third lines. They performed fish-hook maneuvers, whereby they raced beyond defensive positions then turned around, set up machine guns, and fired into the startled defenders' backs. Once they had established isolated strongholds the bulk of the infantry came on, accompanied by dive-bombing airplanes and mobile artillery. The goal was to create confusion, exploit it, and unnerve defenders who would no longer know where the Front was. To do this the stormtroopers needed suicidal bravery, great latitude in taking the initiative, and lots of luck.

On March 21, 1918, everything fell into place. Ludendorff decided to attack over the old Somme battlefield. In the week that followed, it looked as if Germany might win the war.

SENONES IS A logging town and former monastic center that used to be the capital of an independent principality known as Salm-Salm. It was a forested Ruritania that lay sandwiched between Alsace and Lorraine and lived peacefully under its German princes until a stirred-up local populace voted to become a part of France during the revolution. Nowadays, given the banners and pennants festooning its old square, the town seems to regret its vote. As I walk through the wet streets of this lumberjack Versailles, the Front seems farther away than ever. Yet in the wooded ridge to the northwest of town, elaborate concrete bunkers mark the trace of the Great War stalemate.

I set off southward, climbing a gradual slope to a plateau that was once the hinterland of the princes of Salm-Salm. As if to continue a tradition of strange toponymy—Senones is the Front's second palindrome—the Salm-Salm countryside is now known as Ban-de-Sapt. I spend a quiet moment in the French military cemetery of Fontenelle, its Art Deco sandstone statues a marked change from the crumbling concrete memorials evident elsewhere in Lorraine. All around the graveyard is a dense forest, the familiar thicket of rusted picket stakes and barbed wire barring any exploration. By this stage of my journey, seeing a trench does not immediately impress. It is the cumulative effect of having seen so many tortured forest floors that stays in memory. The Front *is* a scar, even in this Lorraine fastness.

Underneath evergreen boughs expectantly outstretched for the snow soon to come, a road marker points out the boundaries of the ephemeral principality of Salm-Salm. Nearby, a worn sandstone marker shows the limits of the German advance in the First World War. A helmet rests on laurel leaves; on the base are inscribed the words: *Ici Fut Repoussé L'Envahisseur* (The Invader Was Halted Here). In the 1920s, veterans' associations and motoring clubs paid for these demarcation stones to be placed along the line of the farthest German advance. Another marker appears just a few miles on, outside the village of Frapelle. Its little valley, through which the River Fave runs, seems to be sadder and more scarred by time than wooded Salm-Salm. Rusting wrought-iron calvaries stand near crumbling bunkers, the door of a wayside chapel creaks in the freshening breeze, great black birds swoop through the rotting rail fences. The rain clouds are closing in once again and the sky darkens. A local delivery van gives me a ride through a three-mile-long tunnel to the town of Ste. Marie-aux-Mines. I'm at the gates of Alsace in the pouring rain. Before I pass them, we must first return to Picardy.

IN THE SPRING of 1918, the Germans got to the gates of Amiens. Their attack on March 21 opened at 4:40 in the morning when close to 7,000 artillery guns fired off steel and gas shells on the unsuspecting British front and rear positions. It was the most massive bombardment of the war. After five hours of this inferno, the *Sturmtruppen* dashed out of their trenches into a thick, protective fog and by noon had smashed through the British lines and were heading into open country. By nightfall, the Germans had gained more in one day on the Somme than the British and French had captured in all of their offensive of 1916—which had lasted 140 days and cost them more than 500,000 casualties. The following days, the feats were repeated as the British were forced to scramble back over the downlands of Picardy in utter disarray. Guillemont fell, as did Beaumont Hamel, Thiepval, even Albert, all the towns and villages so viciously contested two years earlier. Trench warfare was over. My grandfather Bartholomew, caught up in this rout, was made prisoner as half a million German soldiers advanced forty miles into the west.

An Australian friend also had a grandfather involved in that distant turmoil. Private Frank Gordon Turner, a survivor of Passchendaele, celebrated his twenty-first birthday on March 21, 1918, the fateful day of the launching of Ludendorff's so-called *Kaiserschlacht* (Kaiser's Battle). He and his fellow troops from New South Wales, then stationed in Artois, were hurriedly sent south to the Somme and eventually into billets at Villers-Bretonneux, a village just six miles east of Amiens. It was there, on April 4, 1918, that the Australians would finally be the ones to halt the overextended German forces. His journal for that day is a common man's experience of an uncommon day:

> I was awakened by the loud report of a shell which landed just a few yards from the room I was sleeping in & opposite the window. parts of the shell came through the window & splintered wood must have been flying. With my first waking breath I got the fumes from the shell down my throat & to make matters worse a piece of wood hit me in the face making my left cheek bleed a little. the fumes of the shell burnt my throat terribly. I thought I'd snuff it. I got out into the fresh air & slime & slobber streamed from my nose & mouth . . . an officer came up & asked me if I could detect any gas about. I'd a liked to have told him what I thought of him asking me if I could detect gas when I reckon I had got a stumack full of it. That shell wounded 6 . . . & killed one poor chap. One of the fellows . . . had one leg blown off below the knee & the other one partially cut off . . . We stood to at about 7 a.m. we got word fritz was advancing towards Villers Bretonneux & so we got all our gear on & went out to meet him. We had some close goes with shells as we passed down the narrow streets

along the road to the open fields. we had only gone about ¼ of a mile from the town when we could see the Germans coming about ½ to ¾ of a mile away. there was an aerodrome between us & him & as it afforded a bit of cover we made in that direction . . . we went forward again about 300 yds. & got along a road in front of the aerodrome from where we got a very good field of fire. as we got into our position the nearest germans were about 300 yds. in front of us. hundreds of them must have fallen by our rifle shots . . . it was raining all the day; about 2 p.m. there seemed to be some movement on our right. all our men were retreating & we knew no reason for it. we thought fritz must have broken through & was cutting us off . . . Fritz evidently didn't grasp the situation of things on our side & never stirred from his position. we dug ourselves in when it got dark & was fairly comfortable till word came we had to go about 200 yds. further on. The night was pitch black & we went forward once & got lost, found our old position & started out again. this time after a good deal of wandering about we found the place we had to go to. & so we had to dig in for the second time in one night. I was very tired but daybreak was approaching & it rested with ourselves whether we were under cover by daylight or not. My mate Ted Ryan & I dug in together & was quite safe by morning.

Ludendorff then launched a scaled-down but nonetheless murderous attack in Flanders and Artois. The spearhead of his forces encountered a Portuguese unit, who abandoned the Christ of the Trenches at Neuve Chapelle and disappeared behind the lines. Debacle threatened again as stormtroopers raced past the whorehouses of Béthune and Armentières toward Hazebrouck and Bailleul, major supply depots for the British army.

Fatigue now stepped in. Many German soldiers, half-starved after years of fighting on the side that had been successfully blockaded, could not believe their eyes when they saw the relative opulence of British supplies in food and drink. They realized that their leaders had been lying to them about the effect of submarine warfare and the parlous state of Allied economies. In the open countryside behind the old British lines, the conquering Germans busted open wine cellars. The best army on the Western Front began to disintegrate. In just over a month, more than 350,000 German soldiers had been wounded as a result of the attacks in Flanders, Artois, and Picardy; 50,000 had been killed. Mass drunkenness and bouts of long-deferred gluttony stalled Ludendorff's latest advance, as did stiffening British resistance. The ordinary, stoic Feldgrau began to disobey orders. As at the Chemin des Dames in 1917, the human spirit momentarily triumphed.

His Flanders breakthrough thwarted and his army disgruntled, Ludendorff called off the offensive. During May of 1918 the Germans secretly moved thirty divisions to their lines behind the Chemin des Dames, the quiet "sanatorium of the Western Front" ever since the Nivelle disaster thirteen months earlier. The French suspected nothing. Worse yet, the general in charge of this section of the Front, Denis August Duchêne, refused to implement the defense-in-depth system of manning the trenches out of a stubborn belief that every single speck of his beloved France should be defended to the utmost. Thus the bulk of his forces were in front-line trenches—and were consequently annihilated when the awesome German artillery went into action on May 27. Within a day, the attackers had overrun the French line, sprinted down the slopes from the Chemin des Dames, crossed the River Aisne, and gone more than twelve miles. For the French army, which had broken itself in the Nivelle offensive, the German success on this day and over this terrain was a slap in the face felt for many years. It was yet another reason to ensure that the miracle on the Marne and the myth of Verdun became the sole French memories of the war.

The spirit of *Götterdämmerung* had overtaken the military minds in control of the Kaiser's armies. Nothing mattered but the battle, regardless of the future. As the Germans came ever closer to the Marne, even Pershing grew alarmed enough to allow his new doughboy divisions to be put under the temporary control of the French and the British. Eventually the offensive was stopped at Chateau-Thierry.

This astounding spring of 1918 was not yet over. A debilitated Europe came into contact with an influenza strain that would kill millions more than the war itself. It was called "Spanish" influenza, because Spain, as a nonbelligerent country, had allowed its uncensored press to report the multiplying instances of the sickness within its borders. On the Western Front, whole regiments of Allied soldiers fell ill; the underfed and extenuated Germans fared even worse. Ludendorff, unfazed, ordered more attacks. By mid-July of 1918, the German army could do no more. The stage was set for the endgame.

9. Alsace

In Flanders the river that separates the Latin from the Germanic peoples is called the Douve. I crossed that linguistic front on a sunny day in July, just south of the village of Messines, Belgium. Here in the Vosges, the Lièpvrette forms the divide and runs through the town of Ste. Marie-aux-Mines. It is now mid-September and the sky seems to have resigned itself to remaining gray. To the north of the Lièpvrette lived the French-speaking Catholics who owed allegiance to the Duke of Lorraine, to the south, the Alsatian-speaking Lutherans and Calvinists bound to the Count of Ribeaupierre. The political and linguistic division was enshrined in an agreement of 1399; the religious complexities came later, shortly before Ste. Marie-aux-Mines turned into the site of a sixteenth-century silver rush. Hence its name.

On the town's main square, the façades of half-timbered houses form a staircase of gables on either side of steeply pitched roofs. French is definitely not the only *lingua franca* in the streets here. Alsatian drifts out of pastry shops selling rich butter and pound cakes unknown in the Latin lands of petits fours and croissants. Alsace, the smallest of France's regions, is the final staging ground of the Front.

These last days are spent hiking and hitching along the Route des Crêtes, a summit-skirting roadway built in the First World War to help French troops get to and from the diabolically placed battlefields of the Alsatian Front. On peaks such as Tête des Faux and the Linge, men fought each other so as to control vantage points over other peaks. It was inane, even by Great War standards. Wherever the high ground was highest, the loosely organized lines suddenly became full-blown trench systems, in spots just a few yards apart, accessible only to French *chasseur* and German *Jäger* troops on their skis. It sounds more exalted than the trench warfare in Champagne or Artois, but in fact it was as brutal as any other sector of the Front. A relative dearth of artillery meant more hand-to-hand fighting, more desperate bayoneting in sneak attacks, more gas canisters in the still mountain air, more blood on the snow. Thousands of men perished in these fights of 1914 and 1915, until both parties to the pointless savagery realized that stalemate had descended on the mountains and that the war would be won or lost elsewhere. This land was meant not for war but for hikers.

Make that hikers with the legs of a champion cyclist. My second day in the Vosges Mountains has brought me huffing uphill to the Bonhomme Pass, formerly the boundary between France and Germany. The Front passed onto imperial German soil here for the only portion of its entire 450-mile length. Bonhomme, at 3,084 feet in altitude, leads to higher battlefields yet. I take a hiking trail south from the pass and am soon within hollering distance of two mountain lakes, Lac Blanc and Lac Noir. They look cloned from a postcard image of northern Ontario. Great gray rock formations and lone pine trees stick out at odd angles along their shores. As I leave Lac Noir, its green-black waters turn blue in a sudden and brilliant burst of sunshine, and the morning's autumnal chill is banished. Soon the forest thins in the warming air and the first of a series of alpine meadows appears before me. I have somehow gone from Ontario to Austria in a few steps. Cowbells tinkle over great slopes of deep green, which are bordered by hardy bushes the color of rust. I continue on, enchanted, Maria von Trapp–like, forgetting why I am here—until a French tricolor can be seen fluttering incongruously in the distance. I am nearing the Linge, one of the two famous Front sites of Alsace.

The battlefield, or rather battlehump, looks like a garden strung with barbed wire. A strange park suitable only for mountain goats with a metal detector, the Linge stretches on seemingly indefinitely, its trench systems snaking up and down a summit denuded of trees. A level path has been carved out through the topsy-turvy contours; whenever the trail-makers struck a body they put up a cross—white for French, black for German. The resulting random cemetery of black and white against the purples and greens of the thistles and junipers makes the place oddly beautiful.

The attention to appearance continues in the Linge's small museum. In 1914, a French commander gave his assessment of what it took to be a chasseur soldier and wear the broad berets of his regiment with the appropriate swagger. His words are blown up and put on a large cardboard sign. The man should have been writing cover lines for fashion magazines. The original French is worth citing:

> *C'est la rapidité dans l'exécution des gens qui "pigent," qui "galopent." C'est l'allant, c'est l'allure, c'est le chic.*
>
> (It's about doing things fast by people who "get it," who "move it." It's about drive, it's about pace, it's about style.)

The other major battle site in Alsace is far less tony. It spreads like a stain over a peak called Hartmannswillerkopf, a lookout over the valley of the Rhine. On leaving the Linge, the Front runs downhill to the east of Munster, a tourist town now principally famous for its cheese and the storks that nest on its gaily colored rooftops. From there the broken line of bunkers heads into the shadow of the Grand Ballon, the summit of which, at 4,628 feet in altitude, is the highest point of the Vosges. Hartmannswillerkopf, a few miles to the southeast of the Grand Ballon, qualifies as the Alsatian Verdun in both senselessness and empty symbolism. The French chasseurs, unable to get their stylish mouths around the Alsatian, dubbed the place Le Vieil Armand (Old Armand).

In the first two years of the war a horrible game of King of the Castle was waged here by troops destined to perish after each fragile conquest. It became a point of honor to take the summit of Hartmannswillerkopf.

There were attacks and counterattacks in almost every month of 1915. The battles here surpass even the Linge for feral atrocity. At the peak of the mountain the trenches came within four yards of each other. Pumped-up units would capture the height, celebrate their victory, then disappear to the last man in the inevitable reprisal raid a few days later. When in the beginning of 1916 it finally dawned on both sides that neither could dominate the highest point for long, the armies retreated to comfortable trenches slightly downhill and spent the rest of the war awaiting the decision of Picardy, Flanders, and Lorraine. It had taken a murderously long time for this modus vivendi to develop. Aside from Hartmannswillerkopf's huge cemetery of the identifiable dead in their separate plots, there is a mass grave here for more than 10,000 soldiers.

When I walk from the wide lawn of the graveyard up the last two hundred yards to the cross at the summit, the notion of a calvary is inescapable even if that image does not fit. There is nothing holy or sanctified about such tortured ground. The peak is scarred, not sacred. Far from being a national Golgotha, Hartmannswillerkopf is the Front's final testament to the sheer futility of the Great War. Unlike every other part of the Front, however, the trenches here come with a view. Hundreds of feet below the peak, the green and yellow plain of Alsace fans out toward the dark metallic ribbon of the Rhine in the distance. Beyond that, a dozen miles away, the cloud-topped ridges of *Schwarzwald*—the Black Forest—roll in like breakers from the eastern horizon.

The view from this, the last great battlefield of the Western Front, might please some improperly weaned Nietschzean, but it is inconveniently grandiose for my purposes. The war, like the Front, did not end on the heights of exultation, with some clear-eyed view from a mountaintop of acquired wisdom. The war of our grandfathers ended the way it had been waged: sloppily, cruelly, destructive of the past and disastrous for the future. The endgame of the war already partook of the twentieth century's long march into forgetfulness.

SO WHAT HAPPENED? The byword of the regular Allied soldier stuck in France after the last of the Ludendorff offensives was: "Wait for the Americans and the tanks." The former now numbered more than a million and the latter, proven devastatingly effective in a limited engagement at Cambrai at the end of 1917, were rolling off assembly lines. The chief Allied commanders—Foch and Pétain for the French, Haig for the British, Pershing for the Americans—drew up plans for a grandiose offensive in 1919. In the meantime, it was agreed, the exhausted Germans could be kept off balance by a series of attacks until the advent of the wet, cold days of winter.

The French and the Americans began the decisive action on July 18, 1918, by attacking the new German salient that stretched to the Marne. Their superiority in manpower and firepower pushed the Germans back until new defensive lines were formed south of the River Aisne. On August 8, it was the turn of the British army. In a surprise attack out of the village of Villers-Bretonneux in Picardy, Australian and Canadian troops followed a wall of tanks and made ten-mile incursions into the German front. More important, the scale and suddenness of the success revealed to commanders on both sides the demoralization of the Kaiser's armies. Many units surrendered after putting up only token resistance, the Feldgrau soldiers singing in delight as they emerged from their dugouts to surrender.

The Allied attacks then came in quick succession, forcing the German warlords to scramble to send their ever-depleting number of reinforcements to help manage an orderly retreat. On August 20, the French attacked again on the Aisne; the following day the British hit north of Albert. By the time the Americans went into action at St. Mihiel the Germans had retreated in Picardy once again to the Hindenburg Line. Even that could not be held. The Belgians and the British finally broke through at Ypres, as the Americans pressed up in the Argonne in late September. Soon every Allied army was attacking as the German army slowly backed its way through Belgium and northern France.

At home, imperial Germany began to fall apart. The autocratic government and the privations of wartime could be endured no longer. Riots broke out, sailors mutinied, and a new liberal chancellor was appointed to work real reforms with the Reichstag. Ludendorff resigned his post on October 27—and would remain in obscurity until 1923, when he participated in Hitler's failed beer-hall putsch in Munich. In early November, 1918, the Second Reich finally collapsed under the pressure of mounting chaos, and the Kaiser, forced to abdicate, fled to the Netherlands. The newly constituted republic consented to the Allied terms for surrender and the armistice was signed in Field-Marshal Foch's railway carriage in a clearing of the Compiègne forest. The papers were initialed in the early hours of November 11, 1918. A few seconds before eleven o'clock that same morning, one observer with South African troops in Flanders saw a German machine-gunner fire off a scorching hail of bullets toward their trenches. At the stroke of eleven, the gunner stood up, made a deep bow, turned around, and walked away.

The war was over. Princip's bullet had caused some 67 million men to don uniforms and go to fight. One in every six of these men was killed. Of the remainder, approximately half were wounded. On the Western Front alone, more than 4 million had died in their ditches.

I HAVE COME down from the mountain. The Vosges end as abruptly as they begin, and here at their southern extremity vineyards hug the lower slopes near the towns of Thann and Cernay. Once past the twine of roadways connecting the two, the Front leads over slow rises of alternating field and woodland to the Swiss border. I set out alone over this uneven plain, glad to regain the gentle rhythm of level walking after the strenuous trails in the mountains. Left-right, left-right, left-right—there is little to occupy me now except a longing for closure. But for a flurry of movement in 1914, this may have been the quietest part of the entire Front.

The route takes me past a garbage dump, then under an expressway near a village named Burnhaupt. I notice with practiced irony that the expressway's restaurant complex, Les Portes de l'Alsace, is located in no-man's-land. My long afternoon's walk in the fields yields no sign of the distant fighting, just the usual regiment of irritated farm dogs. After a night spent digesting sauerkraut in the market town of Altkirch, the last day of my journey dawns. I decide that there can be no trace of the war left in this land of plump cheeks and gabled domesticity. Rural Alsace is far too house-proud to leave trenches lying about. In a village called Hirtzbach I walk alongside a watercourse overhung with scores of flower-pots. On either side of the stream, half-timbered dwellings strain under the weight of several generations of geraniums. The place has won some sort of award. Evidently, the region's villages try to outbloom each other every year in a competition adjudicated by flower experts. Neatness must count, too—in Hirtzbach, even the dirt doesn't have dirt on it.

The gentle landscape outside the villages here is far prettier than that on the plain near the mountains. Low wooded ridges alternate with paddocks of greenery on which listless horses graze. Signs in the villages now inform the curious that this part of the world may be referred to as the Route of the Fried Carp. The tourist board must have decided that this name was snappier than the End of the Western Front.

At twin villages named Seppois-le-Bas and Seppois-le-Haut, I arrive at a stream called the Largue. On either side of it ran the final trenches of the Front. I scan an old French military map that shows the sector in great detail. The German side was usually better built than either the

French or the British, so I decide to follow the eastern, German side of the Largue. My quest for old bunkers is quickly thwarted. After a mile or so the Western Front becomes a golf course, from which I am shooed away by a party of four annoyed duffers. Reluctantly, I take a road around the links to the hamlet of Mooslargue. Two children stop what they are doing to look at me in openmouthed astonishment. I feel as if I have disturbed a field of sunflowers again.

Muddy little Mooslargue shares with Pfetterhouse, the much larger town on the other bank of the stream, the distinction of being the last built-up area on the Front. On the other end of the ditch is Nieuport. It is said that when news reached the German trenches that a mine had sunk the ship carrying Lord Kitchener, the British military chief, some clever Feldgrau in a trench started banging his mess tin in delight. Soon the clatter spread, until the whole of the German Western Front was smashing metal plates together, all the way from Nieuport to Mooslargue, through Flanders, Artois, Picardy, Champagne, Lorraine, and Alsace, a chain of undergound derision 450 miles long. Today, of course, Mooslargue is deep in anonymous sleep.

The bridge over the Largue between Mooslargue and Pfetterhouse stands about half a mile away from the right angle the Swiss border makes at this extremity of Alsace. The stream has been channeled to the south to create a linear fish pond, around which a dozen or so sportsmen are snoozing on lawn chairs beside firmly planted fishing rods. There are signs posted prohibiting outsiders like me from doing the same, but nowhere does it say that I cannot advance farther upstream. I walk under the shade trees past the fishermen, glad to see they are not as secretive and antisocial as their counterparts on the Somme. Although I'm willing to trade civilities—"Are the carp biting today?"—my presence does not excite any interest. The hiker, apparently, is a transient phenomenon to be endured, like mosquitoes in the heat of summer. After continuing for about eight hundred yards more along the bank of the Largue, I understand why the backpacker must be a common sight here in the high season. My path crosses a trail marked by a sign for a *Grande Randonnée*, a long-haul hiking path that crisscrosses Europe. This one is the E5, which goes from the Atlantic to the Adriatic. It is fitting that my unsignposted summer of walking down a metaphor should end on a track laid out by professional pedestrians. Left foot meets right. There is even a shelter nearby, suitable for sleeping overnight or brewing some tea.

I am about to turn on my heels and head back to the road when I realize that this cannot be the end. The Front went all the way to the border. I started at the seaside in Nieuport, on the strand, in the dunes, on the beach—not at some place hundreds of yards away. If there is to be an end to this walk, let it be a proper one. For the first time in a week, my Great War presences return. Go on—say Cadogan, Aronsohn, Tommy, Bartholomew, Daniel—find the right place.

There is a thicket of trees ahead, which I barge through in the hope of finding something that bespeaks finality. The undergrowth thins gradually until I am walking freely up an ankle-twisting slope strewn with loose rocks and dead leaves. Just as a feeling of foolishness begins to steal over me in this landscape of natural anarchy, I catch sight of three ghostly white markers placed at regular intervals in a row. Two have a straight line painted across their top; one, an L-shaped pattern. This is the border, where Switzerland hangs a right.

This should be enough—the Front stops here. But it isn't. I follow the markers farther uphill and, within minutes, find what I've been seeking. A concrete pillbox crumbles onto the forest floor. The very last in a long line. My grandfathers, Tommy, Cadogan, Aronsohn tell me what to do.

I give it a kick, then walk away.

Journey's End

THE TREES IN the forest have shed most of their colors. Today the sun has come out, a brittle disk hovering tentatively overhead, too weak to burn off the lingering mists and too tired to bring the forest of Compiègne to life. It is November 11, and the Ohio Boomer and I — ten years older than we were during our wintry weekend visit to the Somme — have walked out of the village of Rethondes and into the woods. The only concession made to the passing of a decade is the size of the lunch we've just eaten. It was enormous, a foretaste of French middle age.

The road leading toward La Clairière de l'Armistice (the Armistice Clearing) runs as straight as the bridle paths that crisscross it at regular intervals. A dozen or so buses painted a drab army green are parked on either side of the paved roadway, their uniformed drivers slouched behind steering wheels, smoking cigarettes and reading hardcover comic books with an intensity that is almost religious. They take no notice of us as we pass, two more civilians on the way through the woods for the ceremony. The clearing at Rethondes, formerly a railroad siding, is where the piece of paper was signed that put an end to the war on the eleventh hour of the eleventh day of the eleventh month of 1918.

At a junction in the road the police are preventing a small crowd of about twenty people from going the last two hundred yards to the clearing. We make our way to the front of the group and see a platoon of women soldiers surrounded by rifle-toting gendarmes. The police is protecting the army. A civilian in a dark suit talks into his lapel, a sure sign that bodyguards and politicians are on their way.

"Who's coming?" I ask my neighbor.

"Dunno," he replies. "Maybe the president."

His companion lets out a derisive snort. "If it were the president, sausage-head, we wouldn't be this close."

The first fellow motions toward the police. "Then why are these jerks here?"

It's a good question, we all agree, and within minutes it is answered. A dark trio of Citroën limos, their cat's-eyes headlights shining in spite of the slanting afternoon sunbeams, swings theatrically into the intersection. The women snap to attention, the police tense and face us.

First out onto the pavement, no doubt because of the spring still left in their limbs, are two youthful men dressed in conservative suits. Falling across their chests, in beauty pageant fashion, are sashes, which identify them as mayors of nearby towns. Two fat sash-wearers then struggle out of the second car, followed by an elderly general laden with shiny medals and metallic braid. The beige kepi on his head looks as if it has spent a week in the shop of a playful goldsmith. One man seems not dressed for a costume party. He, we conclude, must be the out-of-town political dignitary. When he steps out of his limo, all of the others mill about him in agitated deference.

No one in our crowd of onlookers stirs. There is a low buzz of whispered questioning and a repetitive exchange of shrugs. Sausage-head turns toward his friend and closes his eyes, as if granting him a debating point. When he reopens them, it is to say, defensively, "Must be a minister." The unknown politico—he is, I learn later, the French minister of veterans' affairs—nods to the small crowd of voters, who look back at him in stone-faced disappointment at his lack of celebrity. He goes to lay a wreath at a monument obscured by the honor guard of soldiers, but already the crowd has lost interest in him. Two dogs somewhere to the back of us have begun fighting, setting up a howling call-and-response that drowns out any attempt at solemnity.

By the time everyone has turned around to face the intersection again, the limos are leaving. They go the last few yards before turning up the drive toward the clearing, where the main ceremony of the afternoon is about to begin. The honking of a brass band can already be heard. The police relax, the women soldiers whip out their cigarettes. The stone monument shows a Prussian eagle, dashed and dying, brought down to earth. Eventually, we are allowed to continue on our way.

THE FRONT HAS changed over the past ten years. More and more people are visiting it, and Western Front associations are booming. All is not so quiet. In the Picard town of Péronne, a new museum and resource center has opened to initiate good Euro-citizens into the history and historiography of the war. It is a radical departure from the private little museums that litter the Front with their mix of undigested nationalism and sly war porn. Péronne's Historial is a stimulating place, giving primacy to cultural studies over the usual military descriptions.

Elsewhere, people are sprucing up the Front. In Alsace, a weekend volunteer group formed in the early 1990s now comes to weed the Linge and other battlefields. Around Soissons, a group calling themselves war archaeologists spends their time digging up old bunkers and tracing the graffiti left by long-dead soldiers. The French state, always keen to improve its tourism infrastructure, has adopted a World War I logo for signs and cemeteries. In some places, the unmarked battlefields I visited on foot have since sprouted officially sponsored signboards giving officially sponsored versions of what happened. The one at the Chemin des Dames, for example, manages never once to mention the most famous military mutinies in French history. At the Somme, the local government has installed directional arrows with poppies on them, so that British visitors don't have to struggle with any foreign iconography. Ten years ago, nothing of this sort existed. As it fades further and further into the past, the First World War, paradoxically, seems to be having a revival.

Whether this renewal of interest will do the cause of truth any good is another question. For those who take even a glancing interest in modern history, the First World War is usually seen as some natural calamity, like the biblical flood. Those who see it otherwise are sometimes crackpots: on November 11, 1993, a group of anarchists took to the streets in my Paris neighborhood and vented their antimilitarist ire by smashing the windows of the local McDonald's. Even I, who had hiked the length of the Western Front in search of connections, found that one a bit of a stretch.

As I walk over to the clearing now, it occurs to me that the Front is losing its hold on my imagination, that this may be my last visit to a site associated with the First World War. As a pastime, I've come to realize, it is decidedly odd, akin to the zealous gardening hobby of the New Zealand couple I had met years earlier in a Belgian graveyard. What matters to me now is less the content of the past than the way it informs the present. That is the one lesson drawn from my days and nights at the Front: the past must be addressed, shaken up a bit, but then it should be relinquished.

"AND THEN FOCH took the armistice and put it in his briefcase. Foch got up from the table. Then Foch got off of the train. Foch, despite the earliness of the hour, went to Paris . . ."

A military man on a platform in the Rethondes clearing is giving the keynote speech. It is all about Ferdinand Foch, to the exclusion of anything else. Out of the loudspeakers pours a weirdly outdated cult of the personality. Change a few names, and we could be in North Korea.

The poor fellow's speech goes on and on. Foch, Foch, Foch, and more Foch. It's almost a comfort to see how consistent the French army is in its tastelessness. A lifetime has passed since the armistice was signed here, and one of its officers can still publicly behave as if a French colossus bestrode the planet. Instead of showing decency for the memory of the poilus, the army spokesman is constructing a new Napoleon. The sclerosis of his institution inspires awe.

I look around the clearing. Aside from the official stand, there are two covered enclosures for special guests. The one closest to me holds veterans and their wives. Only a couple of the men look old enough to have fought in the Great War. The rest, in their seventies and eighties, are witnesses to the Second World War. Some, no doubt, were Resistance fighters. All would know of another railway siding near Compiègne, called Royalieu. It is from there that 53,000 French people were sent to Auschwitz. The trains of Rethondes and Royalieu ran through the darkness of the twentieth century.

As A GENERATION like the Boomers heads into midlife, perhaps it is only natural we develop a longing for context. Hence an interest in the past, and in the century that formed us. Which is a good thing, as long as the tools of our memory become demilitarized.

Many studies, and certainly most official literature, minimize the bumbling and atrocious conduct of the war. Of Passchendaele and Haig's decision to press on I have read in an otherwise literate book: "His decision to continue the offensive after the weather broke may have been wrong but it would have been even more wrong to abandon the attack." This, and other examples like it, make you question the simple humanity of some military historians. Anachronistic anger, of the type I felt at the Chemin des Dames and at Ypres, may not be such a failing after all. If people are still lying, if the statue of Joffre still stands in Paris, the likeness of Haig in London, then perhaps some anger is useful. Why should we accept the party line? If we are to let the past inform our lives, then at least let it be a version that is not a self-serving story issued by some institution like the army or the state.

What really should be remembered and taught about the Western Front is that, for the first time, societies were reorganized to feed a killing machine. It would not be the last. My ghosts from the Great War tell me to get the word out: what happened to them can happen again. On June 10, 1991, I stood on lower Broadway in New York's financial district and saw joyful crowds hang people in effigy, as a way of greeting victorious troops back from Iraq. Celebration was in the air, but so too was the sulfur of hate, thick and unadulterated. Something as degrading as the Western Front no longer seemed so implausible. Lest We Forget— not just the dilemmas of our grandfathers, but the continual siren song of violence in uniform. The Serbs in Bosnia, the Hutus in Rwanda, even the Canadians in Somalia. The next century's short list for enforced amnesia is already lengthening.

THE OTHER GROUP of guests at the ceremony in the Rethondes clearing are schoolchildren. There are perhaps two hundred of them, buzzing around their chairs and squealing for the sheer pleasure of it. Their teachers have almost given up trying to quiet them. The contrast between the two groups of guests opposite the podium is striking. The veterans sit silently, almost motionless with age; the young bounce up and down, in frenzied impatience. One is reflective; the other, unlistening. Don't move, says one; don't preach, says the other. The divide is clear, and eternal. It says more about the transmission of experience than any Western Front ever could. I turn and leave the ceremony, satisfied, at last, that I have seen enough of my metaphor.

The following year the French prime minister will visit Rethondes. By then, I will have learned that there was an unsuspected presence with me when I walked the Front. Another great-uncle, Jeremiah O'Shea, the elder brother of my grandfather, was a soldier in the British army. He was also a forgotten man, until a relative in County Kerry summoned up a vague recollection of him. The archivists at the Commonwealth War Graves Commission did the rest. Jeremiah died at age thirty-two, in his native Tralee, of wounds suffered in the Great War, most probably at Gallipoli. His date of death was July 6, 1916, two days after poet Alan Seeger went to his fated rendezvous and two months, to the day, before yet another great-uncle fell at Guillemont. Thus Jeremiah joins Tommy and the others just when it is time to leave them. I am sorry, Jeremiah.

The French government set about distributing prizes on November 11, 1995. Surviving soldiers from the *guerre de quatorze* had been hunted down in the previous months, with the intention of bestowing on them the Legion of Honor. More than 1,500 poilus were found and informed of the extraordinary decoration they were going to receive. One veteran of Verdun, ninety-nine years old and unimpressed, turned down the proffered medal. "I don't want to be a member of the Legion," he told the press. "What for? Nobody learned anything from our war."

I disagree.

Further Reading

THE GREAT WAR has also been a great war of words. Although the conflict has attracted more than its fair share of bores, there are nonetheless a lot of interesting reads in its massive bibliography. What follows is a brief list of some of the better works that should be easily—and currently—available in bookstores and public libraries to nonspecialists and accidental historians. Scholars, look elsewhere.

There is a holy trinity of superb popularized histories of the First World War. Each deals with a different episode. Barbara Tuchman's Pulitzer Prize–winning *The Guns of August* (Ballantine, 1994), a page-turning account of the war's outbreak, is deservedly a classic. So too are Alistair Horne's *The Price of Glory: Verdun, 1916* (Penguin, 1979) and Leon Wolff's indignant *In Flanders Fields: The 1917 Campaign* (Greenwood, 1984), an account of the Passchendaele campaign. There are other books that almost match this standard of good popular history, but none surpasses it.

For oral history, the work of Lyn Macdonald stands alone as the heavyweight of Great War testimonials. Some of her histories include books on Third Ypres (*They Called It Passchendaele*: Macmillan, 1988), Loos (*1915: The Death of Innocence*: Henry Holt, 1993), the British retreat from Mons to the Marne (*1914: The First Year of Fighting*: Simon & Schuster, 1988), and the work of front-line nurses (*The Roses of No Man's Land*: Macmillan, 1989). To my mind, *1915* is the most interesting. Although sometimes repetitive, Macdonald's books are invaluable resources for recapturing the "voice" of war's participants. Similarly, Martin Middlebrook's *The First Day on the Somme, 1 July 1916* (Allen Lane, 1971) patches together the recollections of those who survived the deadly foray into no-man's-land that ended in disaster.

For the big picture of the war, the most recent hefty tome of note is Martin Gilbert's *The First World War: A Complete History* (Henry Holt, 1996). It is readable and rich in anecdote. This, as a complement to Marc Ferro's translated classic *The Great War 1914–1918* (Dorset, 1990) or A.J.P. Taylor's caustic *The First World War: An Illustrated History* (Berkley, 1972), provides an excellent overall view of the war. The late Jean-Baptiste Duroselle, in his as yet untranslated *La Grande Guerre des Français, L'Incompréhensible* (Perrin, 1994), provides a Gallic counterpoint to the Anglo reference book of the war: Basil Liddell-Hart's *History of the First World War* (Pan, 1970). These last two should be attempted if you've got lots of time on your hands. To those with limited hours to devote to reading, I recommend picking up Taylor's pocket-sized history, if only for the pleasure of smiling at his sardonic photo captions.

Often, the big picture is less interesting than the specialized study. Two brilliant books give searingly scary descriptions of the Western Front. John Ellis's *Eye-Deep in Hell: Trench Warfare in World War I* (Pantheon, 1977) and Denis Winter's *Death's Men: Soldiers of the Great War* (Penguin, 1985) are well-documented, detail-crammed reconstructions of troglodyte trench life. Winter, an impassioned historian with a polemical pen, has also published *Haig's Command: A Reassessment* (Penguin, 1992), a masterful new indictment of high-level bungling that should, but probably won't, silence the stubborn apologists of Douglas Haig in military history circles. Winter's prose on the subject of the field marshal makes mine look like that of a diplomat.

In a class of its own among military histories is John Keegan's *The Face of Battle: A Study of Agincourt, Waterloo, and the Somme* (Penguin, 1983). Instead of dealing with generals and grand plans and the like, Keegan set out to determine how the ordinary soldier experienced the awful ordeal of the battlefield. The result is a felicitous and fascinating masterpiece of scholarship and lively writing.

For those interested less in battle than in beauty, World War I's outpouring of excellent poetry and prose continues to be passed down to modern readers. Anthologies of work from the period abound—I recommend anything compiled by Jon Silkin or Jon Silver, two Brit lit mavens with a cosmopolitan sweep that goes beyond the well-trodden paths of Owen, Sassoon, and other great English war poets. A truly exceptional anthology—and an exception to my stated intention to keep this bibliography limited to readily available books—is Tim Cross's *The Lost Voices of World War I: An International Anthology of Writers, Poets and Playwrights* (University of Iowa, 1988). Cross includes only writers who died in World War I and yet produces a wide-ranging compendium of wasted genius that expressed itself in everything from Serbo-Croat to Breton. The introductory essays to each artist are uniformly excellent, and the overall commentaries about the cultural importance of the conflict are first-rate.

Cultural concerns bring us to yet another trinity of nonfiction classics dealing with the war. Paul Fussell's *The Great War and Modern Memory* (Oxford, 1975), on the lingering influence of British war poetry and its cultivation of irony, is justly famous for its literate treatment of the conflict. Fussell's writing is tendentious, his conclusions bold. Less well known is Samuel Hynes's *A War Imagined: The First World War and English Culture* (Atheneum, 1991), a finely observed study of changing perceptions of the war among British intellectual and artistic elites. More continental in outlook is Modris Eksteins's *Rites of Spring: The Great War and the Birth of the Modern Age* (Houghton Mifflin, 1989), an engaging examination of how World War I was the nightmarish midwife at the birth of a sensibility that eventually matured as Nazism. All three studies are difficult to put down.

The literary pantheon of Great War novelists—Henri Barbusse, Ernst Jünger, Ford Madox Ford, Erich Maria Remarque, Blaise Cendrars, et al.—should not obscure the powerful writing of the conflict's memoirists. In my opinion, Robert Graves's *Good-bye to All That* (Anchor, 1957) remains the most entertaining of the memoirs readily available, although by far the most moving is Vera Brittain's *Testament of Youth: An Autobiographical Study of the Years 1900–1925* (Penguin, 1989). A woman's voice crops up once again in current fiction about the conflict: Pat Barker's trilogy of Great War novels, *Regeneration* (NAL-Dutton, 1993), *The Eye in the Door* (NAL-Dutton, 1995), and *The Ghost Road* (Viking, 1995)—the last won the 1995 Booker Prize—stands as a compelling monument to the distant war's staying power in the imagination. In the same imaginative vein, David Macfarlane's memoir of his Newfoundland family's experience of the war, *Come From Away* (Poseidon, 1991), remains a model of micro-history and writerly evocation of past drama.

Acknowledgments

THERE ARE MANY people to whom I owe a debt of gratitude. Friends and colleagues have given me encouragement, pointed out avenues of research, and, perhaps most importantly, shown forbearance in hearing me go on and on about the Western Front for close to a decade now. Strangers, too, have been helpful—hundreds of people in Belgium and France treated me with courtesy during my journey, if only to give me the time of day, a glass of beer, or directions to the next stop in no-man's-land. A backside full of buckshot was never once even a remote possibility.

At the outset four people—Audrey Thomas, Ernst Herb, Mimi Tompkins, Scott Blair—helped me figuratively lace up my boots and get going. Audrey, in fact, picked out the pair of boots that were made for walking. Scott, a non-accidental historian, badgered me back to the Front and, as deadlines drew nearer, gave freely of his time to act as consultant, traveling companion, reader, fact-checker, and debating partner. He and Mitchell Feinberg sacrificed several glorious spring weekends to hole themselves up in Mitch's Paris office and make accurate maps of the French and Belgian boondocks. Heroic.

Many others lent support, in different ways. My parents, Daniel and Annie, and two brothers, Donal and Kevin, offered encouragement from the start, even when it looked as if I'd never get started. The now widely dispersed gang at *Paris Passion* magazine helped, too. My thanks to Edward Hernstadt for his café counter eloquence, to Heidi Ellison for her bemused support, and to the late Alexandra Tuttle for her character-istically barbed praise of the project. In New York, fellow journalist John Howell constantly dug up weird warfare books for me out of old cata-logues. Even if many of them dealt with Stonewall Jackson and Robert E.

Lee, they were unfailingly stimulating. As were the company and conversation of many others who contributed to my thinking about the Front: Eli Gottlieb, Ben Brantley, Timothy Morrow, Mark Schapiro, Sonia Kronlund, Randall Koral, Olga Vincent, Noelle de Chambrun, Alexander Whitelaw, Elizabeth and Kevin Conlon, Zia Jaffrey, Bruce Alderman, Lenny Borger, Graham Fuller, Kathleen O'Shea, Patrick Cocklin, Alan Tucker, Kate Turner, Stokes Howell, Helen Mercer, Peter Lahey, Carole Tonkinson, Susan Schorr. Thanks are also due to George Galt and Ernest Hillen, who published "All Quiet," the travel article that is the seed of this book, in *Saturday Night* magazine in 1989. And to Matt Cohen, whose timely advice and support eased my way into the waters of book-length composition.

Publishers Scott McIntyre, Patricia Aldana, and George Gibson have been warmly supportive of a first-time author. Editor Barbara Pulling has been gentle—and extremely effective in curbing my worst excesses. Despite her impressive vigilance, the blame for any remaining errors or lapses should be laid squarely on my doorstep.

Which brings me home, to Jill Pearlman, who I sometimes feel must be itching to reread the fine print of our wedding contract. I have shamelessly called on—the unkind might say exploited—her talents as writer, editor, and proofreader in preparing this book, and without her support and understanding would not have finished it in this century. When we met in Manhattan in 1990, it is unlikely that Jill could have foreseen a future of picnics on Belgian battlefields or of tiresome breakfast conversations that begin thus: "Do you realize what happened seventy-seven years ago today?" Finally, a word of gratitude to my baby daughter, Rachel, for having had the exquisite good taste to come into the world the day *after* November 11.

Index